D1860136

DISASTER AND TSUNAMI

Psycho-social Impact

DISASTER AND TSUNAMI
PSYCHO-SOCIAL IMPACT

DR I. JEYANTHI

and

DR A. THOMAS WILLIAM

KALPAZ

©Author

All rights reserved. No part of this work may be reproduced, stored, adapted, or transmitted in any form or by any means, electronic, mechanical, photocopying, micro-filming recording or otherwise, or translated in any language, without the prior written permission of the copyright owner and the publisher. The book is sold subject to the condition that it shall not, by way of trade or otherwise, be lent, resold, hired out, or otherwise circulated without the prior publisher's written consent in any form of binding or cover other than that in which it is published.

The views and opinions expressed in this book are author(s) own and the facts reported by them have been verified to the extent possible, and the publishers are not in any way liable for the same.

ISBN: 978-93-5128-254-9

Price: ₹ 1190

First Published, 2017

Published by

Kalpaz Publications
C-30, Satyawati Nagar,
Delhi – 110052
E-mail: kalpaz@hotmail.com
Ph.: 9212142040

Printed at: G. Print Process, Delhi

Cataloging in Publication Data—DK
Courtesy: D.K. Agencies (P) Ltd. <docinfo@dkagencies.com>

Jeyanthi, I., author.
Disaster and tsunami : psycho-social impact / Dr I. Jeyanthi and Dr A. Thomas William.
pages cm
Includes bibliographical references.
ISBN 9789351282549

1. Indian Ocean Tsunami, 2004—India—Tamil Nadu—Psychological aspects. 2. Indian Ocean Tsunami, 2004—India—Kanniyākumāri (District)—Psychological aspects. 3. Indian Ocean Tsunami, 2004—Social aspects—India—Tamil Nadu. 4. Indian Ocean Tsunami, 2004—Social aspects—India—Kanniyākumāri (District) 5. Child disaster victims—India—Tamil Nadu—Psychology. 6. Child disaster victims—India—Kanniyākumāri (District)—Psychology. 7. Disasters—India. I. Thomas William, A., author. II. Title.

HV603 2004.T36J49 2017 DDC 363.3494095482 23

Contents

List of Tables

List of Figures

ST. ANN'S COLLEGE OF ARTS [Co-Education] **AND SCIENCE**
[Affiliated To Thiruvalluvar University]
Chennai to Trichy Bypass Road (NH-45), Tindivanam –604 001.
Phone: Office: 04147 250 903, Email: st.annscollegetvm15@yahoo.com

Foreword

The book on "DISASTER & TSUNAMI : PSYCHO-SOCIAL IMPACT is the concept relevant in today's context in terms of dangers and consequences on disaster worldwide and specific to India. The aftermath of any disaster or disaster like Tsunami on the life of the individual is to be researched in depth so as to promote prevention, treatment and rehabilitation of the victims. In this venture I appreciate the authors who took special interest to study the victims especially the children in the social work perspective justify great attention and appreciation.

Most of the Disasters could be considered as human-made, simply for the reason that the dangers and damages would have been prevented before it is developing into a disaster. Hence Disaster Mitigation Management strategies shall be developed with latest technology in application.

The significant statement India could naturally be called as "Theater of disasters" As our Nation has encountered almost all types of disasters at different points of time and moreover it is on the increase in the recent period hence it should be considered seriously in order to safeguard India form such disasters.

This book has emphasized that the children who are the vulnerable and the victims of such disasters are seldom cared for and suggest that special focus needs to be given to such children while planning for disaster mitigation. Moreover the role of Professional social workers is crucial and essential and they should form part of the team for disaster management. The government and other stakeholders should come out with a policy statement to include their role to recognize their significance in the disaster work.

I am indeed convinced that this book shall serve as a reference material to various research scholars, Development personnel and the disaster brigadiers who want to do the quality service to the victims of disaster.

01.12.2016

Dr A. J. Christopher
PRINCIPAL
Former Associate Professor and Head in Social Work

Acknowledgements

At the outset, we feel proud to place on record our humble thanks and sense of gratitude to Almighty God for making this piece of research work in a book form for academic and research endevours.

We are indebted to Dr A. Umesh Samuel Jebaseelan, Associate Professor in Social Work, Bishop Heber College, (Autonomous), Trichirappalli for his ready assistance, willing co-operation, endurance, erudition, professional competence, scholarly advice and valuable guidance during the empirical part of this work.

Thanks expressed to Mr A.M. Kennedy Ex-JWO in Indian Air Force, beloved husband of Dr I. Jayanthi; for his moral support and encouragement in making work published.

We are highly grateful to the Principals, Teachers and staff of St. Mary's Higher Secondary School, Colachel, St. Little Flower Higher Secondary School Melamanakudi, St. Alex High School, Kottilpadu and Orient Matriculation Higher Secondary School, Kottilpadu in Kanayakumari District, for their kind permission and facilities provided during the field data collection for the empirical part of this book. Love, affection, and co-operation of the children of these schools have made the work easy and we pray and bless for their success in academic and life accomplishments.

We place on record our thankfulness to Dr S. Gunasekaran, Professor and Head and all other faculty members of Dept. of Applied Research, Gandhigram Rural Institute–Deemed University, Gandhigram, Dindigul District; for their moral support and encouragement.

In a special we thank the children and members of both the families for their encouragement and support.

Kalpaz Publications is sincerely acknowledged with heartfelt thanks for undertaking this smart publication.

Dr I. Jeyanthi

Dr A. Thomas William

Preface

Disaster research has been articulated for more than a century and various studies reflect a common observation that all disasters lead to devastation on human and environment. To some of the researchers; disasters can be seen as being human-made, their reasoning being that human actions before the strike of the hazard can prevent it developing into a disaster. All disasters are hence the result of human failure. Adoption of relevant and appropriate Disaster Mitigation Management strategies could prevent most of the disasters. Hazards are routinely divided into natural or human-made, although complex disasters, where there is no single root cause, are more common in developing countries. A specific disaster may spawn a secondary disaster that increases the impact.

The phases of all disasters are whether natural or man-made, are the same. The disasters often differ in quantity of damage caused or in quality of the type of consequences. Man-made disasters are having an element of threat to human, economy and environment. Sociological disasters have a strong human motive, such as criminal acts, stampedes, riots and war.

India could naturally be called as "theatre of disasters" as almost all types of disaster has strike India at different point of time which is on the increase recently. Natural disasters in India, many of them related to the climate of India, cause massive losses to Indian life and property. Droughts, flash floods, cyclones, avalanches, landslides, snowstorms and Tsunamis are the common disasters that hit India nowadays.

Tsunami is a series of large waves of extremely long wavelength and period usually generated by a violent, impulsive undersea disturbance or activity near the coast or in the ocean. When a sudden displacement of a large volume of water occurs, or if the sea floor is suddenly raised or dropped by an earthquake, big tsunami waves can be formed by forces of gravity. The waves travel out of the area of origin and can be extremely dangerous and brought greater damages to life of human beings.

Destruction by tsunamis on the habitat could normally be inundation, wave impact on structures, and erosion. Strong, tsunami-induced currents lead to the erosion of foundations and the collapse of bridges and seawalls. Flotation and drag forces move houses and overturn railroads and cars. Considerable damage is caused by the resultant floating debris, including boats and cars that become dangerous projectiles that may crash into buildings, break power lines, and may start fire accidents.

The deadliest tsunami prior to 2004 in South Asia was in November 1945, which originated off the Makran coast of Pakistan in the Arabian Sea and caused deaths as far as Mumbai. More than 4000 people were killed on the Makran Coast by both the earthquake and the tsunami. Almost all the countries situated around the Bay of Bengal were affected by the tsunami waves in the morning hours of 26 December 2004 (between 0900–1030 hrs IST). The killer waves were triggered by an earthquake measuring 8.9 on the Richter scale that had an epicenter near the west coast of Sumatra in Indonesia.

The consequences the 2004 Tsunami induced in India is beyond repair in terms of human and finance. There is a loss of economy, environment and health. The impact is sustained for years together and though various machineries, agencies and government is undertaking rehabilitation measures on regular basis; but need to continue for years together. The state of Tamil Nadu has been the worst affected on the mainland, with a death toll of 7,793 and caused greater damage to property, animal life, agriculture and made the life risky.

In the eye of disaster or Tsunami; children becomes the highly vulnerable group. Infants and young children, in particular, are physically vulnerable to both sudden-onset and chronic disaster events due to their partial or total dependence on adults. Older children and adolescents are also at risk for injury or death, and they may develop various behavioural, psychological, and emotional issues in the aftermath of disaster. Recognising the different forms of physical and emotional vulnerability is essential in order to better protect and help children. Knowledge of children's vulnerability is important from a social scientific perspective in order to make the rejuvenation process a sustainable one.

At the end of the twentieth century, children affected by disasters is estimated 66.5 million each year and this number is likely to triple over the second decade of the twenty-first century, with up to 175 million children affected every year by disasters triggered by climate change. Common responses of children to disaster vary by age group and stage of physical and mental development. The children are thrown in to new surroundings all of a sudden. They are unable to lead the life they were doing earlier.

Children may exhibit marked reactions of fear and anxiety, increased hostility with siblings, somatic complaints, and sleep disorders, problems with school performance, social withdrawal, apathy, and reenactment through play, PTSD and anxiety. Adolescents and youth may show decreased interest in social activities and school, rebellion and other behavioural problems, sleep and eating disorders, somatic complains, increased or decreased physical activity, confusion, lack of concentration, a decline in responsible behaviours, engage in risk-taking behaviours and may indulge in bad habits such as alcohol and drug consumption. Disasters, which often destroy school buildings and displace students and teachers, may disrupt children's academic progress and diminish their long-term educational outcomes.

Vulnerable groups for disaster include poor, women, and ethnic minorities, persons with physical or mental disabilities, the elderly and children and are considered more susceptible to damage, loss, suffering, injury and even death. Several social and environmental factors that contribute to children being at risk for death or injury in disaster. These include residing in hazard-prone regions in poorer countries and communities living in and going to school in substandard structures losing a parent or becoming separated from family members.

Natural disasters such as the tsunami can have a devastating impact on the psychological and social well-being of anyone exposed to them. Disasters threaten personal safety, overwhelm defense mechanisms and disrupt community and family structures. Such events may also cause mass casualties and destruction of property and may lead to a collapse of the social networks and daily routines of the individuals affected. Psychological and emotional trauma is very common following any disaster.

Depending on the cultural and social contexts, special measures must be taken to ensure the protection from harm of all children, as well as their equitable access to basic services. During this process of ensuring services to children, there is a high possibility that the support for adolescents may not be addressed effectively. There are great changes in living conditions and daily life activities after a disaster. The routines children were comfortable with and the surrounding they knew no longer exist. Relationships with parents and significant others might undergo changes as caregivers are themselves affected by the disaster and become busy and preoccupied in getting their life back in order.

It is imperative that the mental health problems of the children are recognised as early as possible and supportive actions are put in place at home, school and in society. The family is a vital unit in understanding and meeting the needs of traumatised children. Intimate mother-child, family and relative relationships are important in the healing process.

Children and adolescents are more vulnerable than adults to the traumatic events of disasters. Even in preschoolers, the effects can be serious and persistent and can influence their personality development, but, at the same time, children have plasticity to change if an intervention can be developed to address their coping skills. It is most helpful to train and support health workers from the affected communities about the post-disaster mental health aspects. Cultural competence is an important issue for counselling in post-disaster situations, which can be easily met by local volunteers than people from outside.

Early psychological intervention is recommended following disasters especially when the disaster is associated with extreme and widespread damage to property, ongoing economic problems of the stricken community, violence that resulted from human intent, and a high prevalence of trauma in the form of injuries, threat to life and loss of life. The issue is particularly critical in developing countries. Post-disaster counselling should be made available for extended periods, with shifting emphasis to meet the changing needs of high-risk groups. Supportive interventions include fostering a sense of safety and efficacy, connecting patients with communities and services, and helping parents talk about the trauma with their children.

The components of trauma-focused interventions generally include techniques of stress management such as relaxation, thought-stopping, positive imagery, deep breathing, etc. The evaluation and reconsideration of cognitive assumptions the child would have about the trauma and inclusion of parents and other supportive individuals in treatment. Play can be used both as a medium of assessment and therapy for children. A play interview is essential when examining a child less than seven years old but should be utilised for all pre-pubertal children.

Through play children can express verbally and non-verbally difficult painful emotions, their wishes and fears, concerns, fantasies, reenactments and traumatic experiences. The frequency of natural disasters has increased over the last decade. Tsunamis, tornadoes, earthquakes, and hurricanes have ravaged towns, cities, and countries, leaving thousands dead. Beyond the physical injuries suffered, the survivors of these catastrophes, many of them children, often suffer emotional devastation, and profound losses of routines, friends and family, and a sense of security.

Child-centred play therapy empowers children as they lead the play session with a trained adult, assisting them on their journey. This therapy modality allows the child to be in control, which is paramount for those having experienced natural disasters where they were completely helpless. The child may then begin to heal as they make sense of their trauma through their natural language of play. This article provides literature review supporting a case for child-centred play therapy for children experiencing natural disasters as well as recommendations for future research in this area.

It is extremely important to involve parents in assessment and intervention. Psycho-social education of the family members, relatives, significant others and the children involved in the disaster about the manifestations is particularly helpful in the management of post-disaster mental health programme.

Disasters bring together multiple actors who often differ in terms of sector, expertise and nationality, as well as in terms of their abilities, values, norms and goals. Disasters normally associated with massive structural, economic, and population devastation. Research studies and follow-up reported significant mental health distress among the respondents. Disasters have increased in incidence worldwide nowadays and children and adolescents are especially vulnerable as victims.

While all people living in hazard areas are vulnerable, the social impacts of hazard exposure often fall disproportionately on the most vulnerable people in society–the children, elderly, disabled poor and minorities. These groups are often the least prepared for any emergency, have the least resources with which to prepare for a hazard, tend to live in the highest-risk locations in poor housing and lack knowledge or social and political affiliations necessary to take benefit of resources that would make their recovery appropriate, sustainable and in a rapid manner.

It is evident that frequency and intensity of disaster events increase around the globe, children are among those most at risk for the negative effects of disaster. Psychological consequences at early stage could lead to further damage in future life both in the physiological and psychological wellbeing. Disasters lead to stress, physiological deregulation and subsequent illness in children.

Children and adolescents are exposed to traumatic events that lead to physical injury in many cases, psychological perturbation in most cases, and enduring psychological reactions, notably post-traumatic stress disorder, in a minority of individuals. Eight months after the disaster, interaction in the disaster-affected families was characterised by increased levels of conflict, irritability and withdrawal.

This sequence of events can affect later development, learning, emotions, and behaviour. In the process of caring for the physical injury, it is important for the primary care practitioner (PCP) to correctly interpret these presentations and anticipate the need for specific assessments, immediate intervention, referral, and follow-up.

The issue of adjustment becomes an inevitable problem for children in relation to home, school and environment. Anxiety disorders are the most common psychiatric illnesses in children and adolescents. They are associated with significant distress and impairment. Most of the children and adolescents with anxiety disorders are not detected and only a minority receives adequate treatment. Anxious children and adolescents often follow a chronic course of disease with elevated risk of depressive disorders, substance abuse and even suicide. Social withdrawal, self-blaming, and emotional regulation were linked with more severe depressive symptoms.

Disaster intervention calls for both from the top to down and from the bottom up approach. It is noted that most interventions are based on plausible conceptual assumptions, and convergence often can be seen in the content of interventions derived from diverse theoretical perspectives. A school crisis team need to formed comprising school management, teachers, school social workers, parents, students and the local volunteers. These various stake holders would act in co-ordination in identification, rehabilitation and restoration of children which ultimately aimed at reintegration or rejuvenation in a sustainable way.

However, the immediate attention to schools in the aftermath of the disaster and in the long-term reconstruction planning actually created a push to improve the overall quality of education in the affected region. It is true that Psychological First Aid (PFA) is an evidence-informed modular approach for assisting children, adolescents, adults, and families in the immediate aftermath of disaster and terrorism PFA is designed to reduce the initial distress caused by traumatic events, and to foster short and long term adaptive functioning for the victims and survivors.

School-Based Intervention programme becomes crucial and often found successful. It is essential for Teachers to use familiar psycho-educational strategies in a systematic and goal-oriented way, so that the students' psycho-social needs can easily be met. As a consequence, teachers, through their daily interaction with children, can be able to identify those, who despite their psychosocial efforts, still experience distress, and can thus able to refer them to a mental health-care professional and school social workers.

Although children are at special risk in disasters, they are not passive victims. Children and youth can participate in disaster preparedness activities in their homes, schools, and communities that would likely minimise some of the risks that they face including disaster risk reduction information in school curricula is an excellent way to reach children. These children then may communicate risk information to their peers and family members. In order to educate children about disasters and engage them in preparedness activities, age-appropriate materials must be developed and disseminated through various print and electronic media.

The role of school social workers and teachers should undergo mental health training and involve in school and community prevention, mitigation and educational programming. Play therapy interventions such as art therapy, guided imagery and journaling and their ability to provide a sanctuary for children.

The effectiveness of trained volunteer-delivered mental health support for the bereaved persons observed that participants receiving interventions on a regular basis from trained volunteers were less likely to report depressive symptoms and general psychological distress compared with participants who did not receive the above intervention. Role of community in disaster mitigation is proved fruitful to help understand the local culture, traditions, language, belief systems and local livelihood patterns. They also need to integrate with the network of various governmental and non-governmental organisations to cater to the needs of the survivors.

Role of government is crucial in disaster mitigation for providing infrastructural and financial and professional support for the victims. Social capital has an important role for successful policy implementation, which will lead people to utilise government resources to the optimum level for disaster recovery. Follow up is an important phase any programme so as to make the programme a complete one. As after any disaster, many feel the need to share their experiences and feelings with one another, trying to make sense of what has happened and comfort one another as they grief.

With the above backdrop an empirical research is conducted among the disaster victim children belong to the High Schools of Kanyakumari District of Tamil Nadu, India; to assess the mental health, study habit, study involvement, anxiety, depression, and adjustment. It also attempts to test the relationships and associations of variables upon which hypotheses were formed and to make estimates of precision and generality of the findings descriptive design has been drawn.

The universe of the present study consists of 400 students studying eighth, ninth, and tenth standard from the schools in Kanyakumari district during the year 2006-2007 and were affected by tsunami. The four local schools were covered and census method was used to study all the high school students in the universe.

It has been observed that there is a low level of mental health status observed among more than half (57.3 per cent) of the respondents. More than half of the students (53.3 per cent) have low level of study habit. It has been observed a low level of study involvement among (59.3 per cent) of the students.

It is imperative to have these findings in mind:

- There is a high level of anxiety perceived among all the respondents (100 per cent).
- Similarly almost all the respondents (100 per cent) perceive high level of depression.

- Vast majority of the respondents (79.0 per cent) perceive low level of study habits in the dimensions of reading and notes taking
- Absolutely majority of the respondents (79.8 per cent) have low level of involvement. Majority of the respondents (78 per cent) have habit of concentration at low level.
- Majority of the respondents (72.3 per cent) have low-level impact in the dimension of school environment.
- Low level of self-adjustment has been observed among the vast majority of the respondents (72.3 per cent).
- More than half of the respondents (52 per cent) have low level of adjustment.

When analysed the variables in testing the hypothesis it has been proved that there is a significant association between age of the respondents and overall psycho-social impact in all the dimensions namely, mental health, study habit, study involvement, anxiety, depression and overall adjustment. Moreover the study has established that tsunami influenced the mental health of the high school students in a negative way. A careful examination of the data indicates that close to half of the children had poor mental health, all self-reported a high level of anxiety and depression, and more than half had a high level of depression according to a more objective measure. More than half had poor study habits and a majority had low levels of involvement in their studies. In short the mental well-being of the children is highly correlated with their motivation to stay in school and learn their lessons.

It is learnt that any disaster in general and Tsunami in particular has a devastating consequences on the psycho-social wellbeing of the children. The present study reveals that nearly majority of the high school students have low level of mental health status due to devastating impact of tsunami, it affected the study habit and study involvement of children. Mental well being of the children is directly correlated wherein the child is motivated to stay and learn in the school. Since the schools lack any School Social Workers in Tamil Nadu state; Policy decisions need to be taken to appoint School Social Workers so that the social worker can arrange for mental health programme to bringing about positive mental well being in children as well as providing experience that will strengthen children's coping abilities to address the environmental stressors and disadvantages in future.

It is significant to help these children recover from all these psycho-social implications so that the mental well being could be achieved. Schools provide convenient access to children and families in a developmentally appropriate environment. School personnel are a natural source of support for children and classrooms provide formal and informal opportunities for assessing and addressing psychological responses and for correcting misperceptions of the students.

It has been strongly suggested that school-based programmes can normalise the trauma experience and minimise the stigma associated with mental healthcare. The structure and routine of school are important aspects of the recovery environment for children. The various stakeholders such as parents, teachers, school authorities, social workers, health personnel, etc need to be coordinated for a concerted effort to build a very conducive environment for the children to grow in overall development.

Schools play very crucial role in building one's self esteem and a sense of competence. A Social Work Intervention need to be initiated at the school level as the child's life has profound impact on child's overall growth and development. Large number of children attends school at least in early childhood.

Employing Social Work Methods such as Case work to intervene with psychological problems of the tsunami affected children. Individual counselling should be to remove them from grief. Group work should be used for recreational purpose and educating them. Through community organisation problems awareness can be created about the precautionary measures they have take at the time of disaster. Disaster management can also be another ingredient. Social workers should be appointed on full time basis to mould the personality of the tsunami affected children. A wide publicity of government schemes for the welfare of children in particular should be made through mass media. Crisis intervention for victims of disaster is of paramount importance. The goal of such intervention is to help victims confront the reality of what happened; begin to deal with the crisis, and to go beyond the pain and emotional trauma toward new strength and opportunities for growth and change. There are avenues for future research to undertake a macro study at metropolis level among the children those who became orphan children due to tsunami and other major disaster.

Based on these findings it is strongly recommended that school social work need to be given importance and in each and every school a professional social worker need to be appointed to enhance the psycho-social well being of the children, to provide crisis counselling, crisis intervention and problem solving counselling; family life education, family counselling and mental health programmes in order to rejuvenate the disaster children in to the community.

It is concluded that there is a need school-based intervention team comprising various stakeholders such as teachers, parents, students, management and the community. The high risk factors need to be identified for taking appropriate preventive measures. The rescue, treatment and rehabilitation groups need to be made available and readily accessible when any disaster taking place. The updating of Disaster Mitigation Information System with latest technology and design having networking with various agencies both national and international is crucial and compulsory.

The psycho-social needs of the children- most of the time neglected population either pre- and post-disaster period; should be given utmost importance. Care should also be given to promote appropriate and relevant rejuvenation measures in order to make the children population as the assets of future nation. There is a greater need for the role of NGO's, Government Development Departments, International Development Initiatives, Role of Professional Social Workers, Disaster Mitigation personnel and various stakeholders in prevention, rescue and rejuvenation strategies.

Chapter - 1

Disaster Patterns and Devastation

Disaster–Meaning and Definition

WHO (2002) defines disaster as any occurrence that causes damage, ecological disruption, loss of human life, deterioration of health and health services and on a scale sufficient to warrant an extraordinary response from outside. Centre for Research on the Epidemiology of Disasters (CRED) (2005), defines disaster as a situation or event which overwhelms local capacity, necessitating a request to national and international level for external assistance, an unforeseen and often sudden event that cause great damage, destruction and human suffering.

According to Disaster Management Act, 2005; Disaster is a catastrophe, mishap, calamity or grave occurrence in any area, arising from natural or man-made causes or by accident or negligence which results insubstantial loss of life or human suffering or damage to, and destruction of property or damage/degradation of environment and is of such a nature or magnitude as to be beyond the coping capacity of the community or the affected area (NDMA, 2012).

Thus, Disasters can be understood in different ways:

- A disaster is an overwhelming ecological disruption occurring on a scale sufficient to require outside assistance.
- A disaster is an event located in time and space which produces conditions whereby the continuity of structure and process of social units becomes problematic.
- It is an event or series of events which seriously disrupts normal activities.

Disasters, cause huge loss of life, economic loss and makes the community function with less effectiveness. Countries including developed, developing and underdeveloped countries, faced disaster, either natural or man-made and has come across a huge loss in term of human and economic loss (CRED, 2005).

Disaster–Patterns

Generally, disasters are of two types–**Natural** and **Man-made**. Based on the devastation, these are further classified into major/minor natural disaster and major/minor man-made disasters.

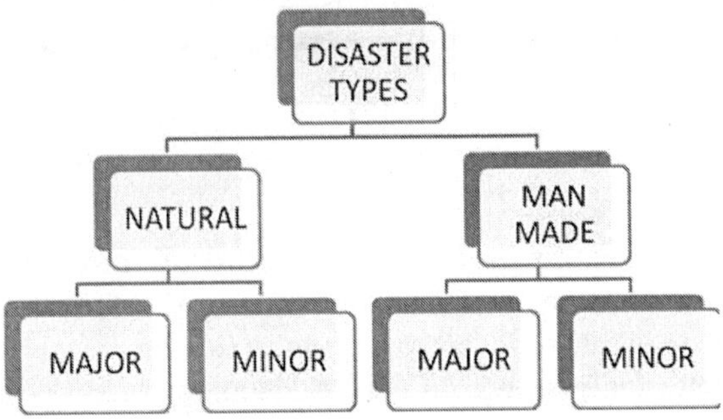

Chart – 1: Disaster Types.

For more than a century researchers have been studying disasters and for more than forty years disaster research has been institutionalised through the Disaster Research Centre. The studies reflect a common opinion when they argue that all disasters can be seen as being human-made, their reasoning being that human actions before the strike of the hazard can prevent it developing into a disaster. All disasters are hence the result of human failure to introduce appropriate disaster management measures. Hazards are routinely divided into natural or human-made, although complex disasters, where there is no single root cause, are more common in developing countries. A specific disaster may spawn a secondary disaster that increases the impact. A classic example is an earthquake that causes a tsunami, resulting in coastal flooding (DRC, 2014).

Natural Disaster Types

It is reported that natural disasters are sub-divided into hydro-meteorological (earthquakes, volcanic eruptions) and geo-physical (avalanches', landslides, droughts, famines, extreme temperatures, floods, forest, windstorms, waves surges) categories, to emphasise the effect on the decade's disasters of the global warming. Today the definition of non-natural

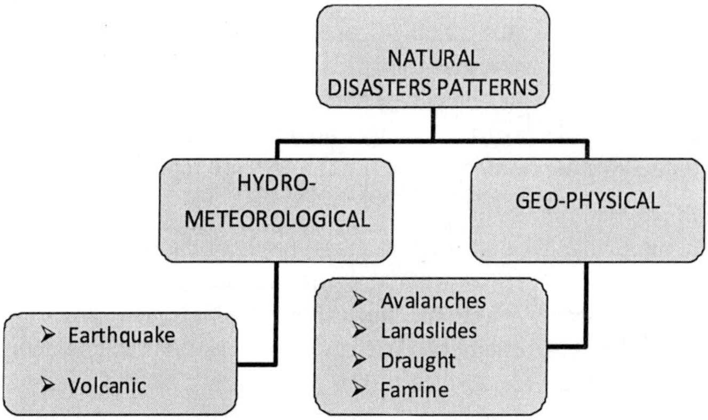

Chart – 2: Natural Disaster Patterns.

(or human-made) disasters has widened to include conflicts, riots, fires, industrial and chemical accidents, building collapses, mass dislocation due to political unrest, insurgency and epidemics such as water-borne diseases, malaria, plague, and so on (IFRC, 2001).

Types of Disaster

It is immaterial that whether a disaster is a natural or man-made but it negatively affects life, property, livelihood or industry often resulting in permanent changes to human societies, ecosystems and environment. Disasters manifest as hazards exacerbating vulnerable conditions and exceeding individuals' and communities' means to survive and thrive. The disasters listed below are compiled from United States Federal Emergency Management Agency and Department of Homeland Security.

Natural Disasters

Planet Earth is our home in space. It is a planet of continuous changes that started billions of years ago and that will continue for billions of years to come. Our vehicle-in-space, this-earth, is restless and in continuous motion.

Most of the great earth changes take place along the interfaces between the lithosphere, hydrosphere, and atmosphere. Two major earth cycles, the petrogenic, or rock cycle, and the hydrologic cycle are operating at the earth's surface. The processes that have taken place during the long history of our Earth, and most of the changes near its surface, come from interactions involving great amounts of matter and energy. The energy either comes from the sun or from processes occurring within the earth.

To understand the earth's changes, one has to understand something about our planet, such as its size, mass, shape, and composition. To understand its evolution, that need to understand the physical laws that govern its behaviour; fortunately, most of the earth's changes are more or less continuous and not catastrophic. Furthermore, many of the changes are repetitive or cyclical in nature.

The rapid changes that occur at inter-phases of the planet which affect the safety and property is termed as natural disasters. These include earthquakes, volcanic eruptions, hurricanes, tsunamis, sea surges, floods, droughts, and other phenomena which are manifestations of interactions of mass and energy on the surface of our planet. Such natural disasters are inevitable because they are beyond the control and thus cannot be prevented (Ready.gov/Natural Disasters, 2013).

Understanding natural disasters can often help mitigate their effects, thus preserving life and property. Some of the changes that take place on our earth, like the rising and erosion of mountains, are very slow, taking millions

Chart – 3: Natural Disaster Types.

of years. Others, like the sudden appearance of storms, are rapid by comparison. The tectonic movements responsible for earthquakes are sudden and unpredictable changes, which are usually catastrophic, particularly if they occur in densely populated regions of our planet. Hurricanes, storms, tsunamis, volcanic eruptions, floods and numerous other hazards are also unpredictable changes that can result in loss of life and destruction to property (www.library.thinkquest.org).

A Natural phenomenon can easily turn into a natural disaster. Appearing to arise without direct human involvement, natural disasters are sometimes called an act of God. A natural disaster may become more severe because of human actions prior, during or after the disaster itself. A specific disaster may spawn different types of events and may reduce the survivability of the initial event. A classic example, is an earthquake that collapses homes, trapping people and breaking gas mains that then ignite, and burn people alive while trapped under debris. Human activity in risk areas may cause natural disasters. Volcanos are particularly prone to causing other events like fires, lahars, mudflows, landslides, earthquakes, and tsunamis.

Avalanche

An avalanche is a slippage of built-up snow down an incline, possibly mixed with ice, rock, soil or plant life in what is called a debris avalanche. Avalanches are categorised as either slab or powder avalanches. Avalanches are a major danger in the mountains during the winter as a large one can run for miles, and can create massive destruction of the lower forest and anything else in its path. For example, in Montroc, France, in 1999, 300,000 cubic metres of snow slid on a 30 degree slope, achieving a speed of 100 km/h. It killed 12 people in their chalets under 100,000 tons of snow, 5 meters deep. The Mayor of Chamonix was charged with manslaughter.

Extreme Cold

Extreme cold snaps are hazardous to humans and their livestock. In a 2003 Mongolian cold snap, almost 30,000 livestock animals perished due to excessive snow and cold. When the temperature drops, caloric intake must increase to maintain body heat to for shivering.

Disease

Disease becomes a disaster when it spreads in a pandemic or epidemic as a massive outbreak of an infectious agent. Disease is historically the most dangerous of all natural disasters. Different epidemics are caused by different diseases, and different epidemics have included the Black Death, smallpox, and AIDS. The Spanish flu of 1918 was the deadliest ever epidemic, it killed 25-40 million people. The Black Death, which occurred in the 14th Century, killed over 20 million people, one-third of Europe's population. Plant and animal life may also be affected by disease epidemics and pandemics.

Drought

A drought is a long-lasting weather pattern consisting of dry conditions with very little or no precipitation. During this period, food and water supplies can run low, and other conditions, such as famine, can result. Droughts can last for several years and are particularly damaging in areas in which the residents depend on agriculture for survival. The Dust Bowl is a famous example of a severe drought.

Earthquake

An earthquake is a sudden shift or movement in the tectonic plate in the Earth's crust. On the surface, this is manifested by a moving and shaking of the ground, and can be massively damaging to poorly built structures. The most powerful earthquakes can destroy even the best built of structures. In addition, they can trigger secondary disasters, such as tsunamis and volcanic eruptions. Earthquakes occur along fault lines, and are unpredictable. They are capable of killing hundreds of thousands of people, such as in the 1976 Tangshan and 2004 Indian Ocean earthquakes.

Famine

Famine is a natural disaster characterised by a widespread lack of food in a region, and can be characterised as a lack of agriculture foodstuffs, a lack of livestock, or a general lack of all foodstuffs required for basic nutrition and survival. Famine is almost always caused by pre-existing conditions, such as drought, but its effects may be exacerbated by social factors, such as war. Particularly devastating examples include the Ethiopian famine and the Irish Potato Famine.

Fire

A fire is a natural disaster that may destroy ecosystems like grasslands, forests causing great loss of life, property, livestock and wildlife. Bush fires, forest fires and mine fires are generally started by lightning, but also by human negligence or arson, and can burn thousands of square kilometers. An example of a severe forest fire is the Oakland Hills firestorm. A mine fire started in Centralia, Pennsylvania in 1962 decimated the town and continues to burn. Some of the biggest city fires are The Great Chicago Fire, The Great Fire of London, and The San Francisco Fire.

Flood

A flood is a natural disaster caused by too much rain or water in a location, and could be caused by many different sets of conditions. Floods can be caused by prolonged rainfall from a storm, including thunderstorms, rapid melting of large amounts of snow, or rivers which swell from excess precipitation upstream and cause widespread damage to areas downstream, or less frequently the bursting of man-made dams. A river which floods particularly often is the Huang He in China, and a particularly damaging flood was the Great Flood of 1993.

Hail

A hailstorm is a natural disaster where a thunderstorm produces a numerous amount of hailstones which damage the location in which they fall. Hailstorms can be especially devastating to farm fields, ruining crops and damaging equipment. A particularly damaging hailstorm hit Munich, Germany on August 31, 1986, felling thousands of trees and causing millions of dollars in insurance claims. Skeleton Lake was named so after 300-600 people were killed by a hailstorm.

Heat

A heat wave is a disaster characterised by heat which is considered extreme and unusual in the area in which it occurs. Heat waves are rare and require specific combinations of weather events to take place, and may include temperature inversions, katabatic winds, or other phenomena. The worst heat wave in recent history was the European Heat Wave of 2003.

Hurricane

A hurricane is a low-pressure cyclonic storm system which forms over the oceans. It is caused by evaporated water which comes off of the ocean and becomes a storm. The Coriolis Effect causes the storms to spin, and a hurricane is declared when this spinning mass of storms attains a wind speed greater than 74 mph. In different parts of the world hurricanes are known as cyclones or typhoons. The former occur in the Indian Ocean, while the latter occur in the Eastern Pacific Ocean. The most damaging hurricane in the United States was Hurricane Katrina, which hit the United States Gulf Coast in 2005.

Impact Event

Impact events are caused by the collision of large meteoroids, asteroids or comets (generically: bolides) with Earth and may sometimes be followed by mass extinctions of life. The magnitude of the disaster is inversely proportional to its rate of occurrence.

Landslide

A landslide is a disaster closely related to an avalanche, but instead of occurring with snow, it occurs involving actual elements of the ground, including rocks, trees, parts of houses, and anything else which may happen to be swept up. Landslides can be caused by earthquakes, volcanic eruptions, or general instability in the surrounding land. Mudslides, or mud flows, are a special case of landslides, in which heavy rainfall causes loose soil on steep terrain to collapse and slide downwards-these occur with some regularity in parts of California after periods of heavy rain.

Mudslide

A mudslide is a slippage of mud because of poor drainage of rainfall through soil. An underlying cause is often deforestation or lack of vegetation. Some mudslides are massive and can decimate large areas. On January 10, 2005 at 1: 20 pm in La Conchita, a massive mudslide buried four blocks of the town in over 30 feet of earth. Ten people were killed by the slide and 14 were injured. Of the 166 homes in the community, fifteen were destroyed and 16 more were tagged by the county as uninhabitable.

Sink Hole

A sinkhole is a localised depression in the surface topography, usually caused by the collapse of a subterranean structure, such as a cave. Although rare, large sinkholes that develop suddenly in populated areas can lead to the collapse of buildings and other structures.

Solar Flare

A solar flare is a violent explosion in the Sun's atmosphere with an energy equivalent to tens of millions of hydrogen bombs. Solar flares take place in the solar corona and chromospheres, heating the gas to tens of millions of Kelvin and accelerating electrons, protons and heavier ions to near the speed of light. They produce electromagnetic radiation across the spectrum at all wavelengths from long-wave radio signals to the shortest wavelength gamma rays. Solar flare emissions are a danger to orbiting satellites, manned space missions, communications systems, and power grid systems.

Storm Surge

A storm surge is an onshore rush of water associated with a low pressure weather system, typically a tropical cyclone. Storm surge is caused primarily by high winds pushing on the ocean's surface. The wind causes the water to pile up higher than the ordinary sea level. Storm surges are particularly damaging when they occur at the time of a high tide, combining the effects of the surge and the tide. The highest storm surge ever recorded was produced by the 1899 Bathurst Bay Hurricane, which caused a 13 m (43 feet) storm surge at Bathurst Bay, Australia. In the US, the greatest recorded storm surge was generated by Hurricane Camille, which produced a storm surge in excess of 25 feet (7.6 m).

Thunderstorm

A thunderstorm is a form of severe weather characterised by the presence of lightning and its attendant thunder, often accompanied by copious rainfall, hail and on occasion snowfall and tornadoes.

Tornado

A tornado is a natural disaster resulting from a thunderstorm. Tornadoes are violent currents of wind which can blow at up to 318 mph. Tornadoes can occur one at a time, or can occur in large tornado outbreaks along a squall line. The worst tornado ever recorded in terms of wind speed was the tornado which swept through Moore, Oklahoma on May 3, 1999. This tornado had wind speeds of 318 mph and was the strongest ever recorded.

Tsunami

A tsunami is a giant wave of water which rolls into the shore of an area with a height of over 15 m (50 ft). It comes from Japanese words meaning harbour and wave. Tsunamis can be caused by undersea earthquakes as in the 2004 Indian Ocean Earthquake, or by landslides such as the one which occurred at Lituya Bay, Alaska. The tsunami generated by the 2004 Indian Ocean Earthquake currently ranks as the deadliest tsunami in recorded history.

Volcanic Eruption

This natural disaster is caused by the eruption of a volcano, and eruptions come in many forms. They range from daily small eruptions which occur in places; like Kilauea, in Hawaii, or extremely infrequent supervolcano eruptions in places like Lake Toba. Recent large volcanic eruptions include that of Mount St. Helens and Krakatoa, occurring in 1980 and 1883, respectively.

Winter Storm

A snowstorm is a winter storm in which the primary form of precipitation is snow. When such a storm is accompanied by winds above 32 mph that severely reduce visibility, it becomes a blizzard. Hazards from snowstorms and blizzards include traffic-related accidents, hypothermia for those unable to find shelter, as well as major disruptions to transportation and fuel and power distribution systems.

Natural Disasters in Oceania

Oceania is a very large region which is difficult to define geographically. It encompasses a very large area of the Pacific. The Pacific Ocean has more islands than the rest of the oceans and seas combined. On a global scale the Pacific Ocean and adjoining seas cover approximately one-third of the earth's surface, or about 70 million square miles. The total area is more than all the land masses of the world combined (www.preventionweb.org).

Anthropologists have defined Oceania as that region of the Pacific Ocean that encompasses three distinct geographical areas - Polynesia, meaning "many islands"; Micronesia, meaning "small islands"; and Melanesia, meaning "black islands." Based on racial migrations, their definition of Oceania includes Papua-New Guinea, Australia and New Zealand, but not Indonesia which has West Iran, the other half of Papua-New Guinea. By that definition, Indonesia and the Philippine islands are not included. Neither are included other countries bordering the Pacific and the Inland seas. However, among the countries of the Pacific, United States of America is considered to be part of Oceania because of its possession of the Hawaiian Islands and other islands in the Pacific. For similar reasons, France, United Kingdom, Ecuador, and Chile are designated as countries of Oceania.

Such an anthropological definition falls short in permitting the description and impact of natural hazards in this large area of the world. Natural disasters do not recognise anthropological definitions of boundaries of geography. A large earthquake in Chile or Peru could generate a tsunami which can be catastrophic in the Hawaiian Islands or in New Zealand. A hurricane generated off the coast of Mexico could affect other areas of Oceania. A catastrophic eruption of a volcano in Indonesia, could affect global climate.

An earthquake along the Sunda Trench could generate a catastrophic tsunami that could affect Australia (www.preventionweb.org). Thus, the following countries that border the Pacific Ocean and the adjacent inland seas south of Latitude 25 North: Australia (Tasmania), Chile (Easter Island), Colombia, Cook Islands, Costa Rica, Guatemala, Ecuador, El Salvador, Federated States of Micronesia, Fiji, France (French Polynesia, New Caledonia, Wallis Island, Futuna), Indonesia (West Iran), Kiribati, Malaysia, Marshall Islands, Nauru, New Zealand (Tokelau), Nicaragua, Niue, Palau, Panama, Papua-New Guinea, Peoples Republic of China, Peru, Philippine Islands, Republic of China (Taiwan), Solomon Islands, Tonga, Tuvalu, United Kingdom (Hong Kong, Pitcairn Island), USA (American Samoa, Guam, Hawaii, Northern Marianas),Vanuatu, Vietnam, and Western Samoa.

Oceania, or the area, is of concern to us because it covers such a large area of the world where we have the highest diversity and highest frequency of all types of natural disasters known to man: Among them some of the most catastrophic disasters are:

- Earthquakes
- Hurricanes
- Tornadoes
- Floods

- Droughts
- Fires
- Landslides
- Volcanic explosions
- Tsunamis

In Oceania, it have the highest diversity and highest frequency of all types of natural disasters known to man such as earthquakes, hurricanes, tornadoes, floods, droughts, fires, landslides, volcanic explosions, and tsunamis. In this section only the major hazards are discussed which that have resulted in loss of life and destruction to property (George Pararas-Carayannis, 2003).

Earthquakes

Earthquakes are inevitable forces of nature which mark a continuous adjustment of the thin and unstable crust of the Earth. Considering the size of the Earth and the thickness of the mantle, the Earth's crust is indeed a thin skin of rock. Underneath the oceans the crust is labeled as oceanic and has an average thickness of about six kilometers. The continental crust (under the continents) is lighter in weight and has a more complicated structure and variable composition because of sediments, mountains, and highly folded layers of material. Crustal material beneath the surface of the earth is also moved, dented, and broken by deformations and changes that take place.

Most of the Earth's great earthquakes occur along the boundaries of oceanic and continental crusts. The downward deflection of the oceanic crust along the boundaries of great crustal plates is called subduction zones and is the regions of extremely destructive earthquakes.

Often these movements may not involve subduction of crustal material, but only lateral movements with practically none or very little vertical movement of the crust. In such instances there is no extensive destruction of the plate material, but simply a gliding of one plate in relation to another. Sometimes the rocks break and slip rapidly, from sudden releases of energy that accumulate in the rocks for many years. These sudden tectonic movements can produce large earthquakes which can be very violent and can cause enormous destruction, particularly if they occur in heavily populated areas.

Around the Pacific Ocean, there is the "Ring of Fire" which is essentially a series of continuous boundaries of oceanic and continental plates where active breaking of the earth's crust occur causing earthquakes. Important plates interacting in the region are defined as Oceania as the South American Plate, the Nasca Plate, the Pacific Plate, and the Philippine Plate. There are a number of many smaller plates in the inland seas that surround the region of Oceania. Many countries in Oceania have been affected by catastrophic earthquakes throughout recorded history. These include the countries of Chile, Peru, Ecuador, Colombia, Central America, Mexico, Philippines, Guam, Republic of China, People's Republic of China, Marianas, Indonesia, Papua-New Guinea, Solomon Islands, Vanuatu, New Zealand, Australia and other regions that border chains of volcanic islands in the Pacific.

Tsunami

The tsunami is a series of ocean waves of very great length and period generated by impulsive disturbances of the earth's crust. Large earthquakes with epicenters under or near the ocean are the cause of the most catastrophic tsunami. Volcanic eruptions and submarine landslides are also responsible for tsunami generation but their effects are usually localised. Although infrequent, tsunami waves are among the most terrifying and complex physical phenomena and have been responsible for great loss of life and destruction of property in Oceania.

Tsunami waves, once generated, travel in all directions at great speeds. Their speed is controlled by the depth of the water. In the deeper parts of the Ocean, the mean velocity of tsunami waves is approximately 700 km/h or 430 mph. These waves cannot be noticed out at sea because of their great wavelengths which may be 200 km or more. They can travel across great expanses of ocean with no loss of energy. When they get close to a coastline, these waves can reach gigantic proportions and can become extremely destructive. Tsunami waves can attain heights of as much as 30 m or 100 ft and may inundate extensive portions of coastlines, particularly those low in elevation.

Volcanic Eruptions

Volcanic eruptions in Oceania are among the greatest of the natural hazards and occur with frequency every few years. Of all the volcanic eruptions in recent history, the most catastrophic have occurred in the Indonesian region. Best known are the great Krakatau eruption in August of 1883, in the Sunda Strait of Indonesia, and the 1815 eruption of Tambora in the same country. The Krakatau eruption resulted in the ejection of about 15-20 cubic km of volcanic material, and the collapse of the caldera. As reported previously, the caldera collapse resulted in a tremendous thirty meter high tsunami wave which killed 36,500 people along the neighbouring coasts of Java and Sumatra.

The 1815 eruption of Tambora resulted in the discharge of almost 100 cubic Km of tephra. A catastrophic tsunami also resulted in killing thousands of people. The volcanic eruption and the tsunami were responsible for the loss of 92,000 people. The depth of ash deposited by this eruption 150 km away was in the order of half a meter.

The greatest volcanic disaster in recent geologic history, in the region, occurred in the Quaternary period of Ice Age, approximately 75,000 years ago. This volcanic explosion devastated the centre of the island of Sumatra. The volume of tephra discharge from this eruption is estimated at 2,000 cubic km, a tremendous quantity considering that the Krakatau catastrophic eruption of 1883 only resulted in 15-20 cubic km of ejected tephra. The collapse crater - the caldera; formed by this giant eruption which must have lasted for several months or even years are filled presently with the waters of Lake Toba on that island.

Fortunately, events of such magnitude as the eruption of Krakatau, or Tambora are relatively rare. Their return periods are infrequent and can be estimated statistically. Volcanic eruptions of the Krakatau magnitude can be expected somewhere in the world, every 300-400 years. Eruptions of the Tambora magnitude may be expected once every 2,000 years. As for the prehistoric event that formed the caldera which is now lake Toba, judging by its tremendous size and the amount of ejected material, a return period of once every 80,000 years can be estimated.

Hurricanes and Storms

Hurricanes

When winds of tropical cyclones in the Atlantic Ocean and the north-east Pacific, reach velocities of hurricane force (64 knots, 73 mph, 118 km/hr, Beauford 12), then these tropical cyclones are called hurricanes. In the Indian Ocean and in the seas around Australia, hurricanes are called "cyclones." In the West Pacific, they are called "typhoons." No matter by what name they go, such tropical cyclones can be extremely catastrophic. If tropical cyclones do not reach hurricane force, and stay below that threshold (39-73 mph, to 63-118 km/h, Bauford 8-11), they are called tropical storms.

Hurricanes - a violent, tropical cyclonic storm, especially of the W North Atlantic, having wind speeds of or in excess of 74 mph. Hurricanes, Cyclones, and Typhoons all have the same characteristics, but they have different names where they appear:

- Hurricanes-North Atlantic Ocean
- Cyclones-Indian Ocean
- Typhoons-Pacific Ocean

Hurricanes, Typhoons, and Cyclones are one of nature's most powerful forces. They are all tropical storms whose winds reach around 74 miles per hour or even more. Their wind blows in a spiral direction around a relatively calm area known as "The Eye." The eye is usually 20 to 30 miles wide. The most violent activity takes place in the area immediately around the eye, called

"The Eye wall." As the hurricane approaches, the sky begins to darken, and the wind gets stronger. As it nears lands, it may bring torrential rain, storm surges, and very high winds. One hurricane can last for more than two weeks in open waters. The heavy rain brought by a hurricane not only threatens coastal areas, but it also hits areas hundreds of miles inland. In some cases, flooding occurs days after a storm actually hits shore.

Months when it occurs include: August and September are the peak months during hurricane season. Hurricane season is between June 1st and November 30th. The name Hurricane was applied to migratory tropical cyclones. They originate over oceans in certain regions near the equator, and particularly to those arising in the West Indian region, including the Caribbean Sea and the Gulf of Mexico. In the North Pacific and Philippines area are "typhoons" while in the Indian and South Pacific Ocean are "cyclones."

Storms

Because of their high frequency and wide distribution, storms are the most significant of the natural hazards in Oceania. Storms are seasonal in nature and include extra tropical (winter) storms and monsoon storms, as well as thunderstorms. They can result in numerous other natural hazards such as flush floods and landslides', squalls, floods, lightning, and tornadoes.

Thunderstorms

Thunderstorms are among the most significant natural hazards in Oceania and adjacent areas. They may occur frequently anywhere within the region. Under extreme circumstances thunderstorms involve heavy rainfall of up to 30 mm per minute, 200 mm in 15 minutes and 600 mm in 3 hours. Such heavy rainfall often may cause heavy flooding in valleys or other topographic depressions. Fortunately, heavy precipitation is usually localised.

Normally a loud crack of thunder is heard after that seen a flash of lightning. Many people don't know how the thunder sound is heard. When lightning strikes the air around it quickly heats to 43,000 degrees, causing the air around it to expand. Then it quickly cools causing the air to contract quickly. The rapid expansion and contraction causes air molecules to move back and forth, creating the noise-thunder.

Each day over 40,000 thunderstorms are taking place on earth. In reality, thunderstorms are the cause of most natural disasters. The lightning they create can result in death and injury and create forest fires. Thunderstorms also create damaging hail, heavy rains, which result in flash, strong downbursts of wind (or very strong winds coming from showers and thunderstorms), including microburst and tornadoes. They even contribute in the formation of hurricanes by several large thunderstorms fusing together.

Typical thunderstorms produce a down pour of rain and can last anywhere from a half-hour to an hour, but if a thunderstorm develops into a more powerful storm, such as a squall line or a super cell they can last for hours. Some storms, called dry thunderstorms which do not produce rain, however, and are often responsible for wildfires.

A thunderstorm is created by warm air rises (this is called an updraft) and condenses into a cumulus cloud. As more warm air collects the cumulus cloud will continue to grow. Soon the water droplets forming in the cloud will become too heavy for the rising air to hold. While this is happening cold air, which is heavier than warm air, starts entering the cloud. The cold air starts to lower beneath the warm (this is called a down draft), pulling the heavy water downwards, resulting in rain. The storm at this point has become a cumulonimbus cloud. Once lightning and thunder starts to occur, it becomes a thunderstorm.

Lightning

Lightning, an electrical discharge, which is released from mature clouds, is an exciting and even beautiful natural phenomenon with many different forms, shapes, and colours. Every minute of every day 1,800 thunderstorms are taking place somewhere on the earth, releasing around 100 lightning bolts apiece. During these storms, it is likely that one person out of every 700,000 will be struck by lightning.

A single lightning bolt is very powerful, releasing enough energy to light a 100-watt light bulb for more than three months. This electrical surge is created by a buildup and discharge of positively charged and negatively charged electrical energy. Air rising and descending from the thunderstorm and water and ice particles separate the positively charged areas and the negatively charged areas. The lightning strike begins as an invisible channel of electrically charged air trying to get to the ground. Then a surge of electricity from the ground moves upwards, creating a lightning strike. Lightning comes in many forms such as:

- Forked Lightning
- Streak Lightning
- Sheet Lightning
- Heat Lightning
- Ball Lightning
- Saint Elmo's Fire
- High-altitude Lightning.

Flush Floods and Landslides

Flush floods and landslides are often the byproduct of such thunderstorms and are common in many areas of Oceania. The strong vertical winds of thunderstorms often can generate hail and lightning. Although lightning is characteristic of virtually every thunderstorm, hail is a less frequent phenomenon, occurring only 10-15 per cent of the time. Both hail and lightning are natural hazards of importance, posing threat to life and property. Historically, both, lightning and hail have been significant hazards to aviation, causing serious disasters. Thunderstorms can be a particularly significant hazard in arid areas and desserts. Because the dried hardened soil of such areas will not allow the rainwater to seep in, extensive and destructive flooding in such areas may occur.

Lahars

Lahar is a term that describes a hot or cold mixture of water and rock fragments flowing down the slopes of a volcano and/or river valleys. When moving, a lahars looks like a collection of wet concrete that carries rock debris ranging in size from gravel to boulders. When lahars rushes downstream from a volcano, the size, speed, and the amount of water and rock debris it carries is always changing. The starting surge of debris erodes rocks and plant life from the side of the volcano or mountain. Lahars can also carry part of a mountain, water, and snow and ice, which can overflow the rivers. By picking up debris as they go downhill, lahars can grow to over 10 times their own size. As lahars moves away from a volcano or mountain, it starts to size down.

Lahars cause serious economic and environmental damage. They can level anything in their path. Buildings can be crushed and completely ruined. Lahars can shear off hills or anything else in their path. The aftermath of lahars is burial of the city or wildlife. Stones, boulders, tree trunks, and building rubble are picked up on the way. Mudflows, a type of Lahar, are often more powerful that rivers, killing thousands of people and causing enormous amounts of damage over a large area. After the mud sets it becomes as hard as concrete.

Drought

Drought is a period of dry weather, especially a long one that is injurious to crops, animals and human beings. There are four different types of drought. They are meteorological, agricultural, hydrological, and socioeconomic.

(a) **Meteorological-**Meteorological drought type is caused from the departure of rain and other usual precipitation for a certain geographical area.

(b) **Agricultural-**Agricultural drought happens when the amount of moisture in the soil does not meet the needs of a regional crop or plant.

(c) **Hydrological**-Hydrological drought happens when surface and subsurface water supplies are below the normal amount of water.

(d) **Socio-economic**- Socio-economic drought happens when a physical water shortage affects the public. It is important to learn how to be safe during a period of drought or when the temperature has become dangerously high.

Squalls

Gail force winds, associated with squalls represent other significant hazards of thunderstorms in Oceania. Squalls usually mark the foremost boundary of an approaching thunderstorm front. They can be visually recognised from a great distance, as they are associated with heavy rainfall. Hail or heavy rainfall which often occur at the same time, increase the potential for damage of the strong squalls.

Avalanches

A rise in temperature or an earthquake may loosen the snow causing it to give way, or because a new fall of heavy snow. The layers of the snow are a way to predict if an avalanche could fall soon or if an avalanche will not be able to stir up. The snow on the surface begins to slide from a single point, collecting more snow as it moves, and widening out into a triangular shape, creating what is commonly called a slough. Once the avalanches start, they are capable of snapping the tops off trees and destroying everything in their path. When the snow falls to the ground and it is at the foot of the hill, the snow hardens giving someone who is trapped under the great amounts of snow a slim chance of survival.

Tornadoes

Tornadoes usually affect a very small area but develop extremely high forces on their path which can be devastating in terms of losses of life and property, if they occur in a highly populated region. They can occur more frequently over large land areas, but tornado like funnels have also been observed over ocean regions. The average diameter of the funnel of a tornado may be approximately 100 meters, and its mean length of path only a few kilometers. However tornadoes with a funnel of as much as 1,000 meter wide, and paths of 300 km long have been reported. At the edge of the funnel of a hurricane, winds of maximum velocity of more than 400 km/h (250 mph) can be generated, and such winds can cause massive destruction even to substantial buildings. Within the funnel of a tornado there may be a reduction in atmospheric pressure of as much as 90 per cent, which will cause glass windows and glass fronted structures to explode, adding to the damage of the hazard.

Tornadoes usually occur over land masses at latitudes ranging between 20 to 60 degrees, north, or south. They are associated with local thunderstorms cells that usually occur in spring or summer. There is no accurate historical record of tornadoes in Oceania, other than in Australia, where damaging tornadoes have been reported. Fortunately, tornadoes do not occur with a great deal of frequency in Oceania. A tornado is a violently rotating column of air extending from a thunderstorm to the ground.

Tornadoes form in a severe thunderstorm called a super cell. In a super cell an updraft can cause wind to rotate horizontally inside the cloud. As the wind speed increases within the storm the updraft blows harder forcing the wind to start rotating vertically. The area of the storms rotation spreads about 2-6 miles wide. It's in this area that a funnel starts to form inside the cloud and because of the winds low air pressure, more air can get sucked into the funnel faster. As the funnel grows larger it can hit the ground and move around on it, while it's still attached to the super cell. The new tornadoes winds can reach speeds from 70 miles per hour to 250 miles per hour.

Tornadoes can basically be categorised into three groups, which are weak tornadoes, strong tornadoes and violent tornadoes. Eighty-eight per cent of tornadoes that hit the ground are weak tornadoes, which only cause five per cent of tornado related deaths. Weak tornadoes usually last for 1 to 10 minutes, but they have been known to last longer, with a wind speed of less than 110 miles per hour. 11 per cent of tornadoes are strong tornadoes. These can last up to 20 minutes or longer and can have winds that are 110-205 miles per hour. Almost 30 per cent of all tornado related deaths are caused by strong tornadoes. Only 1 per cent of tornadoes are violent tornadoes, but 70 per cent of all tornado related deaths are cause by these. Violent tornadoes can last up to one hour or longer and reach winds greater than 205 miles per hour.

Floods

Floods are a significant natural hazard for many regions of Oceania. They are usually associated with rainstorms and hurricanes. Floods kill an average of 140 people a year, making them the leading cause of deaths associated with thunderstorms. Most of these deaths are caused at night, when it may be harder to notice high waters and more confusing for the victim. There are many ways for people to stay safe during a flood, however, and many ways for people to prepare themselves before a flood.

Many factors can affect the way that floods develop. These include deep snow cover, frozen ground, wet soil, high rivers and streams, ice covered rivers, and heavy rain. During a thunderstorm, large quantities of deep snow can affect floods by melting into more water while it is raining heavily. Frozen ground adds to flood development by not allowing water and snow to sink into the ground. If soil is already wet, a large amount of water rising quickly does not allow the ground to absorb more water and excess water pours into rivers and stream, causing them to overflow.

Rivers that are already full of water can overflow easily, which can flood areas around the river. Another common factor in flood development is layers of ice floating on top of a river breaking apart and floating downstream. When this happens, it is common for the sheets of ice to clog up at bridges and other obstacles in the river, which can create a dam. If a dam does form, then water can rise rapidly, causing areas around it to be flooded. A factor that affects all flood formation is heavy rainfall. Heavy rain combined with the above factors can cause large areas to be covered in a layer of water that is dangerously high. Only six inches of floodwater can knock a person off their feet and only two feet of water can lift most cars.

Chart – 4: Man-made Disaster.

Man-made Disasters

Disasters caused by human action, negligence, error, or involving the failure of a system are called Man-made disasters. Human-made disasters are in turn categorised as technological or sociological. Technological disasters are the results of failure of technology, such as engineering failures, transport disasters, or environmental disasters (www.restoreyoureconmy.org).

The phases of all disasters are whether natural or man-made, are the same. The disasters often differ in quantity of damage caused or in quality of the type of medical consequences. Man-made hazard is a threat having an element of human intent, negligence, or error, or involving a failure of a man-made system. Man-made disasters are disasters resulting from the same factors. Sociological disasters have a strong human motive, such as criminal acts, stampedes, riots and war.

Sociological Hazards

Arson

Arson is the criminal intent of setting a fire with intent to cause damage. The definition of arson was originally limited to setting fire to buildings, but was later expanded to include other objects, such as bridges, vehicles, and private property. Arson is the greatest cause of fires in data repositories. Sometimes, human-induced fires can be accidental: failing machinery such as a kitchen stove is a major cause of accidental fires.

Civil Disorder

Civil disorder is a broad term that is typically used by law enforcement to describe forms of disturbance. Although civil disorder does not necessarily escalate to a disaster in all cases, the event may escalate into general chaos. Rioting has many causes, from low minimum wage to racial segregation.

Terrorism

The use or threatened use of violence for the purpose of creating fear in order to achieve a political, religious, or ideological goal. Under this definition, the targets of terrorist acts can be anyone, including civilians, government officials, military personnel, or people serving the interests of governments. In the early twenty-first century, terrorism has been considered by some a constant threat to all people of the world.

War

War is conflict between relatively large groups of people, which involves physical force inflicted by the use of weapons. Warfare has destroyed entire cultures, countries, economies and inflicted great suffering on humanity.

Other terms for war can include armed conflict, hostilities, and police action. Acts of war are normally excluded from insurance contracts and disaster planning.

Technological Hazards

The following disasters are identified as technological hazards and each has its consequence on the environment and community according to its velocity and magnitude (www.episcopalrelief.orgy).

Industrial Hazards

Industrial disasters occur in a commercial context, such as mining disasters. They often have an environmental impact.

Structural Collapse

Structural collapses are often caused by engineering failures. Bridge failures may be caused in several ways, such as under-design (as in the Toy Rail Bridge), by corrosion attack (such as in the Silver Bridge), and by aerodynamic flutter of the deck (as in Galloping Bertie, the original Tacoma Narrows Bridge). Failure of dams was not infrequent during the Victorian period, such as the Dale Dyke dam failure in Sheffield, England in the 1860s, causing the Great Sheffield Flood. Other failures include balcony collapses.

Power Outage

A power outage is an interruption of normal sources of electrical power. Short-term power outages (up to a few hours) are common and have minor adverse effect, since most businesses and health facilities are prepared to deal with them. Extended power outages, however, can disrupt personal and business activities as well as medical and rescue services, leading to business losses and medical emergencies. Extended loss of power can lead to civil disorder, as in the New York City blackout of 1977. Only very rarely do power outages escalate to disaster proportions, however, they often accompany other types of disasters, such as hurricanes and floods, which hampers relief efforts.

Fire

Bush fires, forest fires and mine fires are generally started by lightning, but also by human negligence or arson. They can burn thousands of square kilometers. If a fire intensifies enough to produce its own winds and "weather," it will form into a firestorm. A good example of a mine fire is the one near Centralia, Pennsylvania, started in 1962, it ruined the town and continues to burn today. Some of the biggest city-related fires are The Great Chicago Fire, The Peshtigo Fire (both of 1871) and The Great Fire of London in 1666.

Casualties resulting from fires, regardless of their source or initial cause, can be aggravated by inadequate emergency preparedness. Such hazards as a lack of accessible emergency exits, poorly marked escape routes, or improperly maintained fire extinguishers or sprinkler systems may result in many more deaths and injuries than might occur with such protections. See for example, Category: Fire disasters involving barricaded escape routes.

Hazardous Materials

Radiation Contamination

When nuclear weapons are detonated or nuclear containment systems are otherwise compromised, airborne radioactive particles (nuclear fallout) can scatter and irradiate large areas. Not only is it deadly, but it also has a long-term effect on the next generation for those who are contaminated. Ionizing radiation is hazardous to living things, and in such a case much of the affected area could be unsafe for human habitation. During World War II, United States troops dropped atomic bombs on the Japanese cities of Hiroshima and Nagasaki. As a result, the radiation fallout contaminated the cities' water supplies, food sources, and half of the populations of each city were stricken with disease.

The Soviet Republics of Ukraine and Belarus are part of a scenario like this after a reactor at the Chernobyl Nuclear Power Plant suffered a meltdown in 1986. To this day, several small towns and the city of Chernobyl remain abandoned and uninhabitable due to fallout. In the 1970s, a similar threat scared millions of Americans when a failure occurred at the Three Mile Island Nuclear Power Plant in Pennsylvania. The incident was fortunately resolved, and the area retained little contamination.

CBRN–Chemical, Biological, Radiological and Nuclear

A catch-all initialise meaning Chemical, Biological, Radiological and Nuclear. The term is used to describe a non-conventional terror threat that, if used by a nation, would be considered use of a weapon of mass destruction. This term is used primarily in the United Kingdom. Planning for the possibility of a CBRN event may be appropriate for certain high-risk or high-value facilities and governments. Examples include the Halabja poison gas attack on the Kurdish purported by Saddam Hussein, the Saran gas attacks in Tokyo and the preceding test runs in Matsumoto, Japan 100 kilometers outside of Tokyo, and Lord Amherst giving smallpox laden blankets to Native Americans.

Transportation

Aviation: Air Disasters

An aviation incident is an occurrence other than an accident, associated with the operation of an aircraft, which affects or could affect the safety of operations, passengers, or pilots. The category of the vehicle can range from a helicopter, an airliner, or a space shuttle. One of the more devastating events occurred in 1977 on the island of Tenerife of the Canary Islands, when miscommunications between and amongst air traffic control and an aircrew caused two fully loaded jets to collide on the runway, killing over 500 passengers.

Railroad: Rail Disasters

A railroad disaster is an occurrence associated with the operation of a passenger train which results in substantial loss of life. Usually accidents with freight (goods) trains are not considered disasters, unless they cause substantial loss of life or property. One of the more devastating rail disasters occurred in 2004 in Sri Lanka when 1,700 people died in the Queen of the Sea train accident. Other notable rail disasters are the 1989 Ufa accident in Russia which killed 574, and the 1917 Modena train accident in France which killed more than 500 French Soldiers. The troops were returning from fighting World War-I in Italy.

Space Disasters

Space disasters, either during operations or training, have killed around 20 astronauts and cosmonauts, and a much larger number of ground crew and civilians. These disasters include either malfunction on the ground, during launch, or in orbit with technology, or of natural forces. Not all space disasters result in human fatalities, for example, unmanned orbiting satellites that drop to the Earth can incinerate and send debris spewing across the sky. One of the worst manned space disasters, the Space Shuttle Challenger explosion of 1986, cost all of the lives on board.

The shuttle exploded several seconds after taking off from the launch pad in Cape Canaveral, Florida. Another example is the Space Shuttle Columbia, which disintegrated during a landing attempt over Texas in 2003, with a loss of all seven astronauts on board. The debris field extended from as far as eastern New Mexico to Mississippi. An example of a space disaster killing nearby residents occurred on February 15, 1996, in Sichuan Province, China, when a Long March 3B rocket crashed during takeoff. In 1960 also killed 126 when an R-16 ICBM exploded on the launch pad (www.wikipedia.org/wiki/Man-made_hazard).

Chapter - 2

Disasters and Tsunami in India

India contributes one-sixth of the world's population on just two per cent of its land mass. It suffers heavily from natural disasters of every shade and description that hits the poorest of the poor. In India, 12 per cent of land is vulnerable to floods, 8 per cent of land is vulnerable to Cyclones, 59 per cent of land is vulnerable to earthquakes, and 28 per cent of land is vulnerable to Drought (Bandar, 2006). Of the 35 states and union territories, as many as 27 are prone to disasters which very well explains the disaster profile and extent of impact of disasters in India. India could be called as "theatre of disasters" as almost all types of disaster has hit India at different point of time which was in increase in the last one decade (Gopala krishnan S, 2005).

India's Natural Disasters Proneness

On the basis of geographic and climatic considerations, India can be divided into five zones according to its disaster proneness to natural disasters;

- **Northern mountain region including foot hills**; this region is prone to strong Snow Storms leading to Landslides and strong Cold waves and also is Earthquake prone belt with violent subterranean Volcanic activity.
- **Indo-Gangetic plains**; heavy rains during monsoon make these plains vulnerable to Floods.
- **Deccan plateau**; a Drought prone area.
- **The western desert**; a Drought prone area.
- **Coastal areas**; they are prone to Sea erosion, Cyclones and Tidal waves.

India's Disaster Ridden History (Gopala Krishnan S, 2005)

- About 60 per cent of India's land mass is prone to Earthquakes.
- Over 40 million Hectares are prone to Floods.
- Nearly 3 lak sq. km are at risk of Cyclones.
- The Earthquake in Buhl killed 14,000 people.
- Cyclone in Orissa took away 10,000 lives.
- Between 1990 and 2000 an average of about 3400 people lost their lives annually.
- About 3 core people were affected by Disasters every year.
- About 17,000 people perished by the Tsunami on 26 December, 2004.

Natural Disasters in India

Disaster-prone regions in India

Natural disasters in India, many of them related to the climate of India, cause massive losses of Indian life and property. Droughts, flash floods, cyclones, avalanches, landslides brought on by torrential rains, and snowstorms pose the greatest threats. Other dangers include frequent summer dust storms, which usually track from north to south; they cause extensive property damage in North India and deposit large amounts of dust from arid regions. Hail is also common in parts of India, causing severe damage to standing crops such as rice and wheat (www.ndmindia.nic.in).

Landslides

It is common in the Lower Himalayas. The young age of the region's hills result in labile rock formations, which are susceptible to slippages. Rising population and development pressures, particularly from logging and tourism, cause deforestation. The result is denuded hillsides which exacerbate the severity of landslides, since tree cover impedes the downhill flow of water. Parts of the Western Ghats also suffer from low-intensity landslides. Avalanches occurrences are common in Kashmir, Himachal Pradesh, and Sikkim.

Floods

Floods are the most common natural disaster in India. The heavy southwest monsoon rains cause the Brahmaputra and other rivers to distend their banks, often flooding surrounding areas. Though they provide rice paddy farmers with a largely dependable source of natural irrigation and fertilisation, the floods can kill thousands and displace millions. Excess, erratic, or untimely monsoon rainfall may also wash away or otherwise ruin crops. Almost all of

India is flood-prone, and extreme precipitation events, such as flash floods and torrential rains, have become increasingly common in central India over the past several decades, coinciding with rising temperatures. Mean annual precipitation totals have remained steady due to the declining frequency of weather systems that generate moderate amounts of rain.

Cyclones

Tropical cyclones, which are severe storms spun off from the Inter-tropical Convergence Zone, may affect thousands of Indians living in coastal regions. Tropical cyclo-genesis is particularly common in the northern reaches of the Indian Ocean in and around the Bay of Bengal. Cyclones bring with them heavy rains, storm surges, and winds that often cut affected areas off from relief and supplies. In the North Indian Ocean Basin, the cyclone season runs from April to December, with peak activity between May and November. Each year, on an average of eight storms with sustained wind speeds greater than 63 kilometers per hour (39 mph) form; of these, two strengthen into true tropical cyclones, which have sustained gusts greater than 117 kilometers per hour (73 mph). On an average, a major (Category 3 or higher) cyclone develops every other year.

During summer, the Bay of Bengal is subject to intense heating, giving rise to humid and unstable air masses that produce cyclones. Many powerful cyclones, including the 1737 Calcutta cyclone, the 1970 Bola cyclone, and the 1991 Bangladesh cyclone, have led to widespread devastation along parts of the eastern coast of India and neighbouring Bangladesh. Widespread death and property destruction are reported every year in exposed coastal states such as Andhra Pradesh, Orissa, Tamil Nadu, and West Bengal. India's western coast, bordering the more placid Arabian Sea, experiences cyclones only rarely; these mainly strike Gujarat and, less frequently, Kerala.

In terms of damage and loss of life, Cyclone 05B, a super cyclone that struck Orissa on 29 October 1999, was the worst in more than a quarter-century. With peak winds of 160 miles per hour (257 km/h), it was the equivalent of a Category 5 hurricane. Almost two million people were left homeless; other 20 million people lives were disrupted by the cyclone. Officially, 9,803 people died from the storm; unofficial estimates place the death toll at over 10,000.

Droughts

Indian agriculture is heavily dependent on the monsoon as a source of water. In some parts of India, the failure of the monsoons result in water shortages, resulting in below-average crop yields. This is particularly true of major drought-prone regions such as southern and eastern Maharashtra, northern Karnataka, Andhra Pradesh, Orissa, Gujarat, and Rajasthan.

In the past, droughts have periodically led to major Indian famines, including the Bengal famine of 1770, in which up to one-third of the population in affected areas died; the 1876–1877 famine, in which over five million people died; the 1899 famine, in which over 4.5 million died; and the Bengal famine of 1943, in which over five million died from starvation and famine-related illnesses.

All such episodes of severe drought correlate with El Niño-Southern Oscillation (ENSO) events. El Niño-related droughts have also been implicated in periodic declines in Indian agricultural output. Nevertheless, ENSO events that have coincided with abnormally high sea surfaces temperatures in the Indian Ocean—in one instance during 1997 and 1998 by upto 3°C (5°F)—have resulted in increased oceanic evaporation, resulting in unusually wet weather across India. Such anomalies have occurred during a sustained warm spell that began in the 1990s.

A contrasting phenomenon is that, instead of the usual high pressure air mass over the southern Indian Ocean, an ENSO-related oceanic low pressure convergence centre forms; it then continually pulls dry air from Central Asia, desiccating India during what should have been the humid summer monsoon season. This reversed air flow causes India's droughts. The extent that an ENSO event raises sea surface temperatures in the Central Pacific Ocean influences the degree of drought (www.Wikipedia).

Tsunami

Tsunami is a series of large waves of extremely long wavelength and period usually generated by a violent, impulsive undersea disturbance or activity near the coast or in the ocean. When a sudden displacement of a large volume of water occurs, or if the sea floor is suddenly raised or dropped by an earthquake, big tsunami waves can be formed by forces of gravity. The waves travel out of the area of origin and can be extremely dangerous and damaging when they reach the shore.

The tsunami waves are completely unrelated to the astronomical tides–which are caused by the extraterrestrial, gravitational influences of the moon, sun, and the planets. Thus, the Japanese word "tsunami", meaning "harbour wave" is the correct, official, and all-inclusive term. It has been internationally adopted because it covers all forms of impulsive wave generation.

Origin of Tsunami

Tsunamis arrive at a coastline as a series of successive crests (high water levels) and troughs (low water levels)–usually occurring 10 to 45 minutes apart. As they enter the shallow waters of coastlines, bays, or harbours, their speed decreases to about 50-60 km/hr. For example, in 15 m of water the speed of a tsunami will be only 45 km/hr. However 100 or more kilometers away, another tsunami wave travels in deep water towards the same shore at a much greater speed, and still behind it there is another wave, travelling at even greater speed. As the tsunami waves become compressed near the coast, the wavelength is shortened and the wave energy is directed upward–thus increasing their heights considerably. Just as with ordinary surf, the energy of the tsunami waves must be contained in a smaller volume of water, so the waves grow in height. Even though the wavelength shortens near the coast, a tsunami will typically have a wavelength in excess of ten kilometers when it comes ashore.

Depending on the water depth and the coastal configuration, the waves may undergo extensive refraction–another process that may converge their energy to particular areas on the shore and thus increase the heights even more. Even if a tsunami wave may have been one meter of less in the deep ocean, it may grow into a huge 30-35 meter wave when it sweeps over the shore. Thus, tsunami waves may smash into the shore like a wall of water or move in as a fast moving flood or tide–carrying everything on their path. Either way, the waves become a significant threat to life and property.

If the tsunami waves arrive at high tide or if there are concurrent storm waves in the area, the effects will be cumulative and the inundation and destruction would even be greater. The historic record shows that there have been many tsunamis that have struck the shores with devastating force, sometimes reaching heights of more than 30-50 meters. For example, the 1946 tsunami generated by an earthquake off Unimak island in Alaska's Aleutian Islands, reached heights of more than 35 meters, which destroyed a reinforced concrete lighthouse and killed its occupants.

Finally, the maximum height a tsunami reaches on shore is called the run-up. It is the vertical distance between the maximum heights reached by the water on shore and the mean sea level surface. Any tsunami run-up over a meter is dangerous. The flooding by individual waves will typically last from ten minutes to a half-hour, so the danger period can last for hours. Tsunami run-up at the point of impact will depend on how the energy is focused, the travel path of the tsunami waves, the coastal configuration, and the offshore topography. Small islands with steep slopes usually experience little run-up–wave heights there are only slightly greater than on the open ocean.

This is the reason that islands with steep-sided fringing or barrier reefs are only at moderate risk from tsunamis. However, this is not the case for islands such as the Hawaiian or the Marquesas. Both of these island chains do not have extensive barrier reefs and have broad bays exposed to the open ocean.

Special Features of Tsunami

There are few ways in which tsunami differs from other disasters (www.iaea.org):

- *Time* duration of the attack was very small. The entire attack took place in a matter of a few minutes.
- *Extent of damage was very large*, grossly disproportionate to the duration of attack. Extensive damage took place in a matter of few minutes, which took the people by surprise and awe. Everything seemed to be normal.....All of a sudden water flows in.....Boom! Everything seems different. There was no time for people to adapt to the disaster.
- The victims are either alive and healthy or simply dead. There was *very less physical injury* and hence there was *no great need for medical facilities*, unlike other disasters.
- There have been *no precedents* of this type. People have not even heard of this type of a disaster.
- There were *no outbreaks of any infections*, which are common in floods. This point is of not because in floods, it is freshwater–a good culture medium for organisms. And, when water stagnates, organisms flourish even more.
- But, in tsunami, it was seawater which is hypertonic saline which is unfavourable for microorganisms. Moreover, there was no stagnation as the water receded back completely.

Earthquakes Generate Tsunamis

By far, the most destructive tsunamis are generated from large, shallow earthquakes with an epicentre or fault line near or on the ocean floor. These usually occur in regions of the earth characterised by tectonic seduction along tectonic plate boundaries. The high seismicity of such regions is caused by the collision of tectonic plates. When these plates move past each other, they cause large earthquakes, which tilt, offset, or displace large areas of the ocean floor from a few kilometers to as much as 1,000 km or more.

The sudden vertical displacements over such large areas, disturb the ocean's surface, displace water, and generate destructive tsunami waves. The waves can travel great distances from the source region, spreading destruction along their path. For example, the Great 1960 Chilean tsunami was generated by a magnitude 8.3 earthquake that had a rupture zone of over 1,000 km. Its waves were destructive not only in Chile, but also as far away as Hawaii, Japan, and elsewhere in the Pacific. It should be noted that not all earthquakes generate tsunamis. Usually, it takes an earthquake with a Richter magnitude exceeding 7.5 to produce a destructive tsunami.

Volcanic Eruptions Generate Tsunamis

Although relatively infrequent, violent volcanic eruptions represent also impulsive disturbances, which can displace a great volume of water and generate extremely destructive tsunami waves in the immediate source area. According to this mechanism, waves may be generated by the sudden displacement of water caused by a volcanic explosion, by a volcano's slope failure, or more likely by a phreato magmatic explosion and collapse/ engulfment of the volcanic magmatic chambers. One of the largest and most destructive tsunamis ever recorded was generated in August 26, 1883 after the explosion and collapse of the volcano of Krakatoa (Krakatau), in Indonesia.

This explosion generated waves that reached 135 feet, destroyed coastal towns and villages along the Sunda Strait in both the islands of Java and Sumatra, killing 36,417 people. It is also believed that the destruction of the Minoan civilisation in Greece was caused in 1490 B.C. by the explosion/ collapse of the volcano of Santorin in the Aegean Sea submarine landslides, rock falls and underwater slumps generate tsunamis. Less frequently, tsunami waves can be generated from displacements of water resulting from rock falls, icefalls and sudden submarine landslides or slumps. Such events may be caused impulsively from the instability and sudden failure of submarine slopes, which are sometimes triggered by the ground motions of a strong earthquake.

Major earthquakes are suspected to cause many underwater landslides, which may contribute significantly to tsunami generation. In general, the energy of tsunami waves generated from landslides or rock falls is rapidly dissipated as they travel away from the source and across the ocean, or within an enclosed or semi-enclosed body of water. However, it should be noted, that the largest tsunami wave ever observed anywhere in the world was caused by a rock fall.

Meteorites or Asteroids Generate Tsunami

Fortunately, for mankind, it is indeed very rare for a meteorite or an asteroid to reach the earth. No asteroid has fallen on the earth within recorded history. Most meteorites burn as they reach the earth's atmosphere. However, large meteorites have hit the earth's surface in the distant past. This is indicated by large craters, which have been found in different parts of the earth. Also, it is possible that an asteroid may have fallen on the earth in prehistoric times– the last one some 65 million years ago during the Cretaceous period. Since evidence of the fall of meteorites and asteroids on earth exists, we must conclude that they have fallen also in the oceans and seas of the earth, particularly since four-fifths of our planet is covered by water (www.itic.ioc-unesco.org).

The fall of meteorites or asteroids in the earth's oceans has the potential of generating tsunamis of cataclysmic proportions. Scientists studying this possibility have concluded that the impact of moderately large asteroid, 5-6 km in diameter, in the middle of the large ocean basin such as the Atlantic Ocean, would produce a tsunami that would travel all the way to the Appalachian Mountains in the upper two-thirds of the United States. On both sides of the Atlantic, coastal cities would be washed out by such a tsunami. An asteroid 5-6 kilometers in diameter impacting between the Hawaiian Islands and the West Coast of North America, would produce a tsunami which would wash out the coastal cities on the west coasts of Canada, U.S. and Mexico and would cover most of the inhabited coastal areas of the Hawaiian islands. Conceivably tsunami waves can also be generated from very large nuclear explosions. However, no tsunami of any significance has ever resulted from the testing of nuclear weapons in the past. Furthermore, such testing is presently prohibited by international treaty.

Ring of Fire

Tsunamis are disasters that can be generated in all of the world's oceans, inland seas, and in any large body of water. Each region of the world appears to have its own cycle of frequency and pattern in generating tsunamis that range in size from small to the large and highly destructive events. Most tsunamis occur in the Pacific Ocean and its marginal seas. The reason is that the Pacific covers more than one-third of the earth's surface and is surrounded by a series of mountain chains, deep-ocean trenches and island arcs called the "ring of fire"–where most earthquakes occur (off the coasts of Kamchatka, Japan, the Kuril Islands, Alaska and South America). Many tsunamis have also been generated in the seas which border the Pacific Ocean.

Tsunamis are generated, by shallow earthquakes all around the Pacific, but those from earthquakes in the tropical Pacific tend to be modest in size. While such tsunamis in these areas may be devastating locally, their energy decays rapidly with distance. Usually, they are not destructive a few hundred kilometers away from their sources. That is not the case with tsunamis generated by great earthquakes in the North Pacific or along the Pacific coast of South America. On the average of about half-a-dozen times per century, a tsunami from one of these regions sweeps across the entire Pacific, is reflected from distant shores, and sets the entire ocean in motion for days. For example, the 1960 Chilean tsunami caused death and destruction throughout the Pacific. Hawaii, Samoa, and Easter Island all recorded run ups exceeding 4 m; 61 people were killed in Hawaii. In Japan 200 people died.

Tsunami Energy Travel Across the Ocean

Once a tsunami has been generated, its energy is distributed throughout the water column, regardless of the ocean's depth. A tsunami is made up of a series of very long waves. The waves will travel outward on the surface of the ocean in all directions away from the source area, much like the ripples caused by throwing a rock into a pond. The wavelength of the tsunami waves and their period will depend on the generating mechanism and the dimensions of the source event. If the tsunami is generated from a large earthquake over a large area, its initial wavelength and period will be greater. If the tsunami is caused by a local landslide, both its initial wavelength and period will be shorter. The period of the tsunami waves may range from 5 to 90 minutes (www.mapsofworld.com/Tsunami).

The wave crests of a tsunami can be a thousand km long, and from a few to a hundred kilometers or more apart as they travel across the ocean. On the open ocean, the wavelength of a tsunami may be as much as two hundred kilometers, many times greater than the ocean depth, which is on the order of a few kilometers. In the deep ocean, the height of the tsunami from trough to crest may be only a few centimeters to a meter or more–again depending on the generating source.

Tsunami waves in the deep ocean can travel at high speeds for long periods of time for distances of thousands of kilometers and lose very little energy in the process. The deeper the water, the greater the speed of tsunami waves will be. For example, at the deepest ocean depths the tsunami wave speed will be as much as 800 km/hr, about the same as that of a jet aircraft. Since the average depth of the Pacific Ocean is 4000 m (14,000 feet), tsunami wave speed will average about 200 m/s or over 700 km/hr (500 mph). At such high speeds, a tsunami generated in Aleutian Islands may reach Hawaii in less than four and a half hours. In 1960, great tsunami waves generated in Chile reached Japan, more than 16,800 km away in less than 24 hours, killing hundreds of people.

Destruction by Tsunamis

There are three: inundation, wave impact on structures, and erosion. Strong, tsunami-induced currents lead to the erosion of foundations and the collapse of bridges and seawalls. Flotation and drag forces move houses and overturn railroad cars. Considerable damage is caused by the resultant floating debris, including boats and cars that become dangerous projectiles that may crash into buildings, break power lines, and may start fires. Fires from damaged ships in ports or from ruptured coastal oil storage tanks and refinery facilities can cause damage greater than that inflicted directly by the tsunami. Of increasing concern is the potential effect of tsunami draw down, when receding waters uncover cooling water intakes of nuclear power plants.

Historical Account

A similar tsunami in 1868 from northern Chile caused extensive damage in the Austral Islands, Hawaii, Samoa, and New Zealand. Although not as frequent, destructive tsunamis have been also been generated in the Atlantic and the Indian Oceans, the Mediterranean Sea and even within smaller bodies of water, like the Sea of Marmara, in Turkey. In 1999, a large earthquake along the North Anatolian Fault zone generated a local tsunami, which was particularly damaging in the Bay of Izmir. In the last decade alone, destructive tsunamis have occurred in Nicaragua (1992), Indonesia (1992, 1994, and 1996), Japan (1993), Philippines (1994), Mexico (1995), Peru (1996, 2001), Papua-New Guinea (1998), Turkey (1999), and Vanuatu (1999).

Destructive tsunamis have occurred in all of the world's oceans and seas. In the last half of the twentieth Century, Pacific-wide, destructive tsunamis occurred in 1946, 1952, 1957, 1960 and 1964. (Many more tsunamis in inland seas around the periphery of the Pacific, where extremely destructive locally and claimed thousands of lives. Such localised tsunamis occurred in 1975, 1983, 1985, 1992, 1993, 1995, 1998, 1999 and 2001.

Aleutian Earthquake and Tsunami (1 April 1946)

One of the most destructive Pacific-wide tsunamis was generated by a magnitude 7.8 earthquake near Unimak Island in Alaska's Aleutian Island Chain. A huge wave of 35 meters destroyed completely the U.S. Coast Guard's Scotch Cap lighthouse on Unimak and killed all five of its occupants. The lighthouse was a steel-reinforced concrete structure standing about 30 meters above sea level. Without warning, destructive tsunami waves reached the Hawaiian Islands, five hours later, causing considerable damage and loss of life.

The waves completely obliterated Hilo's waterfront on the island of Hawaii, killing 159 people there. Altogether a total 165 people lost their lives from this tsunami, including children attending school at Hawaii's Laupahoehoe Point, where waves reaching up to 8 m destroyed also a hospital. Damage was estimated at $26 million (in 1946 dollars). In 1948, and as a result of this tsunami, the U.S. established a Pacific Tsunami Warning Centre in Hawaii (www.bom.gov.au › Tsunami Warnings).

Kamchatka Earthquake and Tsunami (4 November 1952)

A strong earthquake (magnitude 8.2) off the coast of Kamchatka Peninsula generated a great destructive Pacific-wide tsunami. Its waves struck the Kamchatka Peninsula, the Kuril Islands and other areas of Russia's Far East, causing considerable damage and loss of life. The tsunami was widely observed and recorded in Japan, but there was no loss of life or damage there. There was considerable damage in the Hawaiian Islands and some damage in Peru and Chile. The tsunami was recorded or observed throughout the islands of the Pacific. In New Zealand waves reached height of 1 m.

In Alaska, in the Aleutian Islands and in California waves of up to 1.4 meters were observed or recorded.

By far the largest waves outside the generating area were observed in the Hawaiian Islands. Fortunately, no human lives were lost in Hawaii from this tsunami, but damage was extensive, estimates ranging from $800,000-$1,000,000 (in 1952 dollars). The tsunami caused damage on Midway Island. Elsewhere in the Hawaiian island chain, the waves destroyed boats and piers, knocked down telephone lines, and caused extensive beach erosion. In some locations, tsunami waves were destructive in certain locations but hardly noticeable at others. The north shore of the Island of Oahu experienced higher waves of up to 4.5 meters. On the south shore of the island, the tsunami was powerful enough to throw a cement barge in the Honolulu Harbor into a freighter.

The island of Hawaii experienced run up to 6.1 meters. In Hilo, one of the tsunami waves lifting it off its foundation, and then smashing it down destroyed a small bridge connecting Coconut Island to the shore. The effects of the tsunami in the generating area in Kamchatka varied significantly. From Kamchatka Peninsula to Kronotsky Peninsula the wave heights ranged from zero to five meters. From Kronotsky Peninsula to Cape Shipursky the heights ranged from 4-13 meters. The highest wave of 13 meters was the third and was observed at Olga Bay, where it caused considerable damage. Travel time of the first tsunami wave to Olga Bay was approximately 42 minutes after the earthquake. From Cape Shipursky to Cape Povorotny, the tsunami waves ranged from 1 to 10 meters and caused considerable loss of life and damage (www.wsspc.org/TsunamiCenter/Tsunami).

Aleutian Earthquake and Tsunami (9 March 1957)

On March 9, 1957, an 8.3 magnitude earthquake south of the Andreanof Islands, in the Aleutian Islands of Alaska–in the same general area as that of April 1, 1946–generated a Pacific-wide tsunami. Although no lives were lost, there was extensive destruction of property in the Hawaiian Islands, with damage estimated at approximately $5 million (1957 dollars).

The waves were particularly high on the north shore of the island of Kauai where they reached a maximum height of 16 meters, flooding the highway, and destroying houses and bridges. This was twice the height of the 1946 tsunami. At Hilo, Hawaii, the tsunami run-up reached 3.9 m and there was damage to numerous buildings along the waterfront. Within Hilo Bay, Coconut Island was covered by 1 m of water and the bridge connecting it to the shore, as in 1952, was again destroyed (www.wsspc.org/TsunamiCenter/Tsunami).

Chilean Earthquake and Tsunami (22 May 1960)

The largest earthquake (magnitude 8.6) of the twentieth century occurred on May 22, 1960 off the coast of south central Chile. It generated a Pacific-wide tsunami, which was destructive locally in Chile and throughout the Pacific Ocean. The tsunami killed an estimated 2,300 people in Chile. There was tremendous loss of life and property in the Hawaiian Islands, in Japan and elsewhere in the Pacific. Destructive waves in Hilo, Hawaii, destroyed the waterfront and killed 61 people. Total damage was estimated at more than $500 million (1960 dollars).

Alaska Earthquake and Tsunami (28 March 1964)

The largest earthquake of the twentieth century in the northern hemisphere, with a magnitude 8.4, affected an area in Alaska that was almost 1600 km long and more than 300 km wide–extending from Valdez to the Trinity Islands, southwest of Kodiak Island in the Gulf of Alaska. The earthquake caused areas to be lifted by as much as 15 m (50 feet) in certain areas, while many other areas subsided greatly. In addition to many local tsunamis generated within the Prince William Sound, vertical crustal displacements averaging 1.8 m (6 ft.) over an area of about 300,000 square kilometers (115,000 square miles) extending in the Gulf of Alaska's continental shelf, generated a Pacific-wide tsunami. Its waves were very destructive in southeastern Alaska, in Vancouver Island (British Columbia), and in the U.S. States of Washington, California and Hawaii. The tsunami killed more than 120 people and caused more than $106 million in damages, making it the costliest ever to strike the Western United States and Canada. Five of Alaska's seven largest communities were devastated by the combination of earthquake and tsunami wave damage. Alaska's fishing industry and most seaport facilities were virtually destroyed. Tsunami waves at Kodiak Island washed away a total of 158 houses and buildings within two blocks of the waterfront.

Fishing boats were carried hundreds of meters inland. The 1964 tsunami waves caused also extensive damage in Vancouver Island (British Columbia), and in the states of Washington, California and Hawaii, in the United States. The waves affected the entire California coastline, but were particularly high from Crescent City to Monterey ranging from 2.1-6.3 meters (7-21 feet). Hardest hit was Crescent City, California, where waves reaching as much as 6 meters (20-21 feet) destroyed half of the waterfront business district. Eleven persons lost their lives there. At Santa Cruz Harbor, the tsunami waves reached as high as 3.3 meters (11 feet) causing some damage. There was extensive damage in San Francisco Bay, the marinas in Marin County and at the Noyo, Los Angeles, and Long Beach harbours. Estimated losses in California were between $1,500,000 and $2,375,000 (1964 dollars), while at Crescent City tsunami damage was estimated at $7,414,000 (www.iitk.ac.in).

Locally Generated Tsunamis

A locally generated tsunami may reach a nearby shore in less than ten minutes. There is not sufficient time for the Pacific Tsunami Warning Centre or for local authorities to issue a warning. For people living near the coast, the shaking of the ground is a warning that a tsunami may be imminent. For tsunamis from more distant sources, however, accurate warnings of when a tsunami might arrive are possible because tsunamis travel at a known speed.

A catalog of about ninety tsunamis in the Indian Ocean has been prepared from 326 BC to 2005 AD. In the nineteenth and twentieth century's tsunamis have occurred once in three years or so. Sunda Arc is the most active region that has produced about seventy tsunamis. The source zones of the remaining tsunamis are Andaman-Nicobar islands, Burma-Bangladesh region in the eastern side, while Makran accretion zone and Kutch-Saurashtra region are in the west. These zones are subduction zones or zones of compression (Science of Tsunami Hazards, 2006).

Tsunamis are not as common in the Indian Ocean as in the Pacific. As compared to average eight tsunamis per year in the Pacific, Indian Ocean has one in three years or so. A catalog of tsunamis presented here includes about ninety tsunamis in the Indian Ocean out of which over 70 tsunamis are from Sunda. Some 20 tsunamis are reported from rest of the Indian Ocean, though source region of five of them may be in Sunda arc. Hence, eighty per cent of the tsunamis of the Indian Ocean originate in Sunda arc covering Java and Sumatra. The Sunda belt extends northward to Andaman-Nicobar Islands where a few tsunamis have originated. Further north, Bangladesh-Myanmar coast has produced some well-documented tsunamis. Makran coast in the northwest is known to have generated at least one major tsunami. Karachi-Kutch coast region has also produced some possible tsunamis. Cause of tsunamis is mostly thrust-type earthquakes with vertical uplift in subduction zones and zones of compression (Science of Tsunami Hazards, 2006).

The seismic gap areas along the subduction zones are possible sites of future great earthquakes. Along the Sunda arc, great earthquakes of magnitude 8.5 or greater can repeat every two centuries at a site but smaller tsunamigenic earthquakes can repeat every few decades. Along Sunda Arc volcanic eruptions have also given rise to large tsunamis. There appears to have been a hiatus in tsunami generation in this region, with a significant gap in events occurring from around 1909 through 1967. The Carlsberg spreading ridge or old oceanic ridges like Chagos Ridge and Ninety east Ridge with normal faulting can give rise to local tsunamis. Many of the tsunamis and their effects are described in some details. However, tsunamis from Java region are not described in detail as they did not affect the countries other than Indonesia (www. tsun.sscc.ru).

Tsunamis from Sunda Arc Region

Newcomb and McCann (1987) compiled historical records of earthquakes and tsunamis from Sunda arc region. Heck (1947), Berninghausen (1966), Litzin (1974) and USGS catalogs list some more. The Sumatra part of the Sunda arc had been much more active than Java part. Detailed description of some of the significant earthquakes and the tsunamis caused by them are given below:

Earthquakes/Tsunamis in Sumatra-Historical Enumeration (Science of Tsunami Hazards, 2006)

- 11 December 1681-"Strong earthquake" shook the Sumatra Mountains near Mentawai Archipelago and a seaquake was observed.
- 3 November 1756-Many houses collapsed in several towns of Sumatra near to Enganno Is. No tsunami was reported.
- 10-11 February 1797-Mw 8.2. A large earthquake and tsunami was observed in ports on the coast of the mainland. Waves of great force near Padang (0.99S 100.37E) the town was inundated and more than 300 fatalities occurred (Heck, 1947).
- 18 March 1818-A very strong shock associated with both tsunami and seaquake near to Enganno Island.
- 24 November 1833-The great earthquake of magnitude > 8.7 had maximum intensities and generated a tsunami over 550 km along the south-central coast of Sumatra that also caused much damage to the coast. Numerous deaths occurred in West Sumatra. This earthquake ruptured the plate margin from the southern island of Enggano to Batu.
- 5 and 6 January 1843-The earthquake caused severe damage, liquefaction and many fatalities in Nias Island. A tremendous tsunami wiped out towns on the east coast of Nias and mainland. The damage and associated tsunami were much localised. The village of Barus and Palan Nias reported large waves on two days.
- 11 November 1852-Earthquake near Nias generated seaquake.
- 16 February 1861-A great earthquake of magnitude 8.5 ruptured a major segment of the plate boundary in northern Sumatra. The tsunami that was generated extended over 500 km along the arc. Tsunami destroyed southern towns of Batu Island, and a town on the southwest side of Nias experienced a tsunami height of 7 m. The earthquake and tsunami caused 1000s of fatalities at west coast of Sumatra.

Subsequent local tsunamis in the Sunda Strait were generated by the 1927 and 1928 eruptions of the new volcano of Anak Krakatau (Child of

Krakatau) that formed in the area. Although large tsunamis were generated from these recent events, the heights of the waves attenuated rapidly away from the source region, because their periods and wavelengths were very short. There was no report of damage from these more recent tsunamis in the Sunda Strait (George, 2003).

- 4 Jan 1907-This event caused tsunamis that devastated Simeuleu, Nias, and Batu Islands of Sumatra and extended over 950km as measured by tide gauges.
- 25 June 1914 - earthquake destroyed buildings in southern Sumatra. No tsunami was reported.

The 2004 Sumatra-Andaman earthquake of magnitude 9.3 generated 30 m-high tsunami when upward slip of the ocean floor was up to 15 m along a 1300 km long and 160 to 240 km wide rupture. It was the deadliest tsunami killing about 300,000 people in 13 countries situated all around the Indian Ocean. The earthquake had created large thrust ridges, about 1500 m high, which collapsed in places to produce large landslides, several kilometers across. The force of displaced water was such that blocks of rocks, massing millions of tons apiece, were dragged as much as 10 km. An oceanic trench several kilometers wide was also formed. The run up in the India was 5 m or less (Science of Tsunami Hazards, 2006).

Magnitude 8.7 great Sumatra Earthquake of 28 March 2005 with an upward movement of 2 m of seafloor in an area of 400 km × 100 km generated locally damaging 4 m-high tsunami that struck nearby islands and coastal Sumatra and was recorded by tidal stations in the Indian Ocean (www.asc.India.org). The earthquake and tsunami killed 665 people. The tsunami struck Nias Island with wave heights of 4-5 m. A 3-4 m wave struck the islands of Banyak and Simeulue and the Singkil district of Sumatra. According to the Pacific Tsunami Warning Centre (PTWC) (www.ptwc.org) tide gauges in the Indian Ocean recorded minor wave activity in the Australian Cocos Island (10-22 cm), the Maldives (10 cm), and Sri Lanka (25-30 cm).

Tsunamis' Impact on India

Though rare, tsunamis have hit India earlier. The oldest record of tsunami is available from November 326 BC earthquake near the Indus delta /Kutch region that set off massive sea waves in the Arabian Sea. Alexander the Great was returning to Greece after his conquest and wanted to go back by a sea route. But a tsunami due to an earthquake of large magnitude destroyed the mighty Macedonian fleet (Lisitzin, 1974).

Poompuhar is a town in the southern part of India in the state of Tamil Nadu. It was a flourishing ancient town known as Kaveripattinam that was washed away in what is now recognised as an ancient Tsunami in about

500 AD this time matches with the Krakatoa explosion. There is mention of tsunami effect in scriptures at Nagapattinam in 900 AD that destroyed a Buddhist monastery. The sea inundated warehouses and sheds and began to flow into the streets. Ships and boats seemed suspended in mid-air, precariously poised on the water peaks. The book also describes how an elephant was swallowed by the gushing water (Science of Tsunami Hazards, 2006).

Tsunami has been observed in the North Indian Ocean on the Iranian coast from a local earthquake between 1st April and 9th May 1008 (Murty *et al.,* 1999). An earthquake occurred during 1524 AD off the coast of Dabhol, Maharashtra and a resulting large tsunami caused considerable alarm to the Portuguese fleet that was assembled in the area (Bendick and Bilham, 1999).

A tsunami is known to have occurred in the Bay of Bengal on April 2, 1762, caused by an earthquake in Bangladesh–Myanmar border region. The epicenter is believed to be 40 km SE of Chittagong, or 61 km N of Cox's Bazaar, or 257 km SE of Dhaka, Bangladesh. The shock caused severe damage at Chittagong and other areas on the eastern seaboard of the Bay of Bengal. The Arakan coast was elevated for more than 160 km. The quake also caused a tsunami in the Bay of Bengal. The water in the Hoogly River in Kolkata rose by two meters. The rise in the water level at Dhaka was so sudden that hundreds of boats capsized and many people were drowned. This is the earliest well-documented tsunami in the Bay of Bengal (www.freejournal.net).

An earthquake on 11th November 1842 near the northern end of Bay of Bengal caused a tsunami by which waters of the distributaries of the Ganges Delta were agitated. Boats were tossed about as if by waves in a squall of wind. Meteorological Department (http://www.freejournal.net), informed that a tsunami struck Sunderbans (Bangladesh) in May 1874, killing several hundred thousand people. It was result of an earthquake in Bhola district. Earthquake and tsunami both played havoc in vast areas of Sunderbans, 24-Parganas, Midnapore, Barishal, Khulna and Bhola. Even Kolkata felt its impact. It was the same year that the meteorological centre in Alipore was set up. However, no written record of such an earthquake or tsunami is available.

Other minor tsunamis of height up to 2 m hit the east coast of India in 1842 and 1861 (from Sumatra), 1881 (from Car Nicobar), 1883 (Krakatau), 1907 (Sumatra) and 1941 (Andaman). The 1881 Andaman earthquake of Mw7.9 caused 1.2-m high tsunami. Indonesian earthquake of 1907 registered about a meter high tsunami in India. Madras Port Trust recorded a 2 m high tsunami due to the eruption of the Krakatau volcano in Indonesia on 27 August 1883. Andaman earthquake of Mw7.7 in 1941 registered a 1.5 m high tsunami (Science of Tsunami Hazards, 2006).

An earthquake of magnitude Mw 7.9 occurred at Car Nicobar Island on 31 December 1881. A tsunami was generated by this earthquake in the Bay of Bengal. Though the run-ups and waves heights were not large, its effects were observed in the Andaman and Nicobar Islands and were recorded on the east coast of India. A meter high wave was recorded at Port Blair on South Andaman Island (Berninghausen, 1966). In the Nicobar Islands, the waves were less than 75 cm high. On the east coast of India, the tsunami first arrived at Nagapatinam at around 10:15 am local time (LT) with 1.2 m high waves.

Tidal gauges at other locations recorded minor variations from normal tidal changes. The tsunami then struck the rest of the Tamil Nadu coast, first hitting Chennai and then progressing north toward Visakhapatnam in Andhra Pradesh at 10:43 LT. Waves arrived at False Point on the Mahanadi delta in Orissa at 11:15 LT and at Pamban in the Gulf of Mannar at 11:32 LT. Waves less than 0.3 meters high were recorded later in the day in West Bengal by tidal gauges at Dublat at the mouth of the Hoogly river at 13:00 LT and then in Diamond Harbour at 15:10 LT (Ortiz and Bilham, 2003). Waves attributed to this tsunami were also observed at Batticaloa and Trincomalee on the east coast of Sri Lanka (Berninghausen, 1966). No tsunami was reported from tidal gauges in Myanmar (Ortiz and Bilham, 2003).

A tsunami was noticed at Dublet (mouth of Hoogly River) near Kolkata due to earthquake in the western part of the Bay of Bengal in 1884 (Murty *et al.,* 1999) that reached up to Port Blair.

June 26, 1941 Andaman earthquake had a moment magnitude Mw 7.7 and was located at 12.1°N and 92.5°E (Bilham *et al.,* 2005). A tsunami was triggered by this earthquake in the Bay of Bengal. Height of the tsunami was reported to be of the order of 0.75 to 1.25 meters. At the time no tidal gauge was in operation. Mathematical calculations suggest that the height could be of the order of 1 m. This tsunami was witnessed along the eastern coast of India. It is believed that nearly 5,000 people were killed by the tsunami on the east coast of India. Local newspapers are believed to have mistaken the deaths and damage to a storm surge, however, a search of meteorological records does not show any storm surge on that day on the Coromandel Coast (Murty, 1984). National dailies like the Times of India, which reported the quake's shaking effects, did not mention any deaths, either as a result of a storm surge or a tsunami.

The deadliest tsunami prior to 2004 in South Asia was in November 1945, which originated off the Makran coast of Pakistan in the Arabian Sea and caused deaths as far as Mumbai. More than 4000 people were killed on the Makran Coast by both the earthquake and the tsunami. The earthquake was also characterised by the eruption of a mud volcano, a few kilometers off the Makran Coast, which are common features in Western Pakistan and

Myanmar. It led to the formation of a four small islands. A large volume of gas that erupted from one of the islands, sent flames leaping "hundreds of meters" into the sky (Mathur, 1988). The most significant aspect of this earthquake was the tsunamis that it triggered.

In 1983 earthquake in Chagos Archipelago, was one of the strongest earthquakes (Mw 7.7) ever recorded in the Indian Ocean. It occurred at 17:46 pm UTC. The earthquake caused some damage (www.NEIC.org) to buildings and piers on Diego Garcia. Diego Garcia is part of the Chagos Archipelago. The 1983 earthquake spawned a tsunami in the region. In the lagoon, on Diego Garcia, there was a 1.5-meter rise in wave height and there was some significant wave damage near the southeastern tip of the island. A 40 cm wave was also recorded at Victoria, Seychelles.

The catalog prepared for tsunamis in the Indian Ocean includes about ninety tsunamis. Eighty per cent of the tsunamis in the Indian Ocean are from Sunda arc region where on an average tsunamis are generated once in three years. In rest of the Indian Ocean tsunamis can be generated once in ten years or so. The Makran accretion zone of southern Pakistan has produced some tsunamis. The 28 November. 1945 (Mw 8.0) earthquake generated the last major tsunami in the Arabian Sea. Indus Delta and may be the Coasts of Kutch and Saurashtra are also potential zones for great earthquakes and tsunami. Tsunami was generated by an earthquake in 1762 in Myanmar and in 1874 by an earthquake near Bangladesh. The Chagos ridge has given rise to a local tsunami due to a normal earthquake of Mw 7.7 on 30 November. 1983 near Diego Garcia. (Science of Tsunami Hazards, 2006).

Impact of Tsunami in Tamil Nadu

Almost all the countries situated around the Bay of Bengal were affected by the tsunami waves in the morning hours of 26 December 2004 (between 0900–1030 hrs IST). The killer waves were triggered by an earthquake measuring 8.9 on the Richter scale that had an epicenter near the west coast of Sumatra in Indonesia.

The first recorded tsunami in India dates back to 31 December 1881. An earthquake of magnitude 7.5 on the Richter scale, with its epicenter believed to have been under the sea off the Coast of Car Nicobar Island, caused the tsunami. The last recorded tsunami in India occurred on 26 June 1941, caused by an earthquake with magnitude exceeding 8.5. This caused extensive damage to the Andaman Islands. There are no other well-documented records of Tsunami in India.

The 2004 Indian Ocean earthquake was an undersea earthquake that occurred at 00:58:53 UTC on December 26, 2004, with an epicenter off the west coast of Sumatra, Indonesia. It is known by the scientific community as the Great Sumatra-Andaman earthquake, and the following tsunami is known as the Asian Tsunami or the Boxing Tsunami. The earthquake was caused by subduction and triggered a series of devastating tsunami along the coasts of most landmasses bordering the Indian Ocean, killing more than 225,000 people in eleven countries, and inundating coastal communities with waves up to 30 meters high.

In 2004, the killer wave-Tsunami , caused by a 9.0 magnitude earthquake, is the most devastating tsunami in modern times, affecting 18 countries in Southeast Asia and Southern Africa, killing more than 250,000 people in a single day, and leaving more than 1.7 million homeless. However, less reported, albeit real, is its impact in the islands of the Indian Ocean more than 1,000 miles away from its epicenter (Georges Ramalanjaona, 2011).

It was one of the deadliest natural disasters in recorded history. Indonesia, Sri Lanka, India, and Thailand were hardest hit. With a magnitude of between 9.1 and 9.3, it is the second largest earthquake ever recorded on a seismograph. This earthquake had the longest duration of faulting ever observed, between 8.3 and 10 minutes. It caused the entire planet to vibrate as much as 1 cm (0.4 inches) and triggered other earthquakes as far away as Alaska. The plight of the many countries prompted a widespread humanitarian response. In all, the worldwide community donated more than $7 billion (2004 U.S. dollars) in humanitarian aid.

In India, 10,136 people, according to official estimates, were killed and hundreds of thousands were rendered homeless when a tsunami triggered by the 2004 Indian Ocean earthquake near the Indonesian island of Sumatra hit the southern peninsular coast on 26 December 2004. The earthquake registered 9.0 in moment and was the biggest in five decades. This was followed by strong aftershocks, including a 7.1 magnitude quake in the Andaman and Nicobar Islands.

It was all quiet on the waterfront on the Sunday morning after Christmas in 2004 at Kanyakumari in Tamil Nadu, the famous Marina Beach in Chennai and elsewhere on the Kerala coast and Andaman Nicober Islands. There was the excitement of a holyday with an offbeat mood with swarms of people on the sea front: children playing cricket and men and women on their morning walk at the Marina. Elsewhere, fishermen were putting out to sea for the day's catch. Then all on a sudden, a curious thing happened. The holiday makers at Kanyakumari were awestruck (DRC, 2005).

In the present tsunami, India was the third country severely battered after Indonesia and Sri Lanka. In India, the State severely affected by tsunami are Tamil Nadu, Pondicherry, Andhra Pradesh, Kerala and Andaman and Nicober Island. The state of Tamil Nadu has been the worst affected on the mainland, with a death toll of 7,793. Nagapattinam district has had

5,525 casualties, with entire villages having been destroyed. Kanyakumari district has had 808 deaths, Cuddalore district 599, the state capital Chennai 206 and Kancheepuram district 124 deaths (Govt. of Tamil Nadu Report, 2005).

Disaster snapshot

State	*Deaths*		*Injured*	*Missing*	*Evacuees*	*Refugees*
	Official	*Estimated*				
Tamil Nadu	7,960	8,000	—	—	500,000	310,000
Andaman and Nicobar	1,310	7,000	200	5,544	17,000	37,000
Pondicherry	590	665	—	75	70,000	6,100
Andhra Pradesh	105	116	—	11	34,000	0 (All returned)
Kerala	171	171	700	—	25,000	25,000
Total	**10,136**	**16,000**	**900**	**5,630**	**650,000**	**380,000**

Source: (NDMA, 2012).

Tsunami damage in India

Factor	*Andhra Pradesh*	*Kerala*	*Tamil Nadu*	*Pondicherry*	*Total*
Population affected	211,000	691,000	2,470,000	43,000	3,415,000
Area affected (km²)	7.9	Unknown	24.87	7.9	40.67
Length of coast affected (km)	985	250	1,000	25	2,260
Extent of penetration (km)	0.5-2.0	1-2	1-1.5	0.30-3.0	
Reported height of tsunami (m)	5	3-5	7-10	10	
Villages affected	301	187	362	26	876
Dwelling units	1,557	11,832	91,037	6,403	110,829
Cattle lost	195	Unknown	5,476	3,445	9,116

Source: (NDMA, 2012).

The death tolls in other districts were Pudukkottai (15), Ramanathapuram (6), Tirunelveli (4), Thoothukudi (3), Tiruvallur (28), Thanjavur (22), Tiruvarur (10) and Viluppuram (47). Those killed in Kanyakumari include pilgrims taking a holy dip in the sea. Of about 700 people trapped at the Vivekananda Rock Memorial off Kanyakumari, 650 were rescued. In Chennai, people playing on the Marina beach and those who taking a Sunday morning stroll were washed away, in addition to the fisher folk who lived along the shore and those out at sea. The death toll at Velankanni in Nagapattinam district is currently 1,500. Most of these people were visiting the Basilica of the Virgin Mary for Christmas, while others were residents of the town. The nuclear power station at Kalpakkam was shut down after sea water rushed into a pump station. No radiation leak or damage to the reactor was reported.

About 100 casualties were reported from Kalpakkam, all power plant personnel and their families (DRC, 2005).

Affected States and Regions

Tamil Nadu

The state of Tamil Nadu has been the worst affected on the mainland, with a death toll of 7,793. Nagapattinam district has had 5,525 casualties, with entire villages having been destroyed. Kanyakumari District has had 808 deaths, Cuddalore district 599, the state capital Chennai 206 and Kancheepuram district 124. The death tolls in other districts were Pudukkottai (15), Ramanathapuram (6), Tirunelveli (4), Thoothukudi (3), Tiruvallur (28), Thanjavur (22), Tiruvarur (10) and Viluppuram (47) (www.tn.gov.in/tsunami).

Wave Arrival Time

The tsunami waves arrived first on the east coast. As can be seen from the tide gauge data, the tsunami waves first reached Kochi at 11:10 A.M., Tuticorin at 9:57 A.M., and Chennai and Visakhapatnam at 9:05 A.M. all Indian Standard Time. Most locations experienced 3–5 waves.

Tsunami Effects

The tsunami effects varied greatly across different parts of the coast according to the number of waves experienced, inundation distance and height of the waves, and density of the area—as well as topological and geographical features that made some areas more vulnerable than others. The number of lives lost was also influenced by the proximity of habitats to the coastline, exposure to previous disasters, and the local disaster management capability.

Effects of 2004 Tsunami in India

The consequences the 2004 Tsunami induced in India is beyond repair in terms of human and finance. There is a loss economy, environment and health. The impact is sustained for years together and various machineries, agencies and government is undertaking rehabilitation measures on regular basis; but need to continue for years together. The following is the short account of impact created on various regions (www.tn.gov.in/tsunami).

- **Southwest coast:** This comprises Kerala, which suffered significant damage that impacted the largest number of people of any affected state but suffered relatively lower loss of life, and the Kanyakumari district of Tamil Nadu, which suffered heavy loss of life due to a large extent, to human-created local topographical features.
- **Southeast coast:** This comprises the rich alluvial delta region of the Tamil Nadu coast and Pondicherry, which experienced maximum

wave heights and recorded the maximum loss of life and damage in mainland India.

- **East coast:** This comprises Andhra Pradesh, which suffered marginal damage and loss of life. Kanyakumari forms the southwest district of Tamil Nadu. Unlike the Kerala coast, the Tamil Nadu west coast has flat land at sea level along the north coast in some areas such as Kolachel, where the soil is rich alluvium, but in other areas and further south, the land is mountainous. It slopes steeply upward from the coastline and is rocky.

Impact in Kanyakumari District, Tamil Nadu State

One of the most affected areas in Kanyakumari district was Kolachel and the surrounding villages, located 30 km west of Nagercoil, which is the capital of the Kanyakumari district. The land near the coast is flat and is at sea level, and no seawall was visible. Water travelled inland by more than 300 m. New streams and estuaries were carved out by incoming waves. When the waves receded, they deepened these features further by scouring. The town and neighbouring villages recorded more than 500 fatalities, of which more than 50 per cent were children. The wave height was reported to be 5 m, and the run-up height was 2.6 m (www.tn.gov.in/tsunami).

A large number of deaths were triggered by the human created topology of this town. Harbour Road, which experienced the maximum number of casualties, had a long, open, dry channel called the Ananda Victoria Marthandam AVM Canal. This canal is more than 2.5 m deep and 6 m wide, running parallel to the shore. The canal was meant to bring in fresh water but was not in use. Besides this canal, there were numerous open trenches laid parallel to each other that catered to the special needs of the coir-making industry, which is the main means of livelihood in this region besides fishing. These trenches were about 1.5-2m deep, 15 m long and 4 m wide. They were used to soak the coconuts and separate the husk for making coir. When the tsunami waves surged into the town, the AVM canal and these trenches became death traps.

More than 300 bodies were found in the slush of the AVM channel and open trenches husk for making coir. When the tsunami waves surged into the town, the AVM canal and these trenches became death traps. The masonry retaining wall of the jetty at Kolachel was badly damaged. A few kilometers from Kolachel is Muttom Beach, and this area did not suffer damage, because it is more than 50 m above mean sea level. A few tourists who had gone down to the sea to watch the tsunami were washed away (www.tn.gov.in/tsunami).

The Mannakudi *panchayat* near Kolachel was a cluster of villages, including Melamanakudi, which was badly affected. A 160-m-long bridge had been commissioned in concrete block house with a reinforced it was observed at Muttom Beach and at the tip of Kanyakumari. On some beaches such as Sothavilai, there are sand dune formations.

In 2002, to connect the villages of Melamanakudi and Kelamanakudi on opposite banks of the Pazhyar River a bridge was constructed. The bridge went missing after the tsunami. It was originally built with four spans, all of which were washed away by the tsunami. The two end spans travelled upstream by 100 m and were beached on the banks; the central spans were not visible, apparently having sunk into the waters. The substructure appeared to be intact except at the apron.

There were no restraints between the superstructure and the foundation. Melamanakudi is a prosperous and picturesque hilly village built on the waterfront. A road from the village of Palam to Melamanakudi was reportedly built by leveling the sand dunes in the region, in violation of the coastal regulation zone CRZ rules. Numerous houses were built on the seashore not more than 50 m from the shoreline, apparently after the leveling of sand dunes. These houses suffered complete devastation structures 250 m from the shoreline suffered little or no damage, because the land sloped upward. About 150 people died at Melamanakudi.

Sothavilai has a beautiful beach and was being actively developed by the state for tourism. The beach slopes upward from the shoreline and folds into sand dunes about 8–10 m high along parts of the beach. A beach resort has been constructed inland beyond the sand dunes. Numerous tea shops and other food stalls lined the path leading to the beach. The tsunami waves lashed and made their way over the ridges of these dunes and beyond them through the numerous small drainage channels running into the sea from the town, causing loss of life and much scouring while receding. An estimated 200 people, mainly stall owners and visitors, died at this beach.

The southernmost tip of mainland India, Kanyakumari, experienced tsunami waves that were over 4.5 m high. Because Kanyakumari is on high land, the damage was limited—street furniture and compound walls were destroyed. About 1,200 people stranded at the rock memorial were successfully evacuated a few hours after the tsunami (www.tn.gov.in/tsunami).

Chapter - 3

Experiences of Children in Disasters

First and foremost; children represent a highly vulnerable group. Infants and young children, in particular, are physically vulnerable to both sudden-onset and chronic disaster events due to their partial or total dependence on adults (Vijayakumar, Kannan and Daniel, 2006). Older children and adolescents are also at risk for injury or death, and they may develop various behavioural, psychological, and emotional issues in the aftermath of disaster (Stevens and Slone, 2008). Recognising the different forms of physical and emotional vulnerability becomes essential in order to better protect and help children. Also, as Anderson (2005) notes, knowledge of children's vulnerability is important from a social scientific perspective, as we attempt to build more robust theories and models that explain the full range of human experiences in disasters.

Second, without a sustained focus on children, their special needs may be neglected. Following a disaster, we cannot assume that children's needs are met if their parents' needs are met (Christina Suboh, 2008). Depending on their age and stage of development, children may require different forms of physical, social, mental, and emotional support than the adults in their lives. Yet research has shown that adults often underestimate children's problems and needs (McFarlane 1987). Moreover, when parents, teachers, and other adults are distracted or distraught, they may not be able to provide children with the care and support that would help reestablish a sense of safety and security. Children may be further disadvantaged by their inability to articulate their distress and subsequently seek help (Silverman and La Greco, 2002).

Third, disasters can affect children's personal growth and development. Disasters not only disrupt children's daily routines, they may also result in missed school and delayed academic progress; missed social opportunities; and increased exposure to various life stressors, such as illness, divorce, family violence, and alcohol and drug abuse (Bhushan and Kumar, 2007; Priya R and G. Kanaga, 2013). Moreover, disasters may separate children from their family members and friends, cause the death of loved ones, or displace children to unfamiliar and unwelcoming environments. These negative effects of disaster may have severe consequences for children's physical health and emotional and intellectual well-being in both the short and long term (Hakeem Irfan, 2013).

Although children are at special risk in disasters, they are not passive victims. Thus, a fourth point worthy of consideration is that children and youth can participate in disaster preparedness activities in their homes, schools, and communities that would likely minimise some of the risks that they face (John H. Ehrenreich, 2001), including disaster risk reduction information in school curricula is an excellent way to reach children. These children then may communicate risk information to their peers and family members (Ronan *et al.,* 2004; Wisner, 2006). In order to educate children about disasters and engage them in preparedness activities, age-appropriate materials must be developed and disseminated through various print and electronic media.

Fifth, children may have practical and creative ideas for helping their families and communities recover from disasters. Disasters harm the physical spaces where children live, learn, and play—their homes, neighbourhoods, schools, parks, and playgrounds (Christina Suboh, 2008). Yet, adults rarely ask children about how they would like these spaces to be rebuilt. Systems can be established to include children's voices in decision-making processes, which would contribute to more holistic community-based disaster recovery planning.

Understanding Vulnerability

In explaining variation in disaster impact, vulnerability scholars consider the intersections between key environmental and social indicators such as exposure to hazard risk, quality of human settlements and the built environment, socio-economic status, gender, race, ethnicity, age, disability and health status, occupation, education, access to resources, social networks, and social dependence (Cutter, Borough, and Shirley, 2003). Researchers working in this area often refer to "vulnerable groups," which typically include the poor, women, and ethnic minorities, persons with physical or mental disabilities, the elderly, and children. These groups are viewed as being more prone to damage, loss, suffering, injury, and death in disasters (Wisner *et al.,* 2004).

The potential risks that young people face in disasters, and the factors that influence those risks. They also acknowledge that all children are not equally vulnerable to disaster impacts.

Types of Vulnerability on Children

Psychological	*Physical*	*Educational*
PTSD	Death	Missed school
Depression	Loss of parents, brothers, sisters and relatives	Poor academic performance
Anxiety	Injury	Delayed progress
Emotional distress	Illness and disease	Failure to complete education
Sleep disorders	Malnutrition	New/temporary class room
Somatic complaints	Heat stress	New play mates New/ unknown peers
Behavioural problems	Physical and sexual abuse	Lack of reading materials
Adjustment problems	Financial crisis	Poor school infrastructure
Insecurity		
Low self esteem		

Source: (Peek Lori, 2008).

Psychological Vulnerability

Over the past 20 years, an increasing amount of scholarly attention has been devoted to children's psychological responses to natural and technological disasters as well as to terrorism and other forms of violent conflict. Thus, much of the research that is available on children and disasters has examined children in a mental health context; in particular, the most widely studied reaction to disasters has been post-traumatic stress disorder (PTSD) or related symptoms (La Greco *et al.,* 2002; Norris *et al.,* 2002).

Common responses of children to disaster vary by age group and stage of physical and mental development. For toddlers and very young children (1-4 years), problems include clinginess, dependence, nightmares, refusing to sleep alone, irritability and temper tantrums, aggressive behaviour, incontinence, hyperactivity, and separation anxiety (Norris *et. al.,* 2002). Older children (5-12 years) may exhibit marked reactions of fear and anxiety, increased hostility with siblings, somatic complaints, and sleep disorders, problems with school performance, social withdrawal, apathy, and reenactment through play, PTSD, and anxiety. Teenagers (13-18 years) may experience decreased interest in social activities and school, rebellion and other behavioural problems, sleep and eating disorders, somatic complains, increased or decreased physical activity, confusion, lack of concentration, a

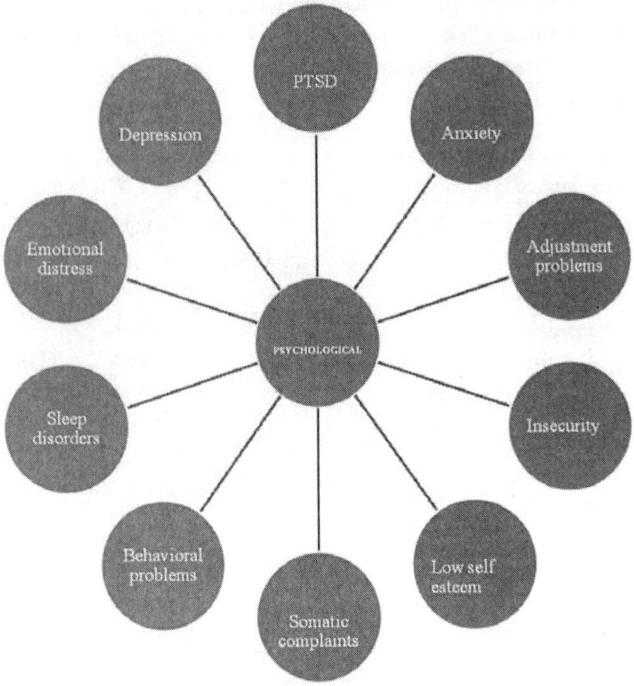

Chart – 5: Psychological Vulnerability.

decline in responsible behaviours, engage in risk-taking behaviours, suffer from PTSD, and be at increased risk for alcohol or drug misuse after disaster.

One of the most critical predictors of children's post-disaster distress is the *extent and intensity of exposure* to the traumatic event. Children who experience life threat, become separated from family members, lose a loved one, suffer extensive damage to their homes and communities, or witness scenes of disaster destruction either directly or through media intake are at particular risk for developing PTSD, anxiety, or depression (Christina Suboh, 2008). The characteristics of the child, including demographic characteristics and pre-disaster functioning, also influence children's reactions to disaster (Kar N, Jagadisha, Murali N. 2001; Kar N, Bastia BK., 2006 and Kar N., 2006).

Girls, racial and ethnic minorities, and children from lower socioeconomic backgrounds seem to be at increased risk for psychological impairment after disaster, although results are not always consistent. Children with poorer behavioural and academic functioning prior to disaster are also likely to suffer higher rates of post-disaster impairment (La Greco *et. al.,* 1998). Family factors and characteristics of the post-disaster environment, including parental distress, lack of access to social support, and the occurrence of additional life stressors (e.g., abuse, poverty, divorce, death or illness of a family member) have been linked to children's adverse mental health outcomes and behavioural problems in the aftermath of disaster (Maida, Gordon, and Strauss 1993; Tuber *et. al.,* 2005; Swenson *et. al.,* 1996; Warhead *et. al.,* 1996; Wasserstein and La Greco 1998).

Finally, the coping skills of the child and the coping assistance received influence children's ability to adapt and respond to traumatic events (Jenney-Gammon *et. al.,* 1993; Grinstein *et. al.,* 1996). It is important to note that most children, when faced with adversity, are capable of coping with one or two major risk factors in their lives without significant detrimental consequences. However, children are highly susceptible to developmental damage and troubling life outcomes when a number of risk factors accumulate.

Physical Vulnerability

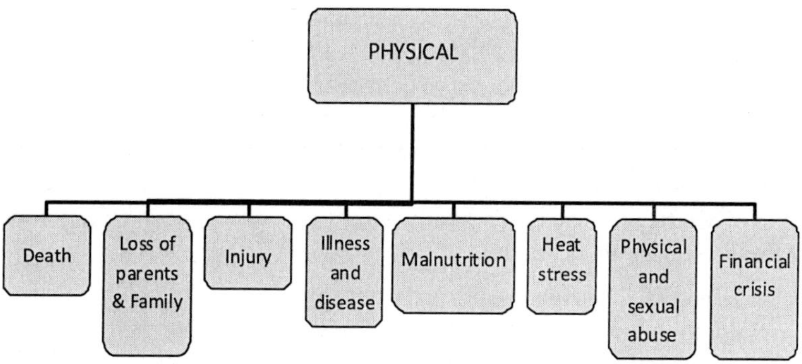

Chart – 6: Physical Vulnerability.

Children and youth are not only emotionally vulnerable to the effects of disaster. As catastrophic events have repeatedly and tragically demonstrated, children are also among those most at risk for illness, injury, and death. More than 18,000 children perished in the 2005 Pakistan earthquake (International Federation of Red Cross and Red Crescent Societies, 2007), and the 2004 Indian Ocean tsunami claimed the lives of at least 60,000 children (Oxfam International, 2005). Compared to the number of studies that examine the mental health effects of disasters on children, much less research has explored children's risk for physical injury or loss of life in disasters of various types.

So, several social and environmental factors that contributes to children being at risk for death or injury in disaster .These include residing in hazard-prone regions in poorer countries and communities living in and going to school in substandard structures (Parasuraman, 1995), losing a parent or becoming separated from family members and experiencing malnutrition and poor diet (Webster, 1994; Young and Jaspers 1995) or artificial feeding (i.e., bottle feeding) (Kelly, 1993). Female children are at higher risk of death (Ramirez *et al.,* 2005; Rivers, 1982; Sapir, 1993) at least in developing nations.

Children are particularly vulnerable to disaster trauma, and this manifests in a variety of complex psychological and behavioural manifestations. However, often the post-disaster psychological reactions in children are not identified. Studies have noted that parents, teachers and even mental health professionals significantly underestimate both the intensity and the duration of the stress reactions in children (AACAP, 1998 and Amaya-Jackson L., 2000).

Common psychiatric manifestations among children include acute stress reactions, adjustment disorder, depression, panic disorder, post-traumatic stress disorder, anxiety disorders specific to childhood and psychotic disorders. Comorbidities and sub-clinical syndromes are also common (Nilamadhab Kar, 2009). There is no consensus in the literature on the age at which children are most at risk for death or injury in disasters, although younger and smaller children are generally considered more vulnerable because of their lesser size and strength to withstand disaster events. Different types of disaster seem to differentially impact children of various age groups (Zahran, Sammy, *et. al.,* 2008).

The potential physical health and safety implications of climate change for children in lower-income countries. Children as a group is likely to be affected by climate change in particular ways, and generally in more extreme ways, than the population at large because of their greater vulnerability to a range of associated stresses. For example, due to their levels of physical development and immature immune systems, children are more susceptible to sanitation-related illnesses, malaria and other vector-borne diseases, malnutrition, heat stress, and respiratory disease (Debra L., (2009).

As an increasing number of children are orphaned (Ehrenreich, 2001) in the developing world, largely as a result of chronic environmental hazards, water and food shortages, violence and conflict, and pandemic, traditional mechanisms for caring for vulnerable children have been severely stressed (Somasundaram DJ, van de Put WA, 2006). Increased rates of abuse may also contribute to children's physical and emotional vulnerability in the aftermath of disaster. In one of the first attempts to empirically examine whether or not child abuse escalates after natural disasters, Curtis, Miller, and Berry (2000) discovered statistically significant increases in child abuse reports in the first six months following Hurricane Hugo and the Loma Pieta earthquake, but found no statistically significant change in abuse rates following Hurricane Andrew.

Keenan *et. al.,* (2004) examined whether there was an increase in traumatic brain injury (TBI—commonly referred to as shaken baby syndrome) among children two years old or younger after Hurricane Floyd. The results showed an increase in the rate of inflicted TBI in the most affected countries for six months following the disaster, possibly reflecting increased injury risk due to prolonged stress. Following the 2004 Indian Ocean tsunami, the media and advocacy organisations drew attention to the risks of sexual violence and human trafficking. That children, and especially girls, faced in displaced person camps. Drawing on interviews with women's advocacy organisations, Fisher (2005) documented incidents of rape, molestation, and physical abuse perpetrated against women and girls in the tsunami aftermath.

Chart – 7: Educational Vulnerability.

Educational Vulnerability

Disasters, which often destroy school buildings and displace students and teachers, may disrupt children's academic progress and diminish their long-term educational outcomes. More than 10,000 school buildings collapsed as a result of the 2005 Pakistan earthquake (Hewitt, 2007), leaving surviving children with few alternatives for an adequate education. In the year following Hurricane Katrina, hundreds of students in New Orleans were turned away from the public schools. As many as 1,150 schools in Indonesia were damaged or destroyed in the 2004 tsunami (UNICEF, 2005). However, the immediate attention to schools in the aftermath of the disaster and in the long-term reconstruction planning actually created a push to improve the overall quality of education in the affected region.

Research on drought in southern Africa reveals that children often leave school to support their parents or siblings during times of chronic disaster. Girls, in particular, are at special risk for being taken out of school because

Factors Influencing Children's Vulnerability in Disaster

Psychological Vulnerability	***Physical Vulnerability***	***Educational Vulnerability***
Life threat Family separation Death of a loved one Material loss Home/school damage Direct exposure or media exposure to disaster Child characteristics (race, age, gender, SES) Poor functioning pre-disaster Parental distress Low levels of social support Additional life stressors Negative coping skills	Living in poor communities in hazard-prone regions Living in/going to school in substandard structures Loss of a parent Family separation Child characteristics (age, gender, SES) Size, strength, stage of development Poor diet Parental distress Unsafe/unsanitary shelter environments Change of home/house	Destruction of school buildings Displacement of students and teachers Loss of vital records Delayed enrollment Multiple school changes Family instability Unwelcoming/unsupportive school environments Poor academic performance Loss of a parent/s Increased work demands Drop outs Loss of peer group

Source: (Peek Lori, 2008).

of cultural expectations and their heavier workloads. Young girls are expected to fetch water, help with household chores, and look after their siblings, while boys are responsible for tending livestock and looking for food. While children understood the importance of helping out with family responsibilities, many young people were unhappy about leaving school as they clearly recognised the importance of attaining a good education for future life chances (Peek Lori , 2008).

Victims and Survivors

Almost everyone in the population is affected by a disaster. No one is untouched by it. Those who suffer damage are called victims. The victims may die or live. Those who manage to live are called survivors.

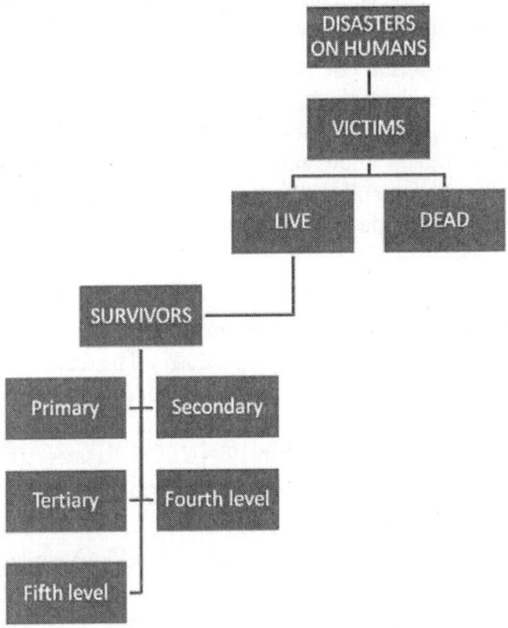

Chart – 8: Disasters on Humans

The survivors can be classified as:

Primary survivor–One who is exposed to the disaster first-hand and then survives. They are called *'survivor victims'*.

Secondary survivor–Person who grieves the loss of his/her primary victims. For example, a mother who lost her child or husband or another person who lost his friend.

Third level survivor–The rescue and relief personnel. These people are also affected due to the disaster as they are at the site of disaster and undergo almost the same mental trauma as the other victims.

Fourth level survivor–Reporters, government personnel, traders, etc.

Fifth level survivor–People who read about or see the event in media reports.

Disasters can result from forces of nature, such as floods, fires, hurricanes, and earthquakes; technological accidents, such as plane crashes, oil spills, and chemical releases; or terrorism and other wilful acts of violence. Disasters may be slow-moving in their onset or sudden and unexpected. What these events share in common is their potential to cause widespread community disruption, displacement, economic loss, property damage, death and injury, and profound emotional suffering.

Disaster risk is on the rise globally, largely as a result of the complex interplay between environmental, demographic, technological, and socio-economic conditions. Climate change, environmental degradation, population growth, increased urbanisation, unsustainable development in hazard-prone areas, risky technologies, and growing social and economic inequalities have all contributed to a dramatic increase in disaster events (Per row, 2006; Swiss Re, 2007).

Indeed, the number of natural disasters recorded globally has increased four-fold over the past three decades, growing from fewer than 100 in 1975 to more than 400 in 2005 (UN-HABITAT, 2007). The resultant financial and human costs have been tremendous. Adjusting for inflation, economic losses associated with natural disasters are now estimated to be 15 times higher than they were in the 1950s, and from 1994-2003, disasters caused approximately US$67 billion in losses each year (Gotha-Sapir, Margit, and Hoboes, 2004; World Bank, 2006).

During the same time period, more than 255 million people were affected annually by disasters, and these events claimed on an average of 58,000 lives every year (Gotha-Sapir *et al.,* 2004; World Conference on Disaster Reduction, 2005). Although disasters occur across the globe, the impacts are distributed unevenly, with as many as 98 per cent of those persons most affected living in developing countries (Un-Habitat, 2007).

Children—here defined according to the United Nations Convention on the Rights of the Child as persons age 18 and younger—represent a significant portion of those who endure the devastating consequences of disasters. At the end of the twentieth century, disasters affected an estimated 66.5 million children each year (Penrose and Tamaki, 2006). This number is likely to triple over the second decade of the twenty-first century, with up to 175 million children affected every year by disasters triggered by climate change (Save the Children UK, 2007).

Despite these figures, researchers and practitioners have historically overlooked children's experiences and needs in disaster. The lack of focus on children may be due in part to the common—and erroneous—assumption that young people are not seriously affected by disasters and that their reactions are fleeting (La Greco *et. al.,* 2002; La Greco, Silverman, and Wasserstein, 1998).

Anderson (2005) contends that social science disaster research on children has lagged in part because of their status in society:

(1) Children do not set the research agenda

(2) Children do not carry out research

(3) Children are not in policy-making or relevant professional positions.

Moreover, children's needs are often excluded from disaster preparedness planning and response activities. This is largely a function of children's lack of power to voice their concerns and the fact that most disaster professionals lack specific child health or child development expertise (Anderson, 2005).

Psychological and Emotional Problems of Survivors

Natural disasters such as the tsunami can have a devastating impact on the psychological and social well-being of anyone exposed to them. Disasters threaten personal safety, overwhelm defense mechanisms, and disrupt community and family structures. Such events may also cause mass casualties and destruction of property and may lead to a collapse of the social networks and daily routines of the individuals affected (Debra L., 2009).

Children and adolescents are more vulnerable than adults to the traumatic events of disasters. Even in preschoolers, the effects can be serious and persistent and can influence their personality development, but, at the same time, children have plasticity to change if an intervention can be developed to address their coping skills. A World Health Organisation (WHO)–funded study conducted in Indonesia (Suresh Bada Math, *et. al.,* 2008), reported that 20 per cent to 25 per cent of children affected by the 2004 tsunami in south and Southeast Asia required professional treatment for psycho-social problems. Depending on the cultural and social contexts, special measures must be taken to ensure the protection from harm of all children, as well as their equitable access to basic services. During this process of ensuring services to children, there is a high possibility that the support for adolescents may not be addressed effectively.

Childhood is a period of growth and development (NCPCR, 2013). It has been seen that the developing years are critical as these years lay the foundation for development into a well-adjusted adult. At each stage of development there are certain tasks that the child must get opportunities to master for a healthy personality development. Relevant and continuous interactions with caregivers, as well as their environment, enable the children to master these tasks and move on to the next phase of development. E H Erikson (1964) highlighted the important role environmental factors play in the normal development of the child and how lack of opportunities to adequately master the developmental tasks can lead to dysfunctional behaviour.

For instance, a child during babyhood must have caregivers who meet the basic needs of the child. Through this the child develops a sense of security and trust or else the child will not feel secure and will develop a general feeling of mistrust about people around him/her (NCPCR, 2013). As the child grows up, he/she needs an environment, which can be explored to enable the development of self-esteem, self reliance, and doing things on his/her own. When the child starts going to school, he/she makes friends and interacts with peers and learns from them.

All these are possible in an environment when the child has caring caregivers who give quality time to the child, a home where the child feels secure, has accessibility to school, and has playmates in the neighbourhood to interact with. A disaster like the tsunami disrupts the process of interaction the child has with his/her environment. It leads to displacement wherein the child loses his familiar environment (home, school, peers, etc). There is a sense of panic and confusion and the caregivers are unable to care for the child or not around for some time; and thus the regular life patterns are disrupted. There can be instances of death of either the parents, or one of the parents or sibling(s) or even a pet, leaving the child with a sense of loss. The child might find it extremely difficult to cope with loss. Disasters hamper the process of healthy emotional and psychological development (Yule, *et. al.,* 1999).

Psychological and emotional trauma is very common following any disaster. In the wake of a major disaster, many people may develop a number of emotional problems, depending on the impact and drama of their individual experiences (Ghodse and Galea, 2006). Many may require psychiatric help. It would be very difficult to estimate the number of people that will develop emotional problems and who may require such help (AACAP, 1998 and Amaya-Jackson L., 2000). No statistics exist presently on the subject.

Children are particularly vulnerable to disaster trauma, and this manifests in a variety of complex psychological and behavioural manifestations. However, often the post-disaster psychological reactions in children are not identified. Studies have noted that parents, teachers and even mental health professionals significantly underestimate both the intensity and the duration of the stress reactions in children. Depending upon the developmental stage, level of cognitive and emotional maturity, and limited coping strategies, the psychological reactions in children are expected to be different from those in adults. This is indeed the case and one cannot generalise adult findings to children besides, methods of intervention for children following disasters understandably vary from those from adults (Stevens and Slone, 2008).

The tsunami that affected thousands of lives including that of children was unexpected and sudden, leaving children confused, shocked and frightened. In a moment, their whole world was disrupted. Some children were orphaned, some lost one parent, some lost their siblings, and some had to adjust to a displaced life as they lost their homes. Some of the children live in the camps with little or no possessions and do not know when they can go back to their places and the adults around them are not in a position to provide much solace or comfort as they themselves are victims of the killer waves (DRC, 2005).

The normal daily routine is disrupted, and often there is no regular school, making it all the more difficult for the children to restore back to normal life. Children in their process of growth are presented with developmental tasks at certain ages that they must achieve in order to move onto the next stage successfully. They need stability and meeting of some basic needs to provide them the nurturance to develop into healthy adults (Christina Suboh, 2008). A disruption of familiar routine and previously secure world leaves children as one of the most vulnerable groups during and following a disaster. Given below are the impacts of the tsunami on the children.

Loss of Relationships

This can be with parents/siblings/caregivers like grandparents or other relatives, teachers, friends, neighbours, or pet. Loss of relationship can be due to death of a person, displacement, and absence since the person is away in a hospital or may still be missing (Kar N, Jagadisha, Murali N., 2001; Kar N, Bastia BK, 2006 and Kar N, 2006).

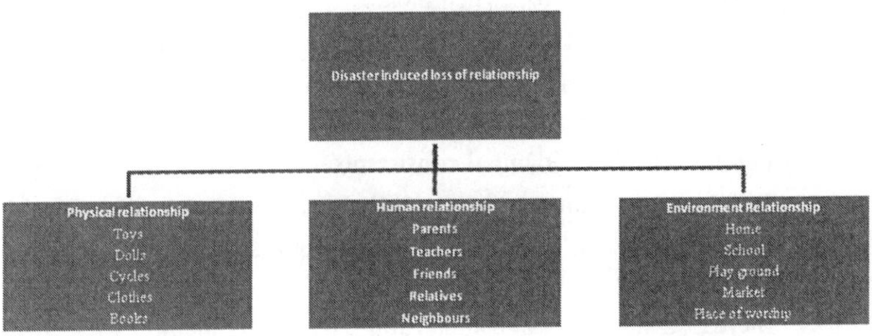

Chart – 9: Disaster Induced Loss of Relationship for Children

- Loss of possessions like toys, dolls, cycles, clothes, books, etc.
- Loss of physical parts or injuries to self or loved ones like a broken.
- Loss of familiar environment. Home, schools, play grounds, market area etc.
- Move out of their surroundings especially into new place with no friends.
- Not going to school.

Disruption of Daily Life

There are great changes in living conditions and daily life activities after a disaster. The routines children were comfortable with and the surrounding they knew no longer exist. Relationships with parents and significant others might undergo changes as caregivers are themselves affected by the disaster and become busy and preoccupied in getting their life back in order (Fetter JC, 2005). The children are thrown in to new surroundings all of a sudden. They are unable to lead the life they were earlier used to. Their life becomes difficult for the following reasons (Peek Lori, 2008):

Psycho-social Care for Children

- Relocation and live in relief camps
- Cramped living spaces
- Unhygienic living conditions
- Little or no personal belongings
- No access to school or having to go to a new school
- Making new friends or not having the old ones
- Being separated from family members
- Financial pressures for the family
- Malnourishment due to lack of proper food and water
- Struggle for food, shelter and other amenities
- Lack of access to proper healthcare
- Not having parents physically or emotionally available
- Parents busy retrieving their lost belongings, trying to look for missing family members
- Parents may face financial constraints
- Parents preoccupied or distressed by disaster related difficulties
- Role substitution to play adult roles (look after siblings, helping with chores, etc)
- Increased alcohol or substance abuse by family members
- Increased conflict amongst adults around them
- Lack of opportunities to participate in normal routines and activities.

Stress of Displaced Living

It is important to understand how children who have been affected by the tsunami would be processing the information gathered and what sort of reactions they show as a result. Since, children have limited capacities to process information, their sense of what happened is often not realistic and they are unable to comprehend the totality of the situation (Peek Lori, 2008).

Often adults tend to overlook the necessity to respond to needs/queries of the child and explain things to him/her, clarify his/her doubts. But the fact remains that children are the worst affected population in any disaster and need extra care and comfort. Children process events around them according to their developmental ages. It is important to try and understand how children of various age groups feel and react to a disaster situation so that they can be understood, reached and helped to feel better (NICE, 2005).

An unexpected disruption of a secure environment results in fear, anxiety, sadness and change of behaviours. Most children simply need time to experience their world as a secure place again and with their parents as nurturing caregivers (Giannopoulou I, *et. al.,* 2006). In the tsunami disaster, many of the children lost loved ones and thus it is important to understand how these children view death since this would be a core issue that children would need to deal with effectively. It is imperative for us to understand how children of different age groups feel and react after a disaster so that when we work with them we are able to relate to them in a better and empathetic way (Jones L., 2008).

Psycho-social Issues of Disaster Children

Small children view their world from the perspective of stability and availability of dependable caretakers. If this is disturbed, they feel anxious and restless. They feel helpless and fearful in the face of a disaster, especially if they are separated from parents. They find it difficult to protect themselves and may feel very insecure without adult caregivers. They are often unable to express their feelings. They typically look to parents, significant others and older siblings for comfort and stability (www.aap.org).

Children who have lost one or both parents need more attention. Loss of a relative, playmate, or a pet can be very disturbing. It is important to understand how children who have been affected by the tsunami would be processing the information gathered and what sort of reactions they show as a result. Since, children have limited capacities to process information, their sense of what happened is often not realistic and they are unable to comprehend the totality of the situation (www.aap.org). Often adults tend to overlook the necessity to respond to needs/queries of the child and explain things to him/her, clarify his/her doubts. But the fact remains that children are the worst affected population in any disaster and need extra care and comfort. Children process events around them according to their developmental ages. It is important to try and understand how children of various age groups feel and react to a disaster situation so that they can be understood, reached and helped to feel better (Nilamadhab Kar, 2009).

An unexpected disruption of a secure environment results in fear, anxiety, sadness and change of behaviours (Pynoos RS, Goenjian *et. al.,* 1993).

Most children simply need time to experience their world as a secure place again and with their parents as nurturing caregivers. In the tsunami disaster, many of the children lost loved ones and thus it is important to understand how these children view death since this would be a core issue that children would need to deal with effectively. It is imperative for us to understand how children of different age groups feel and react after a disaster so that when we work with them we are able to relate to them in a better and empathetic way (AACAP, 1998 and Amaya-Jackson L., 2000).

The following information has been adapted from the psycho-social issues for children and families in Disasters CD HSS series, American Academy of Pediatrics and explains to us about what children think about death at various ages (www.aap.org).

- Children who have lost one or both parents need more attention.
- Loss of a relative, playmate, or a pet can be very disturbing.
- Infants-No comprehension but sense something has happened.
- Recognise that people around are unhappy or worried and hence become afraid.
- May change eating, sleeping and toilet habits in pre-school.
- Death brings confusion and guilt.
- Views illness and death as a punishment for some wrong doing.
- May see death as something that is reversible.

School age children have the ability to understand what the tsunami has done to the people and the environment around them. This makes them sad about the family members being killed in the tsunami and worried about near and dear ones who are injured. School age children have a need to understand what has happened and the concrete steps that they can take to prepare and protect themselves from any such happenings in future (Friedberg & McClure, 2007). Children at this age are much attached to parents, siblings, friends, and their pets. Thus, a loss of any of the aforementioned people causes a great amount of distress to children and they find it difficult to cope. Often children are unable to identify the emotions that they are experiencing. To all appearances they may seem to be all right but there might be lot of turmoil and conflicts within them that requires to be ventilated. They may want to talk about the details of the event over and over again (www.aap.org).

Aged between 5-9 Years

- Often feels responsible for the events and the loss
- Begins to realise that death is final but believes it will never happen to him/her or anyone known
- Tends to personify death

- May associate death with a skeleton or have nightmares.
- Unavailability of other family members to help cope is worrying
- May think about it as magical illusion or punishment
- Develops an interest in the causes of death (violence, old age, sickness)
- Has to cope with social reactions like people at school or others around

Aged between 9-12 Years

- Starts recognising that death are permanent and common to anyone who is alive
- May deny loss and carry on with his/her life
- Curious and interested in the gory details and asks questions
- Starts an interest in biological factors of death
- Wonders who will care for him/her
- May regress to an earlier stage of development
- May feel guilty and overcomes this by attempting to be very good.

Normally, it's during adolescence (12-18 years) that one gains maturity, becomes independent and competent in carrying out his/her daily life activities. They are capable of taking many responsibilities and making decisions. However, when a disaster results in deaths, adolescents are not sure how to handle their own emotions, and may feel guilty and responsible for the deaths that occurred (Kar N, Jagadisha, Murali N., 2001; Kar N, Bastia BK, 2006 and Kar N, 2006).

Adolescents

- Have adult notions and view death as inevitable, universal, and irreversible
- Try to be independent and will feel dependent when forced to face a loss
- Find it very confusing and may have suicidal feelings
- Will question life itself and want a lot of discussions based on life and death
- Need someone to listen; to talk with
- Think about their own deaths which can be frightening
- May withdraw and deny the loss
- May feel guilt, anger, even some responsibility for death that occurred
- Not sure how to handle own emotions in public or private, they need adult guidance.

The manner in which every child processes his/her own experiences will be unique and exclusive to him/her. The age of the child, the events he/she has been through, the amount of exposure to the event, the support and care available to him/her for recovery, will all play important role in how the child is able to cope and deal with his/her emotional reactions. One must remember that;

- These emotional reactions are normal responses to an abnormal experience
- Reactions are common and experienced by everyone
- No one who experiences a disaster is untouched by it
- Reactions manifest differently at different periods of time after the disaster.

After a horrifying disaster like the tsunami, it is inevitable that children will indulge in antisocial acts such as stealing, substance abuse, and use of foul language. This in no way should be interpreted as reflecting the child's character. Instead it is more a reaction of the child to the pain and trauma that he/she has gone through-a response to the event the child has been unable to comprehend and cope with. If one understands this, then one is in a better position to help the child in the recovery process (www.aap.org).

Age-wise Consequences of Disaster

After a disaster, children can show physical reactions, emotional reactions and there can be behavioural changes. These are normal reactions to an abnormal event in their life. Children of different age groups react differently as they perceive the event differently. The reactions are temporary for most children and some support and attention can help them to overcome the trauma and reach their normal level of functioning. Given below are the reactions shown by children of different age groups (NIMHANS, 2005).

Preschool (1-5 years)

- Temper tantrums
- Crying, whimpering or screaming
- Excessive clinging and demanding
- Regressive behaviour (thumb sucking, wanting to be carried, bed-wetting)
- Loss of bowel/bladder control
- Fear of darkness
- Fear of being left alone
- Easily frightened and then angry
- Sleep disturbances-gets up crying, unable to sleep alone, nightmares

- Sensitivity to loud noises
- Fears weather-lightening, rain, strong winds
- Moodiness, irritability
- Helplessness and confusion
- Loss of appetite
- Speech difficulties
- Increased aggression, especially in boys.

School Age (6-11 years)

- Physical complaints-headache, stomach aches, giddiness
- Aggressive behaviour at home or school
- Bed-wetting
- Change in appetite
- Inability to sleep, nightmares
- Sadness and apathy
- Disobedience
- Disruptive behaviour
- Understands loss and becomes anxious
- Withdrawal-does not relate with friends
- Fear of recurrence, fear of darkness, sleeping alone
- Separation from parents
- Fear about weather; water, safety, imaginary fears
- Difficulty in following routines
- Fights with siblings, parents, friends
- Disinterest or difficulties in school work
- Disturbs others, worrying, remains tense
- In-disciplined refusal to go to school, poor concentration
- Feels guilty and responsible for the loss.

Hence, the study was concentrated to study about psychological impact of various factors responsible for the crisis; the following information gives conceptual factors of psychological and social disorder.

Psycho-social Disorder

Children constitute 40 per cent of our total population and the most precious resource of a nation and it would be sensible to assure their welfare, emotional and physical well-being regardless of the prevailing political climate or the priority of the advocacy group. In recent times, the physical wellbeing of children has sought the attention of the national level policies in many countries, but the mental health of the children is yet to gain its due place.

Mental Health

The basic concept of mental health is a controversial notion, based upon the philosophical premise of the separation of mind and body. Even within a medical model this view has distinct limitation. In medicine, health has largely been viewed as the absence of identifiable pathology. An individual is healthy when he or she is not sick. For year's psychologists have pointed to the fact that in behaviour disorders, or so called mental illness, the simple identifications of similar disease entities was the exception rather than the rule some psychologists (Eysenk, 1960) have called for the entire notion of disease entities to be banished from the realm of modern psychology (www.mental health/SAMSHA.gov).

The White House conference, preliminary Report (1930) quotes "mental health may be defined as the adjustment of individuals to themselves and the world considerate behaviour and the ability of facing and accepting the realities of life".

Children and Mental Health

A manual on child mental health and psycho-social development prepared by WHO (1982) identified the following guidelines as important:

- Children need to be healthy and happy to become productive and contented adults
- Understand children on what they do at different ages
- Help them to solve their problems
- Learn that children think, feel, and learn differently at different stages
- Children only grow happy when others around are interested in them
- The general health of a child also affects how he think and feels
- Remember that children of opposite sex behave differently
- Many things children cannot do for themselves and they need help from adults
- If the children feel sad, afraid or anxious much of the time, it is a sign of expecting help
- Children cannot develop their personality to the fuller extent unless they feel at home
- Children who are burdened with anxiety could not learn whole heartedly
- Children with self doubt exhaust their energies in fighting the private battle
- The disturbed child strives continuously to satisfy the needs and to resolve his conflicts

- There are few children; deviant in behaviour to a significant degree found everywhere
- Many children who cannot and do not express their problems and feelings
- Many children need help from a skilled professional
- Teachers must be aware of and sensitive to the needs of these children.

Chapter - 4

Treatment Process–An Overview

A catastrophe such as an earthquake, hurricane, tornado, fire, flood, or violent acts is frightening to children and adults alike. It is important to explain the event in words the child can understand. Parents should also acknowledge the frightening parts of the disaster when talking with a child about it. Falsely minimising the danger will not end a child's concerns. Several factors affect a child's response to a disaster (Nilamadhab Kar, 2009). Therapy can be very helpful to lessen or alleviate ongoing symptoms of adjustment disorder before they become disabling.

Group therapy can be useful to individuals who are enduring similar stress. In some situations the role and participation of community, such as citizen groups, schools, and businesses could be very useful to ease the depression or the anxiety associated with adjustment disorder (Mitchell and Everly, 1996).

Focusing Children

The way children see and understand their parents' responses are very important. Children are aware of their parents' worries most of the time, but they are particularly sensitive during a crisis. Parents should admit their concerns to their children, and also stress their abilities to cope with the disaster (AACAP, 1998 and Amaya-Jackson L., 2000). Helping children overcome emotional problems in the wake of a disaster is a considerable task for parents, teachers, and mental health professionals. Most children have similar fears after a tragic occurrence: that the event will happen again, that someone they love will be hurt or die, and that they may be left alone. First and foremost, all children must have their basic needs met. They need food, clothing, shelter, and to feel safe with someone who cares about them. Assuming that these needs have been met, as well as any health issues addressed, there are actions adults can take to alleviate children's anxiety (www.kellybear.com).

A child's reaction also depends on how much destruction and/or death he or she sees during and after the disaster. A child's age affects how the child will respond to the disaster (AACAP, 1998 and Amaya-Jackson L., 2000). Following a disaster, people may develop Post-traumatic Stress Disorder, which is psychological damage that can result from experiencing, witnessing, or participating in an overwhelmingly traumatic event. Children with this disorder have repeated episodes in which they re-experience the traumatic event. Children often relieve the trauma through repetitive play. In young children, upsetting dreams of the traumatic event may change into nightmares of monsters, of rescuing others, or of threats to self or others (Jones L., 2008). PTSD rarely appears during the trauma itself. Though its symptoms can occur soon after the event, the disorder often surfaces several months or even years later (Friedberg and McClure, 2007).

Psychotherapy

Psychotherapy is a method of treatment for a behaviour disorders, mental illness, or any other condition by psychological means. Psychotherapy may employ insight, persuasion, suggestion, reassurance, and instruction so that patients are helped to understand themselves and their problems more realistically and have the longing to cope up successfully. Psychotherapy is a general term that is used to describe the process of treating psychological disorders and mental distress. During this process, a trained psychotherapist assists the client tackle a specific or general problem such as a particular mental illness or a source of conflict. Depending on the approach used by the therapist, a wide array of techniques and approach is utilised. However, almost all types of psychotherapy involve developing a therapeutic relationship, communicating and creating a dialogue and working to overcome problematic thoughts or behaviours (www.about.psychology/psychotherpy.com).

The primary goals of treatment are to relieve symptoms and assist with achieving a level of adaptation that is comparable to the affected person's level of functioning before the stressful event (Nilamadhab Kar, 2009). The trauma experienced by an individual victimised by a natural disaster or terror attack reverberates through an entire family. Although based in established clinical practice, intervention with survivors of disasters is a different process from other treatments. Most mental health professionals recommend a form of psycho-social treatment for this disorder. Treatments include individual psychotherapy, family therapy, and behaviour therapy (Michael E., 2006).

Pharmacotherapy

Anxiety disorders comprise the most widespread mental health disorders among children and adults. Psychotherapy and pharmacotherapy are effectual in improving clinical impairments from anxiety disorders and maintaining this enhancement. After discussing the clinical guidelines which includes Food and Drug Administration indications and off-label use of medications, and considerations for special populations and youth with comorbidities it has been observed that moderate effectiveness of medication, particularly selective serotonin reuptake inhibitors, in the treatment of anxiety disorders in youth (An Kodish, *et. al.*, 2011). Mental health professionals generally do not use medication to treat this disorder. When medications are used, they are usually in addition to other forms of treatment.

Preventive Measures/Preparedness

Richard Mahapatra (2007) Disasters are not predictable; disaster preparedness is about managing the unknown. If disasters warned in time then there are possibilities to reduce the loss. Hence effective disaster management depends on preparedness, mitigation before the event, relief, and rehabilitation. Disasters are unforeseen, but one can make efforts to prevent the causalities and destruction that it brings. One can plan in future how to prevent the maximum loss of human life and their belongings (Vijayakumar, Kannan and Daniel, 2006).

There are serious limitations in India's state of preparedness. India has no national disaster management policy, the state administration being in charge during a crisis (Richard Mahapatra, 2007).

The Geological Survey of India is mapping 22 cities to review their vulnerability to earthquakes. But what we need most of all is not yet more surveys, but the enforcement of earthquake-resistant building codes, as the standards are not being followed.

The centre has asked the state governments to convert their departments of relief and rehabilitation into disaster management departments. Perhaps the government feels that a change in nomenclature is all that is required. The fact of the matter is that disasters have to be planned for, and that disasters hurt less when planned beforehand.

At present the states are being funded only for relief and rehabilitation; a policy shift is required to allocate funds for disaster prevention and mitigation instead. State governments are still being allocated funds according to their spending during the previous financial year.

Intervention Strategy

Organising the Intervention Process

Disaster workers, involved in rescue and relief measures, need to be trained well in advance in the concepts of emotional first aid, basic communication skills in dealing with traumatised children, and the importance of talking to children about the trauma (Giannopoulou I, *et. al.,* 2006). They need to be sensitised about prevention of abuse and neglect of children in such situations. Mental health support should be blended with other disaster relief work rather than done separately (Kessing LV, 2007).

It is most helpful to train and support health workers from the affected communities about the post-disaster mental health aspects. Cultural competence is an important issue for counselling in post-disaster situations, which can be easily met by local volunteers than the external mental health professionals (Klein DN, Shankman SA, Rose S, 2006). Jyotsana Shukla, (2013), suggested that from the community local volunteers, medical personnel in the primary level of health care and teachers may be trained in handling the psychological impact of disaster on children victims.

The role of mental health professionals is to train the disaster workers, support them in dealing with the mental health issues of the children and help the workers whose own responses may complicate the recovery, besides managing the referred children with complex psychological manifestations (Benight and Bandura, 2004; Ussher, 1992; Chesler, 1972).

It is important that the mental health problems of the children are recognised as early as possible and supportive measures are put in place at home, school and in society. The family context is central to understanding and meeting the needs of traumatised children. Intimate mother-child, family and relative relationships are important in the healing process and in the immediate aftermath children should be close to their families (Rachman S, Wilson GT, 1980). Relatives and foster families adopting orphaned children can be extremely helpful. School-based mental health programmes can provide accessible services to children affected by disaster, reduce trauma-related psychopathology, and emphasise normalisation (Salzman L., Thaler FH, 1981).

Sometimes children may need to be removed from a stressful environment in order to provide them with a comfortable and supportive set up for faster coping and recovery. Recovery of the children from the traumatic experience is also dependent on broad social and economic recovery of the community or country. There is a need to incorporate public mental health approaches, including systematic screening and trauma/grief-focused interventions, within a comprehensive disaster recovery program (Nilamadhab Kar, 2009).

Psychological Support

Early psychological intervention is recommended following disasters especially when the disaster is associated with extreme and widespread damage to property, ongoing economic problems of the stricken community, violence that resulted from human intent, and a high prevalence of trauma in the form of injuries, threat to life and loss of life. The issue is particularly critical in developing countries (Debra L., 2009).

The key factors of post-disaster psychotherapy for children are to listen, clarify, support attachment bonds, facilitate symbolic expression in play and art, and to support the capacity to imagine repair (Nilamadhab Kar, 2009). Many children want to talk about how they and their family are feeling. It is important to help children to make sense of their feelings and to find words for their feelings. It is recommended to follow the child's lead, avoid probing, and respond only to what the child has spontaneously introduced, and to support containment of overwhelming feelings. In the case of the loss of a parent or family member, facilitating the child's need to remember and talk about their lost loved one is needed (Debra L., 2009).

Post-disaster Counselling

Post-disaster counselling should be made available for extended periods, with shifting emphasis to meet the changing needs of high-risk groups. Supportive interventions include fostering a sense of safety and efficacy, connecting patients with communities and services, and helping parents talk about the trauma with their children. A community-based approach with trained grass-root health care workers can provide effective psycho-social support and rehabilitation services (Somasundaram DJ, van de Put WA, 2006).

Cognitive Behaviour Therapy

Cognitive behaviour therapy (CBT) is considered by many to be the mainstay of treatment of children and adolescents with PTSD. The efficacy of CBT in alleviating post-traumatic stress symptoms after catastrophic disaster has been demonstrated (Shooshtary MH, *et al.,* 2008). Short-term group CBT has also been found useful with long-term benefit. Significant improvement was reported in children at an 18-month follow-up, with treatment gains being maintained at a 4-year follow-up (McFarlane AC, 1987 and Kar N, *et. al.,* 2007). For older children with severe post-traumatic symptoms or with severe PTSD, trauma-focused CBT should be offered in the first month after the traumatic event. Where appropriate, families should be involved in the treatment of PTSD in children and young people (Catani C *et. al.,* 2008 and Rutter M., 1987).

Treatment studies in non-disaster related PTSD in children have indicated that cognitive behaviour interventions including direct discussion of the trauma, desensitisation and relaxation techniques, cognitive reframing and contingency reinforcement programs for problematic behaviours would be useful (Silva RR, *et. al.,* 2003 and Donnelly CL, and Amaya-Jackson L., 2002).

Grief-focused Psychotherapy

It seems that trauma-focused interventions have strong clinical and some empirical support despite controversies. Trauma-focused interventions involve exploration of the traumatic event and its impact with the child. However, some clinicians avoid directly discussing the traumatic event for various reasons, e.g., fear of transient increase of symptoms of children, because of their own need to avoid the negative effect associated with such discussion, the idea that repeated questioning may change a child's memory of the event, etc. (Debra L., 2009). But the evidence suggests that direct exploration of the traumatic experience through relaxation and desensitisation procedures has positive effect, helps in mastering anxiety and grief, produces immediate relief and no further distress.

The components of trauma-focused interventions generally include techniques of stress management (relaxation, thought-stopping, positive imagery, deep breathing, etc), evaluation and reconsideration of cognitive assumptions the child would have about the trauma, and inclusion of parents and other supportive individuals in treatment. Few have examined the treatment for PTSD in children faced with disaster in a controlled fashion (Hamblen J., 2006).

Efficacy of a school-based short-term group and individual trauma/grief-focused therapy in adolescents exposed to disaster has been reported it has been found that un-treated adolescents worsened gradually. Brief trauma/grief-focused psychotherapy is not only effective in reducing PTSD symptoms, but it can also halt the progression of depression (McFarlane AC, 1987 and Kar N, *et. al.,* 2007). Emotional First Aid techniques have been used to deal with PTSD in disaster situations. The therapeutic tools include clarification of facts about the trauma, normalising children's PTSD reactions, encouragement of expression of feelings and teaching problem-solving techniques (Catani C *et. al.,* 2008 and Rutter M. 1987; IFRC, 2009).

Group Therapy

Using schools, hospitals and other community settings for this purpose, many authors have focused on the efficacy of group therapy for children affected in a common traumatic event (Mitchell and Everly, 1996). This kind of approach seems to be the best way of dealing with the problem of a number of children being affected in a typical disaster. Interventions in groups have been found to be effective to promote catharsis, support, and a sense of identification with the group. Special groups for children should be considered in post-disaster situations (Ignacio Jarero, *et. al.,* 2008).

Play Therapy

Jordan, *et. al.,* (2013) observed that play can be used both as a medium of assessment and therapy for children. A play interview is essential when examining a child less than seven years old but should be utilised for all pre-pubertal children. Through play children can express verbally and non-verbally difficult painful emotions, their wishes and fears, concerns, fantasies, reenactments and traumatic experiences. The frequency of natural disasters has increased over the last decade (Ignacio Jarero, *et. al.*, 2008). Tsunamis, tornadoes, earthquakes, and hurricanes have ravaged towns, cities, and countries, leaving thousands dead. Beyond the physical injuries suffered, the survivors of these catastrophes, many of them children, often suffer emotional devastation, and profound losses of routines, friends and family, and a sense of security.

Child-centred play therapy empowers children as they lead the play session with a trained adult, assisting them on their journey. This therapy modality allows the child to be in control, which is paramount for those having experienced natural disasters where they were completely helpless. The child may then begin to heal as they make sense of their trauma through their natural language of play. This article provides literature review supporting a case for child-centred play therapy for children experiencing natural disasters as well as recommendations for future research in this area.

Child-centred play therapy (CCPT) is based on the fact that children communicate primarily through play (Landreth, 2002). Jennifer Baggerly *et. al.*, (2010) Children can be supported emotionally through the engagement processes, explained about difficult situations, bereavement and suggested coping methods through the play content. Interaction with an empathic, objective, neither judgmental nor over-indulgent therapist enables the child to reintegrate, reorganise and proceed with recovery. Potentially the child may internalise and identify with those qualities in the therapist.

Involving Parents and Families

It is extremely important to involve parents in assessment and intervention. Psycho education of the family members and the children involved in the disaster about the manifestations is particularly helpful in the management of post-disaster mental health sequel (John H. Ehrenreich, 2001). Parents also need help to understand and accept that the child's perplexing and disturbing expressions and behaviours in the post-disaster situation are "normal" to an "abnormal" situation. They should be more accessible, answering child's questions, directly and honestly, without providing more information than children need. They should turn off the television and not expose children to endless repetition of the images of a traumatic event. The families should be encouraged to try to return to ordinary daily life and customary routines as soon as possible.

Disaster and Psycho-social Concepts

Positive Mental Health

The positive mental health based on the recognition that all children have potentials or talents, sometimes very modest and sometimes great, that may either be allowed to languish or at the other extreme, may be developed to the fullest. It is these abilities cultivated to a higher level that constitute positive mental health (NIMHANS, 2007).

Adolescents' Mental Health

Like adults, children and adolescents can have mental health disorders that interfere with the way they think, feel and act. Mental health influences the ways individuals look at themselves, their lives, and others in their lives. Like physical health, mental health is important at every stage of life (www.mental health/SAMSHA.gov).

Child, Adolescent and Family

The mental health needs of children and their families are met within the context of community-based systems of care. Systems of care are developed on the premise that the mental health needs of children, adolescents, and their families can be met within their home, school, and community environments.

Post-disaster Mental Health

Symptoms of anxiety and depression are most common. Pre-school children can present with features of separation anxiety, stranger anxiety, fears of monsters or animals and avoidance of situations (Nilamadhab Kar, 2009). There can be compulsively repetitive play which represents part of the trauma but fails to relieve anxiety (post-traumatic play). Trauma may also be represented by less repetitive plays like normal play activity (play re-enactment). Both these types of play can suggest re-experiencing. In the place of avoidance/numbing, only constriction of play, social withdrawal, and restricted range of affect or loss of acquired developmental skills can be present. Some children start believing that there are certain signs which predict a traumatic event and if they are alert, they can detect signs such as omen formation (www.mental health/SAMSHA.gov).

Acute PTSD presents more with typical physiological hyper arousal and re-experiencing and sleeps problems; the chronic variety presents with dissociation, restricted affect, sadness, and detachment. Dissociative symptoms may take the form of hallucinations or disorganised thinking and behaviour. The phenomena of re-experiencing, numbing and avoidance and hyper arousal in children are comparable to those in adults. However, there can be major differences in manifestation, for example, in young children, repetitive play may occur, in which themes or aspects of the trauma are expressed; the children may actually re-enact the trauma instead of re-experiencing it; and their dreams may not have any specific trauma-related contents. Numbing or avoidance may take the form of restlessness, hyper alertness, poor concentration, and behavioural problems (Ghodse and Galea, 2006).

Many symptoms of PTSD overlap with other childhood disorders namely, attention deficit hyperactivity disorder (ADHD), depression, conduct disorder, oppositional defiant disorder and substance use (Kar N, Jagadisha, Murali N. 2001; Kar N, Bastia BK, 2006 and Kar N, 2006). Moreover, PTSD is highly co morbid with these conditions (McFarlane AC, 1987 and Kar N, *et. al.,* 2007). Results of studies on course of PTSD in children are unclear and contradictory. There are reports of the prevalence/symptom severity decreasing, remaining the same, or increasing during the follow-ups.

Study Habit

Natural disaster has a consequence on the mental health of children leading to problem in their study habit. It is to be remembered that children study habits play a crucial role in their life for a successful academic career. For a student a study habit is something that is done on a scheduled, regular, and planned basis that is not relegated to a second place or optional place in a students' life. It is not merely to allot time but to dedicate oneself to the application and the task of study which is to become engrossed in a process of learning, practice, and enlightenment-education of one's self. Treating good study habits are essential for success in school, college and throughout life. Study habits that serve the child create better grades, a better relationship with the teacher, a sense of satisfaction and confidence (www.parenting-childdevelopment.com/study-habits).

Anxiety Disorders

Anxiety is a normal reaction to stress. It helps one deal with a tense situation in the office, study harder for an exam, and keep focused on an important speech. In general, it helps one cope. But when anxiety becomes an excessive, irrational dread of everyday situations, it has become a disabling disorder.

Generalised Anxiety Disorder

Generalised Anxiety Disorder, GAD, is an anxiety disorder characterised by chronic anxiety, exaggerated worry, and tension, even when there is little or nothing to provoke it. People with generalised anxiety disorder (GAD) go through the day filled with exaggerated worry and tension, even though there is little or nothing to provoke it. They anticipate disaster and are overly concerned about health issues, money, family problems, or difficulties at work. Sometimes just the thought of getting through the day produces anxiety (www.depression-understood.org).

Obsessive-Compulsive Disorder

Obsessive-Compulsive Disorder, OCD, is an anxiety disorder and is characterised by recurrent, unwanted thoughts (obsessions) and/or repetitive behaviours (compulsions). Repetitive behaviours such as hand washing, counting, checking, or cleaning are often performed with the hope of preventing obsessive thoughts or making them go away. Performing these so-called "rituals," however, provides only temporary relief, and not performing them markedly increases anxiety (Edna B. Foa, 2010). People with obsessive-compulsive disorder (OCD) have persistent, upsetting thoughts (obsessions) and use rituals (compulsions) to control the anxiety these thoughts produce (Mowrer OH, 1960).

Being afraid of social embarrassment may prompt people with OCD to comb their hair compulsively in front of a mirror-sometimes they get "caught" in the mirror and can't move away from it. Performing such rituals is not pleasurable. At best, it produces temporary relief from the anxiety created by obsessive thoughts (Stern RS, 1978).

Other common rituals are a need to repeatedly check things, touch things (especially in a particular sequence), or count things. Some common obsessions include having frequent thoughts of violence and harming loved ones, persistently thinking about performing sexual acts the person dislikes, or having thoughts that are prohibited by religious beliefs. People with OCD may also be preoccupied with order and symmetry, have difficulty throwing things out (so they accumulate), or hoard unneeded items (Valderhaug L, Götestam P, 2007; Abramowitz JS, 2007).

Healthy people also have rituals, such as checking to see if the stove is off several times before leaving the house. The difference is that people with OCD perform their rituals even though doing so interferes with daily life and they find the repetition distressing. Although most adults with OCD (Vogel PA, Stiles TC, Gotestam KG, 2004).

Depression

Depression is a mental health disorder that can affect the way you eat and sleep, the way you feel about yourself, and the way you think about things. A depressive disorder is more than a passing mood. It is not a sign of personal weakness, and it cannot be willed or wished away (Saigh and Bremner, 1999).

The following are the symptoms of depression (also called as major depressive episode) (DSM-IV) (Carrion, *et. al.*, 2002; Levendosky, *et. al.*, 2002):

- Depressed mood for almost every day and for the majority of the day

- Loss of interest or pleasure in activities;
- Considerable weight loss or weight gain;
- Difficulties falling asleep or sleeping too much;
- Feeling constantly on edge and restless or lethargic and slowed down;
- Feeling worthless and/or guilty;
- Difficulties concentrating and/or making decisions;
- Thoughts of ending one's own life.

According to the DSM-IV, to be diagnosed with a major depressive episode, a person must experience 5 of these symptoms all within the same two-week (or longer) period (Anderson, 2005). Depression is different from just feeling unhappy or sad. Everyone feels sad from time to time. However, depression is more intense, lasts longer, and has a large negative impact on a life of human being.

Major Depressive Disorder

There are three common forms of depression are; Major Depression, Dysthymia, and Bipolar Disorder. Even within these types of depression there are variations in the number of symptoms, their severity, and persistence. A diagnosis of major depressive disorder (or unipolar major depression) is made if an individual has five or more of these symptoms during the same two-week period. Unipolar major depression typically presents in discrete episodes that recur during a person's lifetime.

Major depressive disorder is a mood disorder characterised by a depressed mood, a lack of interest in activities normally enjoyed, changes in weight and sleep, fatigue, feelings of worthlessness and guilt, difficulty concentrating and thoughts of death and suicide. If a person experiences the majority of these symptoms for longer than a two-week period, they may be diagnosed with major depressive disorder (Fekadu *et. al.,* 2006).

Dysthymic Disorder

The terms *dysthymia* and *dysthymic disorder* refer to a mild to moderate, chronic state of depression. It is a less severe type of depression that lasts a long time but involves less severe symptoms. If you suffer from dysthymia you probably lead a normal life, but you may not be functioning well or feeling good. People with dysthymia may also experience major depressive episodes at some time in their lives (APA, 2000).

Bipolar Disorder

This is also called as manic-depression; is another type of depressive disorder. Bipolar disorder is thought to be less common than other depressive disorders (www.nimh.nih.gov). The mood swings are sometimes dramatic and rapid, but usually are more gradual. When in the depressed stage, a person can have any or all of the symptoms of a depressive disorder (Fekadu A *et. al.,* 2006).

According to Shibre T (2002); Bipolar disorder (or manic-depressive illness) is characterised by episodes of major depression as well as episodes of mania–periods of abnormally and persistently elevated mood or irritability accompanied by at least three of the following symptoms: overly-inflated self-esteem; decreased need for sleep; increased talkativeness; racing thoughts; distractibility; increased goal-directed activity or physical agitation; and excessive involvement in pleasurable activities that have a high potential for painful consequences.

When in the manic stage, the individual may be overactive, over talkative, and have a great deal of energy (Fekadu A, *et. al.,* 2006). Mania affects thinking, judgment, and social behaviour, sometimes in ways that cause serious problems and embarrassment. A person in a manic phase may feel elated, full of grand schemes that might range from unwise business decisions to romantic sprees. Mania if left untreated may worsen to a psychotic state, where the person is out of touch with reality (Negash A *et. al.,* 2005).

Postpartum Depression

Pregnancy brings about many hormonal shifts. These dramatic shifts can sometimes affect mood. This is commonly known as the "baby blues." Postpartum depression can be more than just a case of the blues, however. It can range from mild symptoms that go away without treatment all the way up to postpartum psychosis, which left untreated, may be responsible for tragic murders of children (WHO, Gender and health in disasters, 2002).

Seasonal Affective Disorder

Seasonal affective disorder, or SAD, also known as winter depression is an affective or mood disorder. Most SAD sufferers experience normal mental health throughout most of the year, but experience depressive symptoms in the winter or summer. SAD is rare, if existent at all, in the tropics, but is measurably present at latitudes of 30 degrees N (or S) and higher. Seasonal mood variations are believed to be related mostly to daylight, not temperature. Prolonged periods of overcast weather can also exacerbate SAD. SAD is a serious disorder (www.sciencedaily.org).

If a person experience depression, sleepiness, weight gain and carbohydrate cravings during the winter months, but feel great as soon as spring returns, then this condition is called as Seasonal Affective Disorder (SAD). Climate change is an emerging challenge to the mental health of entire humanity. Several studies, in recent times, have brought to light the adverse public mental health outcomes of extreme weather events for the suffering communities. The general public and the policy-making bodies need to gain awareness about these impacts. Through such awareness, communities and their governments can institutionalise mechanisms to provide psychological support to the populations affected by climate change, before it becomes a massive public health challenge and starts affecting the social and vocational lives of people (Jyotsana Shukla, 2013).

Pre-menstrual Dysphonic Disorder

The most frequently reported symptoms of premenstrual syndrome (PMS) include irritability, fatigue, anxiety, nervous tension, mood swings, depression, feeling overwhelmed or out of control, physical symptoms of swelling or bloating of the abdomen or extremities, appetite changes and food cravings, aches, and breast tenderness (Kathleen M, *et. al.,* 2010). These symptoms may occur for several days to two weeks before menses but subside with the onset of the menstrual period. When these symptoms, especially those of mood, are severe, a diagnosis of premenstrual dysphonic disorder (PMDD) may be made (www.researchgate.net).

Adjustment disorder

Adjustment disorder caused due to depressed mood, anxiety, mixed anxiety and depressed mood, disturbance of conduct, mixed disturbance of emotions and conduct and unspecified (www.socialworktoday.com). Adjustment Disorder is an abnormal and excessive reaction to an identifiable life stressor. The reaction is more severe than would normally be expected, and can result in significant impairment in social, occupational or academic functioning. The response may be associated to a single event such as flood or fire, disaster, divorce, starting school, new job or due to multiple happenings that occur in school, family, marital, business, job, society and community. Added to that; various stressors such as child witnessing the parents fighting constantly, chemotherapy, financial difficulties, exposure to risky living, etc., (www.psychologytoday.com).

Adjustment disorder often occurs with one or more of the following: depressed mood; anxiety, disturbance of conduct and maladaptive reactions or problems related to job or school, physical complaints, social isolation. More over adjustment disorders are linked with higher risk of suicide and suicidal behaviour; substance abuse; prolonging of other medical disorders or interference with their treatment. Adjustment disorder that persists for a longer time would lead to more serious mental disorder affecting the life of an individual (www. psychcentral.com).

To Conclude

Thus, disasters bring trauma to children and to all others who becomes victims. The consequences of disaster are inevitable unless otherwise prepared for it or else adopt preventive measures and that too to a certain extent. It is essential that children need to be protected both before and after the disasters. Indeed their sufferings and difficulties need to be given at most importance as it is seldom noticed and given less significance. As children belong to the weak and vulnerable sections of the community their issues are to be addressed by professionals to make them the future assets of the nation.

Chapter - 5

Psycho-social Impact on Disaster Children

Disaster and Psycho-social Well-being

Introduction

Natural and man-made disasters affect everyone in their path. Some people are nevertheless more vulnerable than others and suffer in different ways and to different extents. The disasters such as tsunami highlighted a number of pre-existing factors that made some people especially vulnerable and it also brought out the ways in which other people became vulnerable (Manuel carballo, *et. al.,* 2006).

Natural disasters can especially be traumatic for children and youth. Experiencing a dangerous or violent flood, storm, wildfire or earthquake is frightening even for adults and the devastation to the existing environment can be long lasting and distressing. Often an entire community is affected. These factors present a variety of unique issues and coping challenges, including issues linked with specific types of natural disasters. Hence the need is created to relocate when home and/or community have been destroyed (Lazarus PJ *et. al.,* 2003).

CRED, (2005) classified disasters into natural disasters, man-made disasters and hybrid disasters. Man-made disasters are classified into technological disasters, transportation accidents, public places failure, and production failure. No definition of disaster is universally accepted. Several criteria are proposed to define disasters. Understanding the definitions, criteria, types, aids, researchers and agencies in the proper classification, good recording and better analysis of disasters is rather difficult.

Disasters have different characteristics and impact; however, disasters have a common element - the severity.

Disasters bring together multiple actors who often differ in terms of sector, expertise and nationality, as well as in terms of their abilities, values, norms and goals (Alberts DS, 2010). Disasters normally associated with massive structural, economic, and population devastation Research studies and follow-up reported significant mental health distress among the respondents (David Abramson *et. al.,* 2008). Disasters have increased in incidence worldwide and children are especially vulnerable as victims.

Childhood is an important period during which physical, mental and social development and growth take place (Weissbecker, *et. al.,* 2008). After catastrophic natural disasters, post-traumatic reactions in children may reach epidemic proportions, remain high for a prolonged period and jeopardise the well-being of the children in the affected region (Pynoos RS, Goenjian *et. al.,* 1993).

IFRCRC (2001) reported that natural disasters are sub divided into hydro-meteorological (earthquakes, volcanic eruptions) and geo-physical (avalanches/landslides droughts, famines, extreme temperatures, floods, forest, windstorms, waves surges) categories, to emphasise the effect on the decade's disasters of the global warming. The definition of non-natural (or human-made) disasters has widened to include conflicts, riots, fires, industrial and chemical accidents, building collapses, mass dislocation due to political unrest, insurgency and epidemics such as water-borne diseases, malaria, plague, and so on.

While all people living in hazard areas are vulnerable, the social impacts of hazard exposure often fall disproportionately on the most vulnerable people in society–the children, elderly, disabled poor and minorities. These groups are often the least prepared for any emergency, have the least resources with which to prepare for a hazard, tend to live in the highest-risk locations in poor housing and lack knowledge or social and political affiliations necessary to take benefit of resources that would make their recovery quickly (Dunning, 2009; NRC, 2006).

Children can be more susceptible to the toxicity of biologic, chemical, and radioactive agents than adults are and, consequently, can be the first to manifest the effects of these agents. Young children exposed to infectious agents often become ill before adults do because their exposure is greater, because their immune systems are less mature, and because they may not yet be fully immunised (Debra L., 2009).

Common psychiatric manifestations among children include acute stress reactions, adjustment disorder, depression, panic disorder, post-traumatic stress disorder, anxiety disorders specific to childhood and psychotic disorders. Co-morbidities and sub-clinical syndromes are also common (Nilamadhab Kar, 2009).

Informal social support networks were associated significantly with better mental health status. Housing and economic circumstances were not independently associated with poorer mental health (David Abramson, *et. al.*, 2008). Mental health distress and disability are pervasive issues among victims. As time progresses post-disaster, social and psychological factors may play greater roles in accelerating or impeding recovery among affected populations. 'Social vulnerability is most apparent after a hazard event has occurred, when different patterns of suffering and recovery are observed among certain groups in the population' (Cutter *et. al.*, 2003).

Social Vulnerability

Social vulnerability perspective aims at identifying and understanding which groups of people may be more sensitive and susceptible to the impacts of natural disasters and why. This knowledge base will enable more targeted 'solutions' and strategies and will therefore enhance the opportunity for effective mitigation and increasing future social capacity and resilience' (Tapsell, S, *et. al.*, 2010).

Vulnerability can be defined as the state of a system before an event triggers a disaster. Vulnerability can also be defined in terms of the likelihood of the outcome of the losses of a system measured in the form of economic or human life losses. Another view is that 'vulnerability is a combination of a particular state of that system with other factors such as capacity to cope and recover; the latter introducing the concepts of resilience and resistance' (Galderisi *et. al.*, 2010).

'Social vulnerability in itself can be treated as a distinct, multifaceted entity incorporating issues of livelihood, housing, security and gender among many others. Social norms and customs, international, national and private and public law may regulate these' (Parker *et. al.*, 2009). Fekete (2008) comments: 'Social vulnerability is often hidden, complex and nested in various human aspects and contingencies bound to different levels of society'.

Social Vulnerability and Disaster

A term used to define the susceptibility of social groups to potential losses from hazard events or society's resistance and resilience to hazard (Blaikie *et. al.*, 1994 and Hewitt, 1997). 'The characteristics of a person or group and their situation that influence their capacity to anticipate, cope with, resist and recovery from the impact of a natural hazard and it involves a combination of factors that determine the degree to which someone's life, livelihood, property and other assets are put at risk by a discrete and identifiable event' (Wisner *et al.*, 2004).

'Social vulnerability derives from the activities and circumstances of everyday life or its transformations' (Hewitt, 1997). 'The condition of a given area with respect to hazard, exposure, preparedness, prevention, and response characteristics to cope with specific natural hazards. It is a measure of the capability of this set of elements to withstand events of a certain physical character' (Weichselgartner, 2001).

Vulnerability Indicators

S.No.	*Characteristics*	*Vulnerability indicators*
1.	Age	Children and very elderly
2.	Gender	Women
3.	Employment	Unemployment
4.	Occupation	Unskilled (also linked to income and financial status)
5.	Education level	Low educational level
6.	Family/household composition	• Large families • Single parents • Single person households • Home
7.	Ownership of house	Renter
8.	Nationality/Ethnicity	Minorities New migrants
9.	Type of housing	Single storey accommodation mobile housing
10.	Number of rooms	Low number of rooms overcrowding
11.	Levels of risk awareness and preparedness	Low awareness low preparedness
12.	Previous Disaster experience	No experience
13.	Access to decision-making	Little access
14.	Trust in authorities	No trust
15.	Health and differently-abled	Long-term-illness Disability
16.	Length of residence	Linked to short residence
17.	Serviced by warning system	No warning system

Source: (Tapsell *et. al.*, 2005).

'Social Vulnerability is a more complex constructs such as healthcare provision, social capital and access to lifelines' (Cutter and Emrich, 2006). It emanates from social factors that place people in highly exposed areas, affect the sensitivity of people to that exposure, and influence their capacity to respond and adapt (Yarnal, 2007).

'The rationale behind measuring vulnerability and the use of vulnerability indicators has been summarised by Birkmann (2006) who discusses different definitions and conceptual frameworks used by the different schools of thought. At broad level information on social vulnerability helps to:

- Define where the greatest need is and set priorities
- Determine actions e.g. by improving intervention tools
- Monitor progress and analyse trends
- Measure effectiveness of mitigation approaches
- Anticipate undesirable states
- Inform policy-makers and practitioners
- Alert the public and raise awareness
- Stimulate discussion
- Gain funding
- Promote poverty reduction initiatives
- Represent social responsibility
- Look at the social roots of vulnerability.

Reducing Vulnerability

Wisner *et al.,* (2004) emphasized the importance of taking a 'bottom-up' approach and document the weight of local knowledge and action as well as stressing the significance of the skills, capacities and political consciousness of ordinary people. They suggest seven objectives for risk reduction which are at the HEART (CARDIAC) or core of their message:

C = **Communicate** understanding of vulnerability
A = **Analyse** vulnerability
R = focus on **Reverse** of PAR model
D = emphasise sustainable **Development**
I = **Improve Livelihoods**
A = **Add Recovery**
C = extend to **Culture.**

Elements necessary for increasing capacities and reducing vulnerability in Disaster Management (Wisner *et al.,* 2004):

- Positive economic and social trends
- Access to productive livelihoods
- Sound family and social structures
- Good governance
- Established networks regionally/nationally
- Participatory community structures and management
- Suitable physical and service infrastructures

- Local plans and arrangements
- Reserve financial and material resources
- Shared community values/goals
- Environmental resilience.

Five Packages to reduce social vulnerability in disaster management (Tapsell, S, *et. al.*, 2010):

- Capacity building
- Risk governance
- Risk perception
- Risk communication
- Risk education.

The foundations of social vulnerability as identified by (Tapsell, S, *et. al.*, 2010) are:

- What level-individual, household, community, and regional
- Who or what are the elements of social vulnerability
- How to identify vulnerable social groups
- Which groups would benefit the most
- What attributes or capacities people posses that might reduce vulnerability.

Children and Disaster

The review on children and disasters revealed that scholars and practitioners should take careful effort in understanding the experiences of children (Lori Peek, 2008). Response to disaster by healthcare providers must include disaster site, hospital, and community based responses that consider not only pediatric victims but also the facilities to care for them. (Debra L., 2009). Following disaster, systematic screening for psychological problems in children needs to be done. An integrated approach combining psycho-socio-educational aspects added with clinical interventions is proved to be fruitful (Nilamadhab Kar, 2009).

David Abramson *et. al.,* (2008) suggested that efforts to expand disaster recovery and preparedness policies to include long-term social re-engagement efforts. Post-disaster follow up should be considered as a means of reducing mental health. It may be too difficult for others who lack the specialised expertise of mental health training to attend to both the child's physical and emotional needs, and it may be impossible for those without medical training to impress on medical personnel the importance of emotional issues (Pfefferbaum, B., 1998).

Manuel carballo *et. al.,* (2006) contended that major social and demographic shifts occurred, and the social fabric of communities was severely eroded. Gender, age, extent of personal loss, personal experience in terms of how direct or indirect exposure emerged as key factors together with loss of place, problems of temporary and permanent housing, poor income generation and uncertainty about if and when it would be possible to return to original home sites and communities.

It is evident that frequency and intensity of disaster events increase around the globe, children are among those most at risk for the negative effects of disaster (Lori Peek, 2008). Psychological consequences at early stage could lead to further damage in future life both in the physiological and psychological wellbeing. Disasters lead to stress, physiological deregulation and subsequent illness in children (Weissbecker *et. al.,* 2008).

There may be expectation from children from significant adults for guidance on how to manage their reactions after the immediate threat is over (Lazarus P. J., *et. al.,* 2003; Manuel carballo *et. al.,* 2006) further reported that host communities were also affected, albeit indirectly. How and to what extent people were psychologically 'damaged' in, and by, the tsunami nevertheless remains poorly defined because of the paucity of real-time monitoring and the fact that in some countries there was little agreement on the nature and classification of psycho-social problems and morbidity.

Gurwitch, R.H. *et. al.,* (1998) observed that in the past few decades, the study of the impact of trauma and disaster on children has grown; however, information about the effects on very young children is still scarce in the literature. In some regards, the characteristics of stress in young children are similar to those of older children and adults; in other ways, their reactions are unique.

Psycho-social Impact on Children

Richard Spates, C. *et. al.,* (2007) reported that children and adolescents are exposed to traumatic events that lead to physical injury in many cases, psychological perturbation in most cases, and enduring psychological reactions, notably post-traumatic stress disorder, in a minority of individuals. Eight months after the disaster, interaction in the disaster-affected families was characterised by increased levels of conflict, irritability and withdrawal (McFarlane, A. C., 1987).

This sequence of events can affect later development, learning, emotions, and behaviour. In the process of caring for the physical injury, it is important for the primary care practitioner (PCP) to correctly interpret these presentations and anticipate the need for specific assessments, immediate intervention, referral, and follow-up. This report provides the foundation for such actions on the part of the PCP (Richard Spates C. et. al., 2007).

Maternal overprotection was also a common feature of care in these families. Post-traumatic morbidity in parents was the major determinant of the observed changes in family functioning and overprotection. Most of the children who lost both parents have been positioned with community or extended families first and then there is a need to establish a proper monitoring system to ensure that foster families act in the child's best interest and in this regard UNICEF and other agencies are assisting the government in setting up such a monitoring system (Yin Yin New, 2005).

Dhavale, *et. al.,* (2001) noted that research and clinical data on early exposure to violence show that consequence of such an exposure is wide-ranging, leading to emotional and mental trauma. The findings revealed the high prevalence of distress symptoms such as sleeplessness, anxiety, fear of playing found among children and this has a psycho-social impact. Wooding, S., and Raphael, B. (2004) observed the importance of a developmental approach to children understands of disaster, particularly death and the nature of grief and loss are discussed as is the distinction between the phenomenology of bereavement and trauma. Family and community support are highlighted as protective factors, and a number of recent, valuable recommendations for intervention including psychological first aid and cognitive-behavioural therapy are described.

The interaction of long-term conflict and rapid onset 'natural' disaster can provoke severe psychosocial response (Sarah Bradshaw and Maureen Fordham, 2013). It is necessary that a public-health approach that not only prepares for such scenarios, but responds by maximising the use of existing systems and agency linkages, is taken. References and further reading may be available for this article. To view references and further reading you must purchase this article. Children of flood victims were assessed blindly for signs of distress, including fear, depression, and anxiety and observed that children from the flooded area demonstrated more distress than those from the non-flooded area (Burke, J. D., P. Moccia *et al.,* 1986).

Impact of Specific Disasters

It is obvious that disasters bring devastation to human life and there are specific impact attributed to the type of disasters. It is Lazarus P. J, *et. al.,* (2002) categorised the consequences specific to certain disasters.

(a) Hurricanes: Hurricanes can be predicted days to weeks in advance, giving communities time to prepare. These predictions give families time to gather supplies and prepare. At the same time, however, these activities may generate fear and anxiety. Although communities can be made aware of potential danger, there is always uncertainty about the exact location of where the hurricane will impact. When a hurricane strikes, victims experience intense thunder, rain, lightning, and wind.

Immediate reactions to hurricanes can include emotional and physical exhaustion. In some instances children may experience survivor guilt. Research indicates that greater symptomatology in children is associated with more frightening experiences during the storm and with greater levels of damage to their homes.

(b) Earthquakes: Aftershocks differentiate earthquakes from other natural disasters. Since there is no clearly defined endpoint, the disruptions caused by continued tremors may increase psychological distress. Unlike other natural disasters (e.g., hurricanes and certain types of floods), earthquakes occur with virtually no warning. This fact limits the ability of disaster victims to make the psychological adjustments that can facilitate coping. This relative lack of predictability also significantly lessens feelings of controllability. Survivors may have to cope with reminders of the destruction.

(c) Tornadoes: Tornadoes can bring mass destruction in a matter of minutes and individuals typically have little time to prepare. Confusion and frustration often follow. Similar to a hurricane, people experience sensations during tornadoes that may generate coping challenges. Survivor guilt has been observed to be an especially common coping challenge. It is revealed that there is a significant associations between children's disturbances and having been in the impact zone, been injured, and having experienced the death of relatives.

(d) Floods: Floods are one of the most common natural disasters. Flash floods are the most dangerous as they occur without warning; move at intense speeds; and can tear out trees, destroy roads and bridges, and wreck buildings. In cases of dam failure the water can be especially destructive. Research has reported that many children who survive a destructive flood experience psychological distress.

(e) Wildfires: Unlike other natural disasters such as earthquakes, there is often some warning of an advancing wildfire. However, depending upon the wind and terrain the direction and spread of a wildfire can change abruptly. The amount of warning can vary from one neighbourhood to the next. Even if evacuation is not ultimately necessary, preparing for the possibility can be frightening for children. Reactions immediately following a wildfire may include emotional and physical exhaustion. In some instances children may experience survivor guilt.

Impact on School Life

As Janiece De Socio, R.N. (2004) took an integrative review of literature to examine the impact of children's mental health on their school success; it was confirmed that a convergence of problems associated with school performance and child and adolescent mental health. Poor academic functioning and inconsistent school attendance were identified as early signs of emerging or existing mental health problems during childhood and adolescence.

Among the goals of school nursing is to provide a process for identification and resolution of students' health needs as they affect educational achievement. Thus, it is within the scope of practice and goals of school nursing to also address children's mental health needs, as they affect school performance. It is concluded that school nursing is well-positioned to respond to the need for mental health promotion, illness prevention, and early intervention related to children's mental health (Janiece De Socio, R.N., 2004).

Lien L. *et. al.,* (2005) has observed that several studies have shown that children who are relatively young within a school year are at greater risk for poorer school performance compared with their older peers. One study also reported that relative age within a school year is an independent risk factor for emotional and behavioural problems. The objective of this study was to test the hypothesis that relatively younger adolescents in the multiethnic population who have poorer school performance and more mental health problems than their relatively older classmates within the same school year.

After stratifying for gender, the peer problem scores differed significantly between age groups only among boys. The SCL-10 score was significant, but only in girls and in the opposite direction to that expected, with the oldest pupils having significantly higher scores than the other two groups ($p < 0.05$). In adolescents from a multicultural city in Norway, relative age within a school year significantly influenced academic performance (Lien L. *et. al.,* 2005).

Siddiqui, A.Q. *et. al.,* (1983) identified the various factors affecting academic achievement of school children. More over this study assessed the relationship of academic performance with intelligence, socio-economic status, and parental attitude. A sample of 200 students (100 high and 100 low achievers), 12-15 years of age were selected from two different schools of Aligarh city. Examination marks from the two previous years were taken to assess the scholastic achievement of each student. The following standardised tools were used to assess the socio-economic status, intelligence and family relationship:

- G.P. Srivastava's socio-economic status scale (urban)
- P.N. Mehrotra's verbal and non-verbal test of intelligence and
- G.P. Sherry and Sinha's family relationship inventory.

It is concluded that besides intelligence, various psycho-social factors were responsible for better or poor academic performance. Factors such as SES, intelligence, and parent avoidance had a significant influence on academic performance, while parental acceptance did not play an effective role. However, high achievers got moderate parental attention (Siddiqui, A.Q. *et. al.,* 1983).

Singh, R.K. and Singh, P., (1989) examined the social and familial variables in relation to school adjustment. In their study they investigated school adjustment in relation to social and familial variables such as education and occupation of father and number of children, stable-unstable economic conditions, and place of dwelling.

Though sample consisted of 250 high school students; they were classified as high and low groups based on their performance on the High School Adjustment Inventory (HSAT). Findings indicated that the predictors of good school adjustment were higher education and occupational status of fathers, small family size, stable home conditions and higher economic status. Rural-Urban dwelling made no difference (Singh, R.K. and Singh, P., 1989).

Wangoo, M.I. and Khan, M.A. (1991) when assessed the socio-economic status with academic achievement of disaster children they made a comparative study of government schools and private schools and studies its influence on their academic achievement. Three government schools and three private schools rated as highly advanced, advanced and regular, were selected. Thirty girl students (in the age group13, STD VII) from each of the six schools were selected yielding a total of 180 children. The findings of the study make it evident that not surprisingly, the higher the SES, the higher was the academic achievement.

Suneeta, B. and Mayuri, K. (1999) observed the effects of familial factors on academic achievement of school children when they are affected by a disaster. Based on the premise that family performs a crucial role in the academic performance of children, the present study investigated the effect of certain select family variables on the academic achievement of the children. The subjects (N=120) from classes IX and X were recruited from ten private schools. Respondents were selected on the basis of their academic performance in the previous annual examination, and those securing first to sixth ranks from each class comprised the sample.

The parents of the children also formed the sample of the study. The tools used for data collection were an interview schedule for children that gathered information regarding their perception of parental contributions, expectations, sibling assistance from other family members (Suneeta, B. and Mayuri, K., 1999).

Impact on Mental Health

Math, S.B. (2007) while analysing the psychological impact of the Tsunami on Children and Adolescents observed that the most common psychiatric morbidities observed among the primary and secondary survivors were adjustment disorder (N = 5, 13.5 per cent), depression (N = 5, 13.5 per cent), panic disorder (N = 4, 10.8 per cent), post-traumatic stress disorder (N = 4, 10.8 per cent), schizophrenia (N = 1, 2.7 per cent), and other disorders (N = 16, 43.2 per cent).

The background of the study ((Math, S.B., 2007) is that an assessment was made to have a presentation of symptoms and psychiatric morbidity of children and adolescents from the Andaman and Nicobar islands during the first three months following the December 2004 earthquake and tsunami. This study included 37 primary and secondary survivors (aged 8 to 18 years) and 498 tertiary survivors of the tsunami disaster selected from the 10th and 12th grades of schools in Port Blair, India.

Majority of the children (75 per cent) have physical problems, psychological problems. (75 per cent), and face social and adjustment problems (65 per cent). Moreover 61 per cent of children face economic problems (Priya R and G. Kanaga, 2013). A Primary Survivor is one who was exposed directly to disasters like earthquake and tsunami, a Secondary Survivor is one who is closely related either through family bond like kinship or personal ties with primary survivors, and Tertiary Survivors are people belong to the communities beyond the impact area, a majority of which were exposed to disasters.

The following three screening and treatment methods were adopted:

- Mental health clinic
- Art therapy
- Group discussions.

Subclinical syndrome was present in the majority of the primary and secondary survivors. Few tertiary survivors had sub-syndromal symptoms. Only a few of the primary and secondary survivors required intensive individual psychiatric interventions; however, a majority of the primary, secondary, and tertiary survivors required community-based group interventions (Math, S.B., 2007).

It is common that children articulate their distress through their behaviour, as they are often less able to do so verbally. Withdrawal, nightmares, avoiding communication, poor concentration, and aggression were common such features (Ghodse and Galea, 2006). Many children between the ages of four and seven also displayed regressive behaviours, including clinging, fearfulness, bedwetting, startle reactions, as well as separation anxiety (Becker, 2007).

Community-based group interventions and group discussions are simple, easy to implement using local resources and effective in all groups, and provide important components of psycho-social rehabilitation. This kind of approach should be started as early as possible, targeting all children and adolescents affected by any disaster in developing countries (Math, S.B., 2007). When suffering occurs too early in life, when young brains are not equipped to withstand the experience, or if the pain is beyond the tolerable level, it can make people less sensitive and more focused on self-preservation, such as often occurs in cases of child abuse and neglect (Maia Szalavitz and Maiasz Time, 2013).

Several child rights groups involved in the post-disaster relief work have expressed concern over the possibility of the trafficking of the large number of children who are left 'vulnerable' by the devastation caused by the floods. They cautioned that the child traffickers swarm into relief and rehabilitation camps posing as relief workers and try to traffic children (Hakeem Irfan, 2013). The National Commission for Protection of Child Rights directing various authorities to take steps to safeguard unclaimed, unattended and vulnerable children (NCPCR, 2013).

The importance of Psycho-social Care for disaster victims has been stressed by Susan M. Becker (2007) as she proclaimed that the tsunami disaster in South Asia affected the mental health and livelihoods of thousands of child and adult survivors, but psychological aspects of rehabilitation efforts are frequently neglected in public health initiatives. It was a professional teams from the National Institute of Mental Health and Neurosciences in Bangalore, India, travelled to the worst-affected areas in South India and implemented a mental health programme of psycho-social care for child and adult survivors Susan M. Becker (2007). The feeling of guilt is common in all ages but especially prominent in young survivors (McDougall, 2005).

A train-the-trainer community-based model was implemented for teachers and community-level workers to respond to the emotional needs of children and adults. In resource-poor settings with few trained mental health professionals, community workers were taught basic mental health interventions by teams of psychiatrists, nurses and social workers as promulgated by Susan M. Becker (2007).

Reactions of Children

It is normal for many children to cope over time with the help of parents and other caring adults. However, some children may be at risk of more extreme reactions. The severity of children's reactions will depend on their specific risk factors. Most children experienced that their symptoms vanished within a few days or weeks of post-tsunami. On the contrary, there are children however, continued to exhibit psychological problems beyond the initial distress (Ghodse and Galea, 2006). Common post-disaster psychiatric morbidities among children are acute stress reactions, adjustment disorder, depression, panic disorder, PTSD, anxiety disorders specific to childhood, and phobias (Kar N, Jagadisha, Murali N., 2001; Kar N, Bastia BK, 2006 and Kar N, 2006).

Young people may also exhibit diverse symptoms than adults, and there is variation between children and adolescents (Hamblen, 2006). These include exposure to the actual event, personal injury or loss of a loved one, dislocation from their home or community, level of parental support, the level of physical destruction, and pre-existing risks, such as a previous traumatic experience or mental illness. Children, who were separated from their families, were at risk of human traffickers - trying to exploit surviving children through labour and sex work. The undertaking of illegal adoptions was also of concern (McDougall, 2005).

Symptoms may differ depending on age and according to Lazarus P. J., *et. al.,* (2003) could include for:

Preschoolers

- Thumb sucking
- Bedwetting
- Clinging to parents
- Sleep disturbances
- Loss of appetite
- Fear of the dark
- Regression in behaviour
- Withdrawal from friends and routines.

Elementary School Children

- Irritability
- Aggressiveness
- Clinginess
- Nightmares
- School avoidance
- Poor concentration
- Withdrawal from activities and friends.

Adolescents

- Sleeping disturbances
- Eating disturbances
- Agitation

- Increase in conflicts
- Physical complaints
- Delinquent behaviour
- Poor concentration.

Tsunami and Mental Health

Derogatis, *et. al.,* (2007) reported the prevalence of severe emotional distress and depressive symptoms using the Hopkins Symptoms for tsunami-affected communities that had experienced armed conflict arising from the ongoing independence movement. The data were collected for the purposes of a mental health assessment. In the sample of 262, 83.6 per cent demonstrated severe emotional distress, and 77.1 per cent demonstrated depressive symptoms. In multivariate regression models, severe emotional distress was positively associated with the number of tsunami-related deaths among household members.

Save people and their home from disasters is a great challenge. In 2004, the Sumatra Tsunami in the Indian Ocean killed more than 14,000 people and left 50,000 people homeless (Abhay Joshi and Aoki Misa, 2013). It is to be remembered that children are an especially vulnerable group in the event of a mass disaster like the Indian Ocean tsunami in 2004 (Vijayakumar, Kannan and Daniel, 2006). McFarlane, A.C. *et. al.,* (1987) in a longitudinal study of the psychological morbidity declared that rather than decrease with time, the prevalence of psychological morbidity increased significantly, after the disaster as at eight months.

Disasters greatly affect the mental health of children and adolescents, but quantification of such effects is difficult. Using prospective pre-disaster and post-disaster data for affected and control populations, we aimed to assess the effects of a severe disaster on the mental health and substance use of adolescents (Reijneveld, S.A., M.R. Crone, *et. al.,* 2003).

Initial assessment by Math, S.B., *et. al.,* (2006) revealed that 5-8 per cent of the populations were suffering from significant mental health problems following the early phase of the disaster. This may increase in the aftermath of the early relief phase. Psychiatric morbidity is expected be around 25-30 per cent in the disillusionment phase (Math, S.B. *et. al.,* 2006). Reijneveld, S.A., M.R. Crone, *et. al.,* (2003) suggested that mental health interventions after disasters should address anxiety, depression, thought problems, aggression, and alcohol abuse of directly affected adolescents and their peer group.

Adjustment Disorder

The issue of adjustment becomes an inevitable problem for children in relation to home, school and environment. The following are some of the prominent features of adjustment disorder observed by various researchers:

- Feelings of depression or anxiety or combined depression and anxiety.
- Acting against the rules and regulations of family, work, or society.
- Manifestation of behaviours like skipping school.
- Unexpected fighting, quarrel and recklessness.
- Withdraw socially.
- Isolating themselves.
- Suffer from physical illness.
- If suffering from a medical illness, that condition may worsen.
- Often poor performance in school or at work.
- Having more difficulty in their close and personal relationships.
- Depressed mood, hopeless feelings, and crying spells.
- Experience anxious feelings, nervousness and worry.
- Have a mixture of anxious and depressed feelings.
- Emotional disturbance.
- Behaviour problems.

Adjustment disorders can occur at any age. People are particularly vulnerable during normal transitional periods such as adolescence, mid-life and late-life.

Adjustment Disorder-Diagnosis

A mental health professional makes a diagnosis of an adjustment disorder by taking a careful personal history from the client/patient. It is important to the therapist to learn the details that surround the stressful event or events in that person's life. No laboratory tests are required to make a diagnosis of neither adjustment disorder nor are there any physical conditions that must be met (APA, 2000).

It is very important for the therapist not to overlook a physical illness that might mimic or contribute to a psychological disorder. If there is any question whether the individual might have a physical problem, the mental health professional should recommend a complete physical examination by a medical doctor. Laboratory tests might be necessary as a part of the physical workup (Casey, 2008).

The conditions associated with adjustment disorder develop within three months of the beginning of the stressful problem. An adjustment disorder usually lasts no longer than three to six months. The condition may persist, however, if an individual is suffering from chronic stress such as that caused by an illness, a difficult relationship, or worsening financial problems. It is appreciable that children often cope well when they face a trauma of a low or moderate scale. In fact there are three main factors involved in determining the child's experience of the trauma and the risk of long-lasting distress (Christina Suboh, 2008):

(1) Proximity to the event

(2) Relationship to victims and

(3) Extent of emotional distress in the moment of exposure.

Adjustment disorder may have number of symptoms and could include (APA 2000):

- Feeling of hopelessness
- Sadness
- Frequent crying
- Anxiety (nervousness)

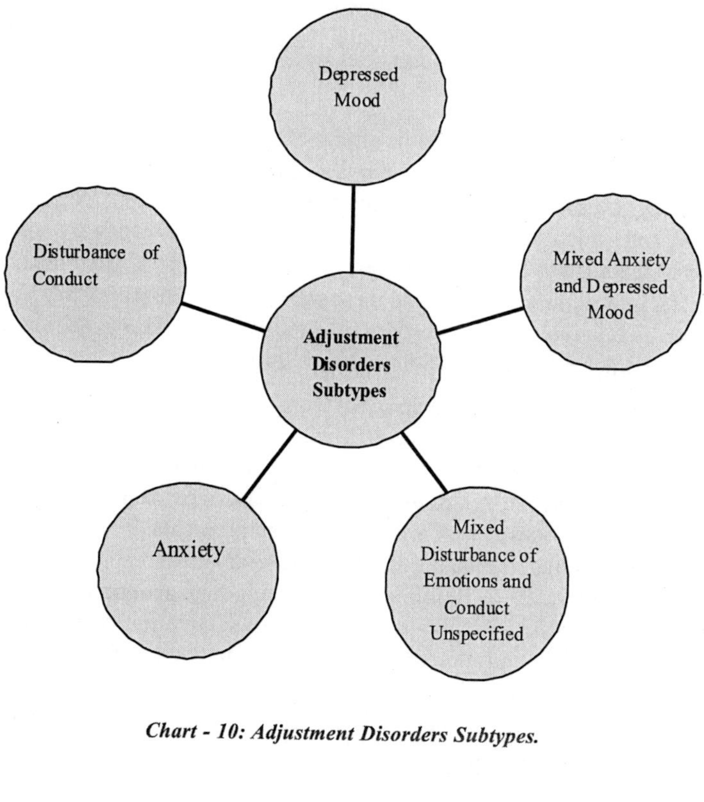

Chart - 10: Adjustment Disorders Subtypes.

- Worry
- Headaches or stomachaches
- Palpitations (an unpleasant sensation of irregular or forceful beating of the heart)
- Withdrawal or isolation from people and social activities
- Absence from work or school
- Dangerous or destructive behaviour, such as fighting, reckless driving, and vandalism
- Changes in appetite, either loss of appetite, or overeating
- Problems sleeping
- Feeling tired or without energy
- Increase in the use of alcohol or other drugs.

Disaster Induced Anxiety

Anxiety disorders are the most common psychiatric illnesses in children and adolescents. They are associated with significant distress and impairment. Most of the children and adolescents with anxiety disorders are not detected and only a minority receives adequate treatment. Anxious children and adolescents often follow a chronic course of disease with elevated risk of depressive disorders, substance abuse and even suicide (Rotberg B. *et. al.*, 2008).

On the other hand, six months after the disaster, a series of focus group studies found that the level of fear was still high and that people were still presenting severe physical and cognitive reactions (ICMH, 2005). Nightmares, anxiety and panic attacks, disbelief, and survivor guilt and anger were reported to be widespread in the communities directly affected by the tsunami. It is not clear how persistent or chronic these were, but in themselves they should be seen as relatively normal responses to the traumatic events people went through (Bracken, Giller and Summerfield, 2005).

Arunya Tuicomepee and John L. Romano (2007) proved that youth behaviour problems were positively associated with tsunami experiences and negatively associated with positive family functioning. Tsunami exposure, school connectedness, religious beliefs and practices, and availability of mental health services did not predict behaviour problems. Rotberg B. *et. al.*, (2008) identified the risk factors for anxiety disorders are complex and consist of intricate interplay of multiple factors, including genetic makeup and environmental risks. Effective, evidence-based treatments for anxiety disorders in children and adolescents consist of cognitive-behavioural therapy and pharmacotherapy with serotonin specific reuptake inhibitors. Further research is needed to design high-quality screening tools for anxiety disorders in the primary care setting.

Axelson D.A., Birmaher B. (2001) observed that there is a relation between anxiety and depressive disorders in childhood and adolescence of victims of disaster. Current research indicates that there is a strong relationship between pediatric anxiety disorders and depression. Assessment measures show high rates of correlation between depression and anxiety and much of the overlap may be related to a common domain of negative affectivity. Anxious youth and depressed youth share a cognitive style marked by a negative bias in information processing. Anxiety disorders and depression are frequently comorbid in children and adolescents.

Pediatric anxiety disorders and depression may share a genetically determined neurobiological component that could involve neural circuits that include or are modulated by serotonergic neurons. This component could contribute to the negative affective temperament that appears to be common in both pediatric depression and anxiety disorders (Axelson D.A., Birmaher B., 2001).

Jonathan Watts (2005) found that some of the child survivors in Tsunami tragedy say they are plagued by recurring nightmares about walls of water. So it leads to increase the suicide rates of the survivors of Tsunami children. Greg Miller (2005) reported that most survivors of the Indian Ocean disaster have shown remarkable resilience. Another research group (David A, *et. al.,* 2000) identified various symptoms of Depression and Anxiety among children. Differences between parent and child factor structures suggest that parents' and children's reports focus on somewhat different aspects of child psychopathology, and they can make qualitatively different contributions to the multiracial assessment of children (David A, *et. al.,* 2000).

Ratnin Dewaraja, *et. al.,* (2005) conducted a multidimensional assessment of the psychological condition of trauma-affected children in the Matara district in southern Sri Lanka. As a part of this assessment, the Synthetic-House–Tree–Person Test (S-HTP), and the Revised Children's Manifest Anxiety Scale (RCMAS) were administered to children (10–16 years old) studying in a school in an area affected by the tsunami, and in a school in a close by area that was not affected. Analysis of RCMAS data indicated that there were no significant differences in the overall anxiety scores of children in the two schools.

Swenson, C.C., C.F. Saylor, *et al.,* (1996) examined the duration of emotional and behavioural problems among children (aged 2-6 yrs) after they had experienced hurricane Hugo and assessed factors that predicted longevity of these problems. Respondents who had experienced the storm showed significantly higher anxiety and withdrawal and more behaviour problems than did children who had not. Behavioural problems decreased steadily over the six months following the storm.

The total anxiety scores of male children in the tsunami-affected school were significantly higher than in the non-affected school. Anxiety was significantly different only in male children between the two schools. (Ratnin Dewaraja, *et. al.*, 2005). Children showed various psychiatric disorders, such as enuresis and disturbance of behaviour/conduct or epilepsy and childhood psychosis (Sharma, R.G. 1984).

Major syndromes, depression, generalised anxiety disorders and alcohol abuse for dependence are the other major syndromes that were detected among the population. Somatoform pain disorders, mixed anxiety depressive disorders and exacerbation/ relapse of mental illness were also diagnosed in small percentage in the target group. While women worry about the recurrence of the tsunami, men are concerned about the future, the study has identified. While most of the fear had vanished by the fourth month, and appetites had largely improved, some of the fear had morphed into concern about the future and alarm on hearing loud noises Ramya Kannan (2005).

Disaster Induced Depression

Social withdrawal, self-blaming, and emotional regulation were linked with more severe depressive symptoms. Lower levels of symptomatology were found among the respondents who sought social support and engaged in cognitive restructuring. The overall symptom level in the sample did not exceed that of normative samples (Jeney-Gammon, P. *et. al.,* 1993). McDermott, B.M.C. and L.J. Palmer (1999) recommended that emotional distress was significantly associated with trait anxiety and evacuation experience and depressive symptoms. Depressive symptoms were associated with total distress core, trait anxiety and perception of threat to the parents. Substantial mental health morbidity was identified even after 6 months a disaster. Robert M. Glickman, M.D (2004) suggested that more numbers of children were affected by trauma and a state of hyper vigilance.

Externalizing symptoms such as behaviour problems and social skills deficits can also result from trauma. Even years after the trauma, children may continue to exhibit high rates of PTSD (26 per cent-95 per cent) and depressive disorder (28 per cent-76 per cent) (Robert M. Glickman, M.D., 2004). GAD is diagnosed when a person worries excessively about a variety of everyday problems for at least six months. Other anxiety disorders, depression, or substance abuse often accompany GAD, which rarely occurs alone. GAD is commonly treated with medication or cognitive-behavioural therapy, but co-occurring conditions must also be treated using the appropriate therapies (Crits-Christoph, P., 2011).

People with GAD cannot seem to get rid of their concerns, even though they usually realise that their anxiety is more intense than the situation warrants. They can't relax, startle easily, and have difficulty concentrating (Albano, A. M., 2003). Often they have trouble falling asleep or staying asleep. Physical symptoms that often accompany the anxiety include fatigue, headaches, muscle tension, muscle aches, difficulty swallowing, trembling, twitching, irritability, sweating, nausea, lightheadedness, having to go to the bathroom frequently, feeling out of breath, and hot flashes (ACA, 2005).

When their anxiety level is mild, people with GAD can function socially and hold down a job. Although they don't avoid certain situations as a result of their disorder, people with GAD can have difficulty carrying out the simplest daily activities if their anxiety is severe (Wood, J.J., 2003). The following are symptoms need to be included for depression such as a persistent sad mood; loss of interest or pleasure in activities that were once enjoyed; change in appetite or body weight; difficulty sleeping or oversleeping; physical slowing or agitation; loss of energy; feelings of significant worthlessness or inappropriate guilt; difficulty thinking or concentrating; and recurrent thoughts of death or suicide (Barlow, D. H., 2002). Research has found that (Hoehn-Saric, 1993) parents are even less likely to identify major depression in their adolescents than are the adolescents themselves.

Depression is a common and under-recognised problem in children and adolescents and is thought to affect upto 5 per cent of children. Untreated, depression can create problems at home, school and problem in relating with others. This may even lead to lead to drug abuse, behaviour problems and even suicide (APA, 2010). Although boys and girls are equally at risk for depression in early childhood, adolescent girls are twice as likely to become depressed as boys. Adolescents and children are also more likely to become depressed if they have a family history of depression, especially having a parent who was depressed at a young age. Children may lead to losing faith in the future or the feeling that the future might be short. It is clear that their previous picture of the world is questioned (Yule, *et. al.,* 1999).

Other risk factors can include being under a lot of stress, cigarette smoking, suffering the loss of a parent or loved one or a breakup of a affair with opposite sex, having attention, conduct or learning disorders or a chronic illnesses, such as diabetes, suffering abuse or neglect or some other trauma (Flannery-Schroeder, E. C., 2004). One of the most challenging problems in depression research and clinical practice is refractory which is otherwise difficult to treat. While approximately 80 per cent of people with depression respond very positively to treatment, a significant number of individuals remain treatment refractory. It has been estimated that disasters have a distressing effect on children, which represent 39 per cent of the overall population in the hardest-hit countries of the tsunami. Children are physically less able to outrun the water or withstand its' force. Hence, children depicted a huge proportion of casualties (UNICEF, 2005). Generally they also display more severe distress after a disaster when compared to adults (Stevens and Slone, 2008).

Disaster Induced Anxiety and Depression

Larger numbers of children were affected trauma, and a state of hyper vigilance. Severe depressive reactions are also common responses to disasters and often occur with PTSD (Robert M. Glickman, M.D., 2004). In addition to internalising symptoms such as depression and anxiety, externalising symptoms such as behaviour problems and social skills deficits can also result from trauma. Even years after the trauma, children may continue to exhibit high rates of PTSD (26 per cent-95 per cent) and depressive disorder (28 per cent-76 per cent) (Robert M. Glickman, M.D., 2004). However, while the literature suggests the majority of children and adolescents will eventually cope successfully for some, there will be an increased risk of higher levels of anxiety and depression compared to children who have not experienced a disaster (Benight and Bandura, 2004).

GAD is diagnosed when a person worries excessively about a variety of everyday problems for at least six months. People with GAD can't seem to get rid of their concerns, even though they usually realise that their anxiety is more intense than the situation warrants. They can't relax, startle easily, and have difficulty concentrating (Flannery-Schroeder, E. C., 2004). Often they have trouble falling asleep or staying asleep. Physical symptoms that often accompany the anxiety include fatigue, headaches, muscle tension, muscle aches, difficulty swallowing, trembling, twitching, irritability, sweating, nausea, lightheadedness, having to go to the bathroom frequently, feeling out of breath, and hot flashes (APA, 2010). GAD is commonly treated with medication or cognitive-behavioural therapy, but co-occurring conditions must also be treated using the appropriate therapies (ACA, 2005).

GAD is diagnosed when a person worries excessively about a variety of everyday problems for at least six months. People with GAD can't seem to get rid of their concerns, even though they usually realise that their anxiety is more intense than the situation warrants. They can't relax, startle easily, and have difficulty concentrating (Robert M. Glickman, M.D., 2004). Often they have trouble falling asleep or staying asleep. Physical symptoms that often accompany the anxiety include fatigue, headaches, muscle tension, muscle aches, difficulty swallowing, trembling, twitching, irritability, sweating, nausea, lightheadedness, having to go to the bathroom frequently, feeling out of breath, and hot flashes. It has once again been proved by researchers that there is an increased level of depression among traumatised youth. If the depression is severe, it can lead to suicidal thoughts and attempts many years after the traumatic event (Yule, *et. al.,* 1999).

When their anxiety level is mild, people with GAD can function socially and hold down a job. Although they don't avoid certain situations as a result of their disorder, people with GAD can have difficulty carrying out the simplest daily activities if their anxiety is severe (Robert M. Glickman, M.D., 2004). It is diagnosed when someone spends at least six months worrying excessively about a number of everyday problems. There is evidence that genes play a modest role in GAD (ACA, 2005). Other anxiety disorders, depression, or substance abuse often accompany GAD, which rarely occurs alone. GAD is commonly treated with medication or cognitive-behavioural therapy, but co-occurring conditions must also be treated using the appropriate therapies (APA, 2010).

Disaster Induced Depression and Mania

The following is the list of symptoms of depression and the list is not conclusive; more over and not everyone who is depressed or manic experiences all of the following symptoms. The severity of symptoms depends upon with individuals and varies over time.

Depression

- Persistent sad, anxious or feeling of emptiness
- Feelings of hopelessness
- Pessimism
- Feelings of guilt, worthlessness and helplessness
- Loss of interest or pleasure in hobbies
- Lack of interest in activities that were once enjoyed
- Decreased energy and fatigue
- Difficulty concentrating, remembering and making decisions
- Insomnia, early-morning awakening or oversleeping
- Appetite and/or weight loss or overeating and weight gain
- Thoughts of death or suicide; suicide attempts
- Restlessness and irritability
- Persistent physical symptoms that do not respond to treatment
- Consistent symptoms of headaches, digestive disorders and chronic pain.

Symptoms of Mania

- Abnormal or excessive elation
- Unusual irritability
- Decreased need for sleep
- Grandiose notions

- Increased talking
- Racing thoughts
- Increased sexual desire
- Markedly increased energy
- Poor judgment
- Inappropriate social behaviour.

Symptoms of Depression in Children

The diagnostic criteria and key defining features of major depressive disorder in children and adolescents are the same as they are for adults. However, recognition and diagnosis of the disorder may be more difficult in youth for several reasons. The way symptoms are expressed varies with the developmental stage of the youngster (Lazarus P. J, *et. al.,* 2003). In addition, children and young adolescents with depression may have difficulty in properly identifying and describing their internal emotional or mood states.

Symptoms of Major Depressive Disorder

- Persistent sad or irritable mood
- Loss of interest in activities once enjoyed
- Significant change in appetite or body weight
- Difficulty sleeping or oversleeping
- Psychomotor agitation or retardation
- Loss of energy
- Feelings of worthlessness or inappropriate guilt
- Difficulty concentrating
- Recurrent thoughts of death or suicide.

Five or more of these symptoms must persist for two or more weeks before a diagnosis of major depression is indicated.

Signs of Depression in Children

- Frequent vague and non-specific physical complaints
- Symptoms of headaches, muscle aches, stomachaches or tiredness
- Frequent absences from school or poor performance in school
- Talk of or efforts to run away from home
- Outbursts of shouting, complaining, unexplained irritability or crying
- Being bored
- Lack of interest in playing with friends

- Alcohol or substance abuse
- Social isolation and poor communication
- Fear of death
- Extreme sensitivity to rejection or failure
- Increased irritability, anger or hostility
- Reckless behaviour
- Difficulty with relationships.

Symptoms Shown by School-Aged Children according to John H. Ehrenreich (2001):

- Depression
- Withdrawal
- Generalised fear, including nightmares,
- Highly specific phobias of stimuli associated with the disaster
- Defiance
- Aggressiveness, "acting out"
- Resentfulness, suspiciousness, irritability
- Disorganised, "agitated" behaviour
- Somatic complaints: headaches, gastrointestinal disturbances, general aches and pains.
- Difficulties with concentration
- Intrusive memories and thoughts and sensations
- Repetitive dreams
- Loss of a sense of control and of responsibility
- Loss of a sense of a future
- Loss of a sense of individuality and identity
- Loss of a sense of reasonable expectations with respect to interpersonal interactions
- Loss of a realistic sense of when he or she is vulnerable or in danger
- Feelings of shame
- Ritual re-enactments of aspects of the disaster in play or drawing or story telling
- Kinesthetic (bodily) re-enactments of aspects of the disaster
- Omen formation
- Regression: bed wetting, soiling, clinging, heightened separation anxiety.
- Post Traumatic Stress Disorder syndromes.

While the recovery rate from a single episode of major depression in children and adolescents is quite high, episodes are likely to recur. In addition, youth with dysthymic disorder are at risk for developing major depression. Prompt identification and treatment of depression can reduce its duration and severity and associated functional impairment (ACA, 2005). Depression is a common and under-recognised problem in children and adolescents and is thought to affect up to five per cent of children. Untreated, depression can cause problems at home, school and with social interactions and can lead to drug abuse, behaviour problems and even suicide (Yule, *et. al.,* 1999).

Other risk factors can include being under a lot of stress, cigarette smoking, suffering the loss of a parent or loved one or a breakup of a romantic relationship, having attention, conduct or learning disorders or a chronic illnesses, such as diabetes, suffering abuse or neglect or some other trauma, including natural disasters (APA, 2010).

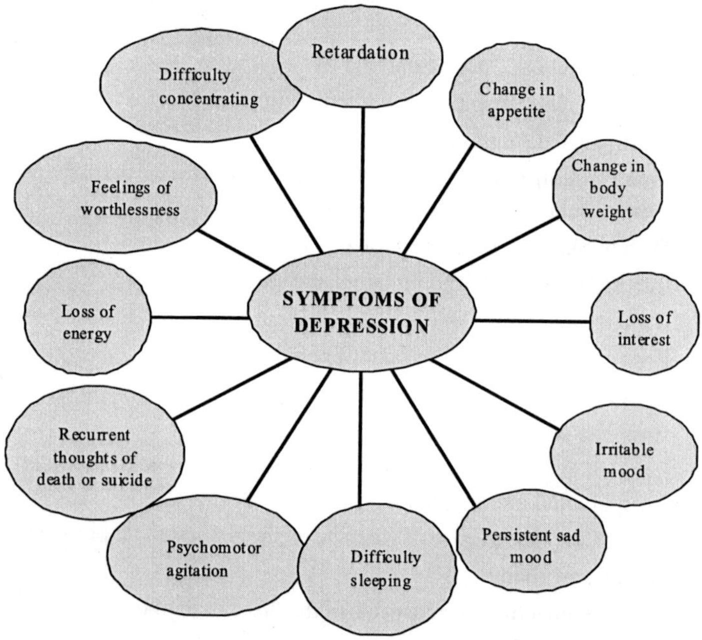

Chart - 11: Symptoms of Depression.

One of the most challenging problems in depression research and clinical practice is refractory–hard to treat–depression. While approximately 80 per cent of people with depression respond very positively to treatment, a significant number of individuals remain treatment refractory.

Chapter - 6

Post Traumatic Stress Disorder (PTSD)

It is proved that PTSD symptoms can be identified both in adults and in children across cultures and the rates of depression, anxiety, and PTSD found among the affected people by the tsunami and the number of people with symptoms may be estimated at several millions (JAMA, 2006). The Asian earthquake and subsequent tsunami of December 2004, one of the largest natural disasters, resulted death toll over 250,000 people and massive destruction in eight countries. It is reported that children are at risk for developing short- and long-term psychological consequences, including post-traumatic stress disorder (John P.B., *et. al.,* 2007).

Most of the children were able to cope with their distress, while some developed mental disorders such as PTSD (Ghodse and Galea, 2006). One area particularly affected by this disaster was southern India. Five hundred twenty-three juvenile survivors of the tsunami were studied to determine the prevalence of PTSD. The survey was conducted in two waves. Interviews were conducted by postgraduate psychiatric social work students and observed the prevalence of post-traumatic stress disorder among children (John P.B., *et. al.,* 2007). Psychotic disorders, even schizophrenia, have also been reported in the survivors (Math, S.B., 2008). Comorbidities and subclinical psychiatric syndromes are also common (Kar N., 2006). Research studies confirmed that following natural disasters (earthquakes, cyclone, hurricanes, flood, tsunami, etc), PTSD symptoms are more common than the syndromal PTSD (McFarlane AC, 1987 and Kar N, *et. al.,* 2007).

In another disaster; approximately 20,000 children were directly affected by the tsunami that struck the six south-western Thailand (CDC, 2006). When assessed the prevalence of symptoms of post-traumatic stress disorder (PTSD) and depression among children in these areas, found that traumatic events experienced during the tsunami were significantly associated with symptoms of PTSD and depression. Children from affected villages were more than twice as likely to report PTSD symptoms as children from unaffected villages. The prevalence of PTSD in high exposure areas is significantly higher than in low exposure areas (Kar N, *et. al.,* 2007).

The prevalence of 70.7 per cent for acute PTSD and 10.9 per cent for delayed onset PTSD. PTSD was more prevalent among girls and more severe among adolescents exposed to loss of life or property. (Susan M. Becker, 2007). McFarlane, A. C. (1987) confirmed that the prevalence of post-traumatic phenomena (PTP) found among school children who are being exposed to an Australian bushfire.

Green B.L. *et. al.,* (1991) analysed through multiple regression analysis showed that life threat, gender, parental psychopathology, and an irritable and/or depressed family atmosphere all contributed to the prediction of PTSD symptoms in the children. There is a comparative assessment is made among boys and girls and observed that fewer PTSD symptoms in the youngest age group and higher symptom levels for girls than boys. In an another study it is confirmed that significantly higher anxiety scores and significantly more PTSD symptomatology were found for children experiencing more or more severe exposure to the hurricane (Lonigan, C.J., *et al.,* 1991).

Psycho-social Impact and PTSD

Nevertheless, natural disasters can be extremely traumatic for children and adults alike. Symptoms of distress, including PTSD, depression and anxiety, were observed in several studies conducted in the affected regions. Risk factors include: level of exposure to the event, personal injury or loss of loved ones, level of parental support, dislocation from community and previous exposure to traumatic events (Christina Suboh, 2008).

Lonigan, C.J., M.P. Shannon, *et. al.,* (1994) stated the presence of PTSD symptoms was strongly related to children's reported severity of the hurricane, degree of home damage sustained, and continued displacement; however, children's level of trait anxiety and their reported emotional reactivity during the hurricane were more strongly related to the presence of PTSD symptoms than were the exposure factors.

Jones, R.T., *et. al.,* (2002) noted that PTSD symptoms reported by parents were generally significantly correlated with (but not concordant with) PTSD symptoms reported by their children. Hamada, R.S., *et. al.,* (2003) reported the first and second stage results of a project to establish the psychometric properties of a post-traumatic stress disorder symptom scale for children designed to be used community-wide after disasters.

Lonigan, C.J., J.L. Anthony, *et. al.,* (1998) suggest which symptoms should be conceptualised as central versus peripheral to the disorder and which symptoms and symptom combinations clinicians should attend to most when diagnosing or screening PTSD in children. Bolton, D., *et. al.,* (2000) argued that children and adolescents exposed to trauma can suffer major adverse psychological effects including not only post-traumatic stress but also other psychological disorders. The highest rates were among the survivors who had developed Post-Traumatic Stress Disorder (PTSD) to a higher level.

Added to that measures of the degree of exposure to the disaster and of subjective appraisal of life threat, and ratings of anxiety obtained five months post-disaster; best predicted whether survivors developed PTSD (Udwin, O., *et al.,* 2000). There is an association between psycho-social factors (life events, lifestyles choices, availability of help during occurrence and long the course of the disaster) and PTSD (Murthy and Karki, 2001).

Follow-up assessments must be conducted to assess the long-term mental health outcomes and the long-term need for mental health services (Thienkrua Warunee, *et. al.,* 2006). In contrast, the corresponding rates of PTSD and depression among children who had not been displaced were at that time "too small for meaningful statistical analysis (Thienkrua Warunee, *et. al.,* 2006).

Gender and PTSD

Girls reported more anxiety and PTSD symptoms than boys (Lonigan, C.J., M.P. Shannon, *et al.,* 1991). The risks are more if they have been suffering from psychological or behavioural problems (Somasundaram DJ, van de Put WA, 2006; Vijayakumar L, et.al, 2006). Accumulation of multiple stressors (Catani C *et. al.,* 2008 and Rutter M., 1987), previous experience of stressful events and their outcome, and coexisting adverse circumstances have also been noted as risk factors (Hoare P., 1993).

At the symptom level, females reported more symptoms associated with emotional processing and emotional reaction to the trauma. Males were more likely to report symptoms related to cognitive and behavioural factors (Shannon M.P., *et. al.,* 1994); in addition to that younger children were more likely to report symptoms overall. Children exposed to a high magnitude natural disaster report sufficient symptoms to establish a DSM-III-R derived classification of a PTSD syndrome. There are differences between gender, age, and race groups appear to be related to differential risk of exposure, reporting biases, as well as a differential risk for developing post-traumatic symptoms. As projected, children with more severe levels of PTSD symptomatology reported more Emotional Processing and Distraction coping assistance (Prinstein, M. J., *et al.,* 1996).

Disasters may lead to an added distress to those with mental health issues and to aggravate emotional distress to those that have not suffered previously. Post-Traumatic Stress Disorder (PTSD) is one well known, although contested, post-disaster disorder and one increasingly recognised as an issue in the developing as well as 'developed' world context (Sarah Bradshaw and Maureen Fordham, 2013). In fact Boys' behaviour tends to be more aggressive and anti-social, and they may take longer to recover. Girls are more verbal and show more distress (Hamblen, 2006).

In gender terms across the globe in 'normal' times there are greater numbers of women than men in therapy, on psychiatric medication, or in mental hospitals (Ussher, 1992; Chesler, 1972). Udwin, O., *et. al.,* (2000) reported that developing PTSD following the disaster was significantly associated with being female, with pre-disaster factors of learning and psychological difficulties in the child and violence in the home, with severity of exposure to the disaster, survivors' subjective appraisal of the experience, adjustment in the early post-disaster period, and life events and social supports subsequently.

McDermott, B.M., E.M. Lee, *et. al.,* (2005) stated that younger children and individuals with greater exposure to and perception of threat experienced higher levels of PTSD and general psychopathology. Female students reported a greater perception of threat but did not report higher levels of PTSD or other symptoms. Screening was well received by students, parents, and staff and proved feasible in the post-disaster environment.

Culture and PTSD

The psycho-social impact of disasters may be gendered and generational but how symptoms are displayed may depend on the culture in question and may not always be negative and who is impacted, and how, is likely to depend in part on existing socio-economic as well as health inequalities (Sarah Bradshaw and Maureen Fordham, 2013). J.D. Burke *et al.,* (2002) identified that visits by Health nurses to the school were significantly reduced following treatment. Psycho-social intervention appears useful for children suffering disaster-related PTSID. Conducting controlled studies of children's treatment in the post-disaster environment appears feasible and reduces the post-traumatic stress disorder. Childhood and adolescence have been identified as particularly vulnerable age for post-disaster psychological morbidity (Somasundaram DJ, van de Put WA, 2006).

Russell T. *et al.,* (2007) noted that PTSD symptoms reported by parents were generally significantly correlated with PTSD symptoms reported by their children. Proportions of children having post-traumatic symptoms or syndromal diagnoses vary in different studies depending on various factors like nature and severity of disaster, diagnostic criteria used, cultural issues regarding meaning of trauma, support available, etc. (Nilamadhab Kar, 2009).

In children, the rates of depression and PTSD were also elevated at two months and remained high at nine months, according to the findings from two Thailand Post-Tsunami Mental Health Study Group studies as reported by Mary Ann Moon (2006). The researchers surveyed a random sample of 371 adults and 371 children living in the three provinces most severely affected by the tsunami in an effort to identify vulnerable populations and to develop culturally appropriate mental health interventions.

At two months after the storm, the rate of anxiety was 37 per cent, the rate of depression, 30 per cent, and the rate of PTSD 12 per cent, in those who had been displaced from their homes (van Griensven, 2006) and for those who had not been displaced, the corresponding rates were lower at 30 per cent, 27 per cent and 7 per cent, respectively. Severe depressive reactions are also common responses to disasters and often occur with PTSD (Robert M. Glickman, M.D., 2004). Van Griensven (2006) found that after nine month follow-up, the rates of anxiety, depression, and PTSD had declined significantly among displaced adults, at 25 per cent, 17 per cent and 7 per cent, respectively. For those who had not been displaced, less significant declines to 26 per cent, 14 per cent and 2 per cent, respectively, were observed. More over grief, loss, uncertainty about the future, and the prospect of a possible recurrence of the tsunami may all play a role in the higher levels of depression and anxiety.

The significant decrease over time in the prevalence of stress reactions, particularly among the displaced, may be attributable to "spontaneous recovery under improved social and environmental conditions," the authors wrote. In the interval between the first assessment and the follow-up, numerous programmes were established for mental health support, occupational training, restoration of livelihoods, and provision of more permanent housing (Mary Ann Moon, 2006).

Risk Factors for PTSD

Childhood and adolescence have been identified as specifically vulnerable age for post-disaster psychological morbidity (Yule, *et. al.,* 1999). The risks are more if they have been suffering from psychological or behavioural problems. Risk factors for PTSD have been female gender, degree of exposure, extent of loss of family members, separation anxiety, trauma-related parental distress, temporal proximity to traumatic events, lower educational level and middle socio-economic status (APA, 2010). Accumulation of multiple stressors, previous experience of stressful events and their outcome, and coexisting adverse circumstances have also been noted as risk factors.

Lonigan, C.J., *et al.,* (1991) through a Self-report analysed the level of Anxiety among 5,687 children to the reactions to a natural disaster. The data (aged 9-19 yrs) were collected approximately for three months after a hurricane devastated the children's community. Information about the children's perceptions of hurricane severity, degree of home damage suffered as a result of the hurricane, and hurricane-related parental job loss was used to categorize children into four levels of hurricane exposure. Anxiety was measured via the Revised Children's Manifest Anxiety Scale, and reports of post-traumatic stress disorder (PTSD) symptoms were found among these children.

Social withdrawal, self-blaming, and emotional regulation were connected with more severe depressive symptoms. Lower levels of symptomatology were found among the respondents who wanted social support and engaged in cognitive restructuring (Jeney-Gammon, P., *et. al.,* 1993).

McDermott, B.M.C. and L.J. Palmer (1999), suggested that emotional distress was significantly linked with trait anxiety and evacuation experience and depressive symptoms. Depressive symptoms were associated with total distress core, trait anxiety and perception of threat to the parents. Substantial mental health morbidity was identified six months after a disaster. The usefulness of post-disaster service provision influenced by proactive screening is discussed and reasons for further research highlighted.

Shioyama A., *et. al.,* (2004), when analysed the anxiety among older children who have a greater tolerance for depressive mood and psychophysical symptoms, but those symptoms occurring in older children have a tendency to continue for a longer time. More over comparatively girls are more heavily affected and need more time to recover from trauma than boys.

There was no difference in the way of decrease according to the severity of disaster, age, and gender. It may be natural that, since the interest in the earthquake decreased as time passed, consideration for the victims decreased. The problems of mental health of children and adolescents after the disaster may consist of at least two different components; "fear and anxiety," which appeared just after the disaster and decreased earlier. In addition to that depressive and psychophysical symptoms appeared at later stage and stayed for longer period of time (Shioyama A., *et. al.,* 2004).

Chapter - 7

Intervention Strategy

Intervention strategies shall be designed and classified in temporal sequence in relation to the disaster event such as pre-disaster phase, impact phase, short-term adaptation phase, and long-term adaptation phase (U.S. Children's Bureau, 1995). Math S.B., *et. al.,* (2006) contended that the activities comprised mental health consultation at camps, community sensitisation, mental health services to the students and children, teachers' orientation sessions and training of NGO functionaries would yield results. Intervention has to address basically the physical and emotional needs. More over a consistent well resourced and accessible mental health network is also necessary for an effective intervention (Vijaykumar, L., *et. al.,* 2006).

Children are particularly vulnerable to disaster trauma, and this manifests in a variety of complex psychological and behavioural manifestations. However, often the post-disaster psychological reactions in children are not identified. Studies have noted that parents, teachers and even mental health professionals significantly underestimate both the intensity and the duration of the stress reactions in children (AACAP, 1998 and Amaya-Jackson L., 2000).

It is noted that most interventions are based on plausible conceptual assumptions, and convergence often can be seen in the content of interventions derived from diverse theoretical perspectives (U.S. Children's Bureau, 1995). Vijaykumar, L., *et. al.,* (2006) while contenting about the psycho-social interventions after tsunami visualised that the mental health needs of the affected community following any disaster depends upon a number of factors, including disaster preparedness, availability of mental health services, both financial and non-financial resources, along with the magnitude, cause, and suddenness of the event. Post-disaster counselling felt to be necessary, and it should be made available for extended periods, with shifting emphasis to meet the changing needs of high-risk groups (Covell NH, *et. al.,* 2006).

Issues Addressed

Sugar, M. (1989) contented that intervention programmes should include issues such as anger, reenactment, verbal repetition, regression, and resumption of development. A counter-transference of helplessness occurred, which may be a central issue posing difficulties in evaluating and treating disaster victims. Care also should be taken as children's' psychopathological reactions to disasters are individually-based and vary according to age, developmental level, proximity to family members, specifics of their situation, losses during and after the disaster and the responses of the family and community (Grunewald F, 2010) Intervention treatment should be individualised as each children's needs and emotional status is different (Comfort, LK., 2007).

Galante, R. and D. Foa (1987) concluded that treatment alleviated symptoms but that the number of children at risk seemed to be related to the length of time needed for the community to reorganise after the disaster. Claude M. *et. al.,* (2002) highlighted that natural disasters negatively affect children's emotional and behavioural adjustment. Although treatments to reduce psychological morbidity following disasters are needed, it has been difficult to conduct treatment research in post-disaster environments because of the sensitivity of victims to perceived intrusiveness and exploitation. It has been reported that the prevalence of PTSD varied from around 5 per cent to over 43 per cent. (Kar N and Bastia BK, 2006).

After treatment, children reported significant reductions in self-reported trauma-related symptoms. This symptom reduction was maintained at the one-year follow-up. Clinical interviews also indicated that treated children had fewer trauma symptoms compared with untreated children. School-based community-wide screening followed by psycho-social intervention seems to effectively identify and reduce children's disaster-related trauma symptoms and may facilitate psychological recovery. While group and individual treatments did not differ in efficacy, fewer children dropped out of the group treatment. This approach may be applicable to screening and treating children exposed to a variety of large-scale disasters (Claude, M. *et. al.,* 2002).

Systematic Screening–Essential

Systematic screening of the children in the disaster affected areas is preferable to routine clinical evaluation as the young survivors may never be brought to the attention. Systematic screening of children can provide critical information for a rational public mental health programme after a disaster. Access to information and capacity for self-protection are typically distributed unevenly within populations (Richard Eiser, *et. al.,* 2012).

Screening should be broad-based to include not only trauma-related clinical syndromes, but also other disorders, sub-clinical symptoms, psycho-social, educational and daily life impairments. It is important that the assessment is age appropriate, culturally sensitive and valid. The needs of children with pre-existing psychiatric disorders should be specifically assessed. The assessments can be done by the primary healthcare workers; however, training is recommended for this in most instances (Jones, L., 2008).

Understanding how people interpret risks and choose actions based on their interpretations is vital to any strategy for disaster reduction (Richard Eiser, *et. al.,* 2012). To make it scientific structured or semi-structured interview schedules either for children and/or parent used for assessment. Formal and objective assessment of play can also aid in the assessment in children.

Development of a broad-based, culturally valid instrument to evaluate sequel in various domains such as psychopathology, behaviour, psycho-social functioning, education, extracurricular activities, and activities of daily life etc is recommended. Attention needs to be paid to how people's interpretations of risks are shaped by their own experience, personal feelings and values, cultural beliefs and interpersonal and societal dynamics (Richard Eiser, *et. al.,* 2012).

The assessments can be done by the primary healthcare workers; however, training is recommended for this in most instances (Jones L., 2008). It is highlighted that considerable amount of time may be required to elicit symptoms from the children. The assessments should be undertaken as soon as possible, repeated periodically and continued for a long period (Richard Eiser, *et. al.,* 2012).

Divs (2005) observed that due to disasters many young children died, families suffered and people became homeless. Innocent people are suffering; they have taken shelter in a cemetery, sleeping in open ground in such a cold weather. There is scarcity of food, first-aid, doctors, water, and clothing to protect them from cold. At this point of time government should take initiative to implement intervention programmes immediately (Comfort, LK, 2007; Nolte, IM, *et. al.,* 2012; Groupe, URD, 2011 and Grunewald, F, 2010). The assistance of defense personnel could be sought in this regard as they are doing their service with full dedication in emergency relief and rehabilitation (Nolte, IM, *et. al.,* 2012; Groupe, URD, 2011). They also help in clearing up debris and taking out trapped people from inside. Those photographs shown on the news channels shake our hearts for once. Still many affected areas are not provided with the required help, people are searching for their relatives and family members (Grunewald F, 2010).

Psychosocial Interventions

Murthy and Karki (2001) noted that for successful psycho-social interventions; polices should take a multi-disciplinary approach in addressing gender, socio-economic status, and culture-specific issues. Mental health professionals should be regularly trained and be 'ordinary' populations, especially at primary health-care levels so as to increase the access, availability and to reduce the rigorousness of the event. Although field-level coordination is important for facilitating efficient use of available resources and for limiting potential duplication of efforts, donor-level coordination is equally vital as there may be other driving forces influencing actors' behaviour than the overall effectiveness of the operation (Emmanuel Raju, N and Per Becker, 2013).

Laor, N., *et. al.,* (2003) observed that while disasters, war, and terrorism are destructive phenomena that usually show up precipitously and involve massive damages and human suffering intervention for child-oriented comprehensive emergency care system be given utmost importance. The future research on disasters should not only concentrate on the prevalence of mental health effects, but also help to establish and evaluate the mental health methods utilised (Christina Suboh, 2008). In 2005, the UNTRS office was set up in Chennai (Tamil Nadu) with a team of professionals along with the UN tsunami coordinator.

These professionals brought with them different expertise such as education, health, livelihoods etc. (Emmanuel Raju, N and Per Becker, 2013). In Tamil Nadu state, Nagapattinam was the worst affected district in terms of social and economic loss. Following the tsunami, the NGO coordination centre was formed to facilitate a coordinated response in the district. This was initiated by three local organisations. Later, the government administration established a relationship with the NGO Coordination Centre. As many NGOs started to register with the NGO Coordination Centre, there was a need felt to coordinate information on the tsunami response in the district. The NGO Coordination Centre was transformed into the NGO Coordination and Resource Centre (NCRC). (Emmanuel Raju, N and Per Becker, 2013) Evaluation of the intervention efforts following the Indian Ocean tsunami is necessary. Until now, little has been done in evaluating and assessing the effectiveness of interventional techniques and methods employed (Christina Suboh, 2008).

Disaster intervention calls for both from the top to down and from the bottom up approach. More over based on ecologic systems theory and principles borrowed from public health, preventive medicine, communal welfare, education and urban planning; Laor, N., *et. al.,* (2003) proposed a common intellectual matrix for medical, psychological, educational, and social interventions. Coordination with local hospitals is essential for efficient use of resources and, for those institutions that are not pediatric centres, should include planning and training for pediatric disaster victims (Debra L., 2009).

A governance approach may be particularly appropriate for grasping and facilitating coordination of recovery, also since it is widely established to be a "window of opportunity" for implementing risk reduction (Christoplos, I., 2006), and closely associated with development (Kennedy, J, Ashmore, J, Babister, E and Kelman, I., 2008). A practical intervention approached was suggested consisting of members from various child care and welfare agencies to act as intervention personnel to implemented a community mental health programme to implement the intervention programmes in a successful manner.

Judith, A. Myers-Walls (2005) listed down the Issues to be discussed with disaster children:

- Reassure them.
- Let the children know that it is normal to talk about unpleasant events.
- Sharing of feelings can help children feel better and better.
- Recognise their fears.
- Support your children's concern for people they do not know.
- Children often are afraid for themselves, their family and friends.
- Children also afraid for people they do not know.
- Make the children aware of others' emotion.
- Look for feelings beyond fear.
- Let the children help others take action.
- Allow Children to take action even it is very simple.
- Let the children get involved with disaster preparedness organisation.
- Give chance to express all emotions of children.

Changes in a Child's Behaviour

- Refusal to return to school.
- Clinging behaviour such as shadowing the mother or father around the house.
- Persistent fears related to the catastrophe.
- Sleep disturbances such as nightmares, screaming during sleep and bedwetting.
- Loss of concentration and irritability.
- Misbehaving in school or at home in ways that are not typical for the child.
- Physical complaints (stomachaches, headaches, dizziness) for which cause is not known.
- Withdrawal from family and friends.
- Sadness, listlessness, decreased activity and preoccupation with the events of the disaster.

Phases of Intervention Work

There is also immense potential in employing cognitive-behavioural strategies, especially since they can easily be adapted to various cultural contexts. Cognitive-behavioural methods also have great relevance to the psycho-educational context of the school-setting (Christina Suboh, 2008). Basically a teacher could work through the following phases in order to contribute substantially in the intervention process of children.

Articulation Phase

In this phase communication is given importance, especially in the post-crisis period, where children face many uncertainties regarding the event and their subsequent feelings. Teachers should try to facilitate the expression of the students' thoughts and emotions associated with the event so as to facilitate better understanding.

Information Phase

It is rather difficult to inform a child that the loved ones are no more. Many a time it is convenient for people to give untruths, such as explaining that the child's parent has gone abroad to find work or gone to the God and things like that. This lie was upheld even when the child had witnessed the parent drown in the wave. To avoid that children become subjects to these fictions, it is important to discuss to which degree children have an understanding of death. Children have the right to obtain information and receive support (Christina Suboh, 2008).

Action Phase

Children are given opportunity to take part actively in collecting and organising information regarding the disaster. Moreover in this phase children are engaged to become aware of disaster preparedness. Important issues to convey to children are how they can detect early warning signs, and how they should act, in the event of a recurring disaster. Hence children are not only informed but also could reduce fearfulness, as well as anxious about a possible reoccurrence of disaster in the near future. Giving pupils insights about natural disaster detectors and how they function may contribute to the reduction of children's insecurity. In this action phase emphasis was given to instill a sense of empathy, compassion, and companionship in their pupils by helping them become engaged in caring for one another, and others who are suffering (Christina Suboh, 2008).

For instance, the Indian Ocean tsunami of 2004 was one of the worst disasters to have affected India. Tamil Nadu was the worst affected mainland state, after the Andaman and Nicobar islands. Following the immediate impact of the disaster, coordination structures were established at the district and state level to facilitate the relief and recovery activities (Emmanuel Raju N and Per Becker, 2013).

Multipronged Approach

Parasuraman and Unnikrishnan (2001) disasters are shared reality spanning individuals, villages, blocks, districts, states, nations, and even regions and have to be responded to with a multi-pronged approach. The poorest are becoming more exposed risks. The consequences of disasters are multiplied further by factors such as political insensitivity, increasing poverty, climate changes, and globalisation (Parasuraman and Unnikrishnan, (2001). They emphasises that disasters set back the development process by decades. It was strongly advocated that there need to be a regional disaster policy for each region specifically taking into consideration each regions' disaster proneness.

Ball, J., and K. Allen (2000) discussed the consensus recommendations for responding to children's emergencies in disasters that emerged from the 1998 Children's Emergencies in Disasters. The disaster relief team should include. Emergency physicians, pediatricians, nurses, emergency medical service and disaster planners, school representatives, and mental health professionals developed the pediatric disaster recommendations. Optimal pediatric disaster planning and response requires a private and public partnership of all provider groups at local, state, and national levels and should include all professional organisations, government agencies, and advocacy groups that have a role in the welfare of children and the training of health-care personnel, first responders, and volunteers (Debra L., 2009). The consensus recommendations include information on medical capabilities, managed care, mental health, community planning, data collection, volunteer services, school and child care, public awareness, and family empowerment.

For those survivors who developed PTSD, its duration, and severity were best predicted by pre-disaster vulnerability factors of social, physical, and psychological difficulties in childhood together with ratings of depression obtained five months post-disaster. Linda Evans Judy and Oehler-Stinnett (2006) emphasised role of school psychologists and reiterated that School psychologists should understand natural disaster effects, such as economic loss, relocation and health concerns and mental health issues. While most children are able to cope, a significant minority develops severe symptoms and Post Traumatic Stress Disorder (PTSD).

1. Play Therapy

Ahmed and Siddiqi (2006) suggested to use of art as part of play therapy in helping children work through trauma following natural disasters such as the Asian tsunami and hurricane Katrina. The authors stated that art provides a means of communication for children and can facilitate healing. Daniels *et. al.,* (2007) discussed the importance of school counsellors developing relationships with children and receiving crisis intervention training.

Villalba and Lewis (2007) profound that considerations is to be accorded for marriage and family therapists working with children who have experienced trauma. They highlighted that while the reactions may differ, children can be affected by trauma through direct exposure or exposure via television. More over play therapy was advocated as an effective and beneficial intervention as well as the importance of involving family members in the process. Henry, Tolan, and Gorman-Smith (2004) conducted a longitudinal study one hundred days prior to and following September 11th and discussed long lasting impacts on inner city children and parents. Findings that may be of interest to play therapists were that beliefs about the importance of family as well as parental supervision.

Dripchak (2007) promoted a therapy called post traumatic play (PTP), a method that incorporates Milton Erickson's principles. Using a directive approach and involving family members in the process, the therapist assists the child to express emotions, through play, working to alter the negative aspects of the trauma.

2. Cognitive-Behavioural Group Therapy

Cognitive Behaviour Therapy (CBT) is considered by many to be the mainstay of treatment of children and adolescents with PTSD (Silva RR, *et. al.,* 2003; Donnelly CL, Amaya-Jackson L., 2002). It was hypothesised that the group experience would lead to bonding and support that would persist beyond the time limits of the group. A group-based intervention programme for adult and child survivors is described, including its administrative structure, therapeutic objectives and interventions, and group process Stubenbort, K., G.R. Donnelly, *et. al.,* (2001).

It is evident that the efficacy of CBT in alleviating post-traumatic stress symptoms after catastrophic disaster has been demonstrated (Shooshtary MH, *et. al.,* 2008). Short-term group CBT has also been found useful with long- term benefit. Significant improvement was reported in children at an 18-month follow-up, with treatment gains being maintained at a four year follow-up (Giannopoulou I, Dikaiakou A, Yule W, 2006).

Lieberman, A.F., van Horn, P. (2004) have analysed about Assessment and treatment methods for disaster affected children and proclaimed that assessment strategies have to be designed to identify traumatic responses in a developmental and contextual framework, and presents forms of intervention aimed at alleviating traumatic responses in the present and at preventing the consolidation of these responses into chronic patterns of emotional, social, and cognitive dysfunction.

3. School Crisis Team

A school crisis team need to formed comprising school management, teachers, school social workers, parents, students and the local volunteers. These various stake holders would act in co-ordination in identification, rehabilitation and restoration of children which ultimately aimed at reintegration or rejuvenation in a sustainable way. The various strategies a school crisis team need to be undertaken is given below (Lazarus P. J., *et. al.*, 2003).

(a) Identify Children at High Risk

Risk factors are outlined in the above section on children's reactions. Interventions may include individual counselling, small group counselling, or family therapy. From group crisis interventions, and by maintaining close contact with teachers and parents, the school crisis response team can determine which students need supportive crisis intervention and counseling services. A mechanism also needs to be in place for self-referral and parental-referral of students.

(b) Support Teachers and Staff

Provide staff members with information on the symptoms of children's stress reactions and guidance on how to handle class discussions and answer children's question. As indicated, offer to help conduct a group discussion. Reinforce that teachers should pay attention to their own needs and not feel compelled to do anything they are not comfortable doing. Suggest that administrators provide time for staff to share their feelings and reactions on a voluntary basis as well as help staff develop support groups. In addition, teachers who had property damage or personal injury to themselves or family members need leave time to attend to their needs.

(c) Engage in Post-Disaster Activities that Facilitate Rehabilitation

La Greca *et. al.,* (1994) have developed a manual for professionals working with elementary school children following a natural disaster. Activities in this manual emphasise three key components supported by the empirical literature:

(a) Exposure to discussion of disaster-related events
(b) Promotion of positive coping and problem-solving skills and
(c) Strengthening of children's friendship and peer support.

(d) Encourage Children to Talk about Disaster-Related Events

Children need an opportunity to discuss their experiences in a safe, accepting environment. Provide activities that enable children to discuss their experiences. These may include a range of methods (both verbal and non-verbal) and incorporate varying projects (e.g., drawing, stories, audio and video recording). Again provide teachers specific suggestions or offer to help with an activity.

(e) Promote Positive Coping and Problem-Solving Skills

Activities should teach children how to apply problem-solving skills to disaster-related stressors. Children should be encouraged to develop realistic and positive methods of coping that increase their ability to manage their anxiety and to identify which strategies fit with each situation.

(f) Strengthen Children's Friendship and Peer Support

Children with strong emotional support from others are better able to cope with adversity. Children's relationships with peers can provide suggestions for how to cope with difficulties and can help decrease isolation. In many disaster situations, friendships may be disrupted because of family relocations. In some cases parents may be less available to provide support to their children because of their own distress and their feelings of being overwhelmed. It is important for children to develop supportive relationships with their teachers and classmates. Activities may include asking children to work cooperatively in small groups in order to enhance peer support.

(g) Create Effective Study Habits

- Homework to be done first.
- Offer them compliments and sops to do their homework.
- Homework needs to be immediately after-school sports.
- Talking with friends, watching Television or the web etc., only after homework.
- Getting their homework done frees the children to enjoy activities.
- The unfinished homework create a pre-occupied mind and lessens the enjoyment.
- Parents should not do the homework for their children.
- Doing home work for them makes no learning for the child.
- Guide the child how to struggle with challenging problems.
- Facilitate to achieve a sense of competence.
- Better teach the child how to do something, explain why it is important.
- Make the child understand that Reading & Writing is important for child's success in life.
- When a child encounters unsolvable problem/ issue do not simply provide the answer.

- Teach the child the various strategies available and make the child to choose the best.
- Show a step-by-step procedure on how to implement the strategy to achieve success.
- Ask questions at each step that are designed to help him.
- Allow the child to learn, think and reason on his own.
- Help the child in challenging/ difficult subjects.
- Caring parents take action to help their children do well in school.
- Help the child to use available resources.
- Role of a parent is to teach the child how to use all the resources available.
- After the task is accomplished appreciate the child.
- Help the child to review the work done.
- If anything to be corrected or modified help the child to do it.
- It is important to share the knowledge with the child.
- Finally positive stroke sustains the sense of competency and improves the study habit.

(h) Emphasise Children's Resiliency

Focus on their competencies in terms of their daily life and in other difficult times. Help children identify what they have done in the past that helped them cope when they were frightened or upset. Tell students about other communities that have experienced natural disasters and recovered.

(i) Support Members

All crisis response team members need an opportunity to process the crisis response. Providing crisis intervention is emotionally draining. This is likely to include teachers and other school staff if they have been serving as crisis caregivers for students.

(j) Secure Additional Mental Health Support

Although more than enough caregivers are often willing to provide support during the immediate aftermath of a natural disaster, long-term services may be lacking. School psychologists and other school mental health professionals can help provide and coordinate mental health services, but it is important to connect with community resources in order to provide such long-term assistance. Ideally these relationships would be established in advance.

(k) Social Skills Training

It helps children gain knowledge of new skills with the help of direct instruction, psycho-educational materials and demonstration of the skill.

Then the skill is practiced, often in form of role play, and feedback is given. Role plays should strive to represent a realistic situation. After the child has grown confident by rehearsing the skill, it is applied in the real context. It is important that positive reinforcement is given as an incentive so that children could be encouraged (Christina Suboh, 2008).

(l) Problem Solving

There are five fundamental steps identified by Christina Suboh (2008):

- Identifying the problem.
- Brainstorming various solutions.
- Evaluating the options for both short-term and long-term consequences.
- Implementing the best solution.
- Rewarding the child for solving the problem.

Bhushan and Kumar (2007) concluded their research with four hypotheses related to stress:

- Children will score high on post-traumatic stress and emotional distress.
- Gender difference observed in regard to post-traumatic stress and emotional stress.
- Family support system will affect post-traumatic stress and emotional distress.
- Loss of family members- the main cause to post-traumatic stress and emotional distress.

Bhushan and Kumar (2007) reported that the high percentages of many survivors were still experiencing many struggles and challenges to re-build their lives and overcome the grief and devastation that the tsunami brought.

Psychological First Aid (PFA)

NCTSN & NC for PTSD (National Child Traumatic Stress Network and National Centre for PTSD), (2005) insisted for Psychological First Aid for disaster victims. It is true that Psychological First Aid (PFA) is an evidence-informed modular approach for assisting children, adolescents, adults, and families in the immediate aftermath of disaster and terrorism PFA is designed to reduce the initial distress caused by traumatic events, and to foster short- and long-term adaptive functioning.

PFA is designed for delivery by mental health specialists who provide acute assistance to affected children and families as part of an organised disaster response effort. A team may be formulated consisting of specialists in a variety of response units, including first responder teams, incident command systems, primary and emergency healthcare providers, school crisis response teams, faith-based organisations, Community Emergency Response Teams (CERT), Medical Reserve Corps, the Citizens Corps, and disaster relief organisations. If teachers are given the right tools and guidance; they could bring about therapeutic effect which would lead to reduced trauma-related symptoms and improved well-being of children (Raundalen and Schultz, 2006).

Principles and Techniques of PFA

- Consistent with research evidence on risk and resilience following trauma.
- Applicable and practical in field settings.
- Appropriate to developmental level across the lifespan.
- Culturally informed and adaptable.

Betancourt and Kashif T. K. (2008) while conducting a study about the mental health of children affected by armed conflict recommended that further research on war-affected children should pay particular attention to coping and meaning making at the individual level; the role of attachment relationships, caregiver health, resources and connection in the family, and social support available in peer and extended social networks. Cultural and community influences such as attitudes towards mental health and healing as well as the meaning given to the experience of war itself are also important aspects of the larger social ecology. The IFRC recommends that meeting psycho-social needs should be based on the principle that most acute stress problems during emergencies are best managed without medication, following the principles of 'psychological first aid' (IFRC, 2009).

Phases of Disaster Aid

Disaster aid is normally categorised into four phases, with each phase catering to different needs of the affected communities.

(1) Rescue Phase

One of the key issues in recovery post-Mitch in Nicaragua on behalf of the international community was a failure to understand local institutional frameworks (Christoplos I, 2010). Recovery literature has noted that top-down institutional approaches may not be viable for recovery, whereas inter-organisational relationships are crucial (Berke PR, *et. al.,* 1993).

The phase begins immediately after a disaster, continuing for about two weeks or more depending on the scale of the event. It can also be defined as the "heroic phase", a time where altruism is at its peak and people come together for a common goal: to prevent loss of life and property. The priorities are to provide food, water, shelter and sanitation, to identify bodies and arrange their burials (Ashraf, 2005). Separated children have been registered, and efforts are ongoing to place them with families in their communities (Yin Yin New, 2005).

A key guiding principle high-lighted by UNDP post-disaster recovery guidelines (UNDP, 2011) relates to coordination. As there are no distinct boundaries between response and recovery, the Gujarat earthquake of 2001 showed that it is important to "improve coordination between a wide range of local, regional, national and international partners" (UNDP, 2001) during the transition.

Many factors can be identified as influencing the change in approach to hazard and disaster management and response, including (Tapsell, S, *et. al.*, 2010):

- Increasing economic and financial cost of disasters
- Rising impact potentials
- Perception that it is not possible to protect against all natural disasters
- Density of infrastructure
- Number of people living in at risk areas
- Expansive and intensified land use
- Increasing conflicts between socio-economic land
- Use and hazard mitigation policy
- Need for better understanding of interrelations
- Social dynamics of risk perception
- Preparedness and impacts
- Disparities in wealth and socio-economic status
- Realisation of the importance of the intangible impacts disasters
- Need for increased post-disaster support and recovery and
- Shouldering of responsibilities, resilience and social capacity building.

Psychosocial care in this phase consists of psychological first aid, which aims to supply those in need with immediate physical and medical assistance. This includes identifying those who are most vulnerable and at risk. Thus, setting up clinics is important, as well as providing them with credible information, which they can rely on. Caution is necessary on rumors which can lead to panic and other undesirable consequences (Rao, 2006).

In this process, an Oxfam study post-tsunami highlights that communities urge to be equal partners in recovery. Further the study reveals that "local knowledge, capacity and priorities were overlooked" (Oxfam International,

(2009). Disaster recovery is one of the under-researched subjects of disaster research (Smith G, Wenger D, 2007). Also, as stated earlier, the subject of coordination in disaster recovery is much neglected as it has been an area of study in disaster response.

(2) Relief Phase

This phase takes place about two to six months after a disaster. It is also referred to as the "honeymoon phase", where the tremendous amount of help, support and promises result in a high level of hopefulness in the affected populations is poured in. However, many people are probable to be still living in relief camps at this stage. The result of living in camps is often loss of identity and disorientation. Thus, psychosocial care is supportive and directed at problem solving, reducing emotional discomfort and normalising the situation in the relief phase (Rao, 2006) could prove better results. As number of resources poured in or mobilised it is not easy to many them both in terms of resources and stakeholders especially as this mix of stakeholders involves very different roles and responsibilities (Kulatunga U, 2011).

(3) Rehabilitation Phase

This phase lasts up to one or two years after a disaster, or longer. It is also known as the "disillusionment phase", where it is exposed that promises are not kept and expectations not met in several cases. This, added with delays and legal barriers, often leads to skepticism and criticism, often directed at international aid agencies and governments. The disaster-affected people recognise that they need to take their problems into their own hands, instead of waiting for assistance that might not come. In comparison to the relief phase, most survivors would have moved to their homes again and established a sense of normality and thus making the rehabilitation to work.

(4) Rebuilding Phase

This phase is the longest of all four phases. Rebuilding the homes and lives destroyed by a disaster can take many years, even a life time. It is also known as the "reconstruction phase" where individuals work together with the community to restore normal functioning. This includes coming to terms with the disaster and its effect-realising that life must continue despite the great loss (Christina Suboh, 2008).

The most essential aspect in this period is to develop disaster preparedness that can prevent a future disaster or minimise its devastating impact. This can be achieved by strengthening the communities' resources and increasing the people's resilience. Developers of psychosocial support programmes will thus devote their time in building competence-training staff who can act quickly in the event of a natural disaster or after an otherwise traumatic event

(Rao, 2006) in order to increase people's participation for prevention as well as promotion.

Trying to meet all needs of a community, or wanting exclusive privilege of working with a specific survivor group can often lead to gaps in the services provided (Ganesan, 2006). Most trainers only remained at the site for a short period of time, preparing project proposals, give training and then moving on to a different project. Hence, there was very little supervision, if any at all (Ganesan, 2006).

In Tamil Nadu the Tamil Nadu Tsunami Resource Centre (TNTRC) was a joint venture of seven organisations, including the United Nations Development Programme (UNDP) and the state government. The main role and functioning of this platform was to ensure coordination (Emmanuel Raju N and Per Becker, 2013).

Stage-wise Tasks Following Disaster Suggested by John H. Ehrenreich (2001):

I. The Rescue Stage (Immediate Post-Impact):

- Provide "defusing" and crisis intervention services for relief workers.
- Ensure safety of victims.
- Ensure that physical needs (housing, food, clean water, etc.) are met.
- Seek to reunite families and communities.
- Provide information, comfort, practical assistance, emotional "first aid".

II. The Early Inventory Stage: First month

- Continue tasks of Rescue Stage.
- Educate local professionals, volunteers, and community on effects of trauma.
- Train additional disaster counsellors.
- Provide short-term practical help and support to victims.
- Identify those most at risk and begin crisis intervention, "debriefing," and similar efforts.
- Begin reestablishing community infrastructure: jobs, housing, community and institutions.

III. The Late Inventory Stage: Months two onwards

- Continue tasks of Rescue and Early Inventory Stages.
- Provide community education.
- Develop outreach services to identify those in need.

- Provide "debriefing" and other services for disaster survivors in need.
- Develop school-based services and other community institution-based services.

IV. The Reconstruction Phase

- Continue to provide defusing and debriefing services for disaster survivors.
- Maintain a "hot line" or other means by which survivors can contact counsellors.
- Follow up those survivors treated earlier.

Chapter - 8

School-based Intervention

Just after the tsunami, UNICEF warned that protection mechanisms must be put in place for children who had either been separated from their parents or orphaned by the tsunami. Teams made up of the government, UNICEF and NGO partners traced and reunified families, assessed the situation and took the best possible care option for children whose parents were missing (Yin Yin New, 2005). Children benefit from learning cognitive and behavioural skills that would bring equilibrium in their emotions, cognitions, behaviours and their social relationships. In addition, cognitive-behavioural strategies can assist children in feeling safer and modify their behaviour. Following are the strategies advocated to better the school intervention programmes (Christina Suboh, 2008).

(a) Storytelling

Many clinicians are of the opinion that storytelling has therapeutic effect with children. It is true that childhood is characterised by stories and imaginary play that have natural narrative themes. Therefore, children's interest in pretend play makes storytelling an unforced activity for them (Trad and Raine, 1995). More over the stories give insight to the child's thoughts and emotions (Friedberg and McClure, 2007) in a better way.

(b) Storybooks

Encouraging children to make a storybook can be a good follow-up activity to the storytelling method, where children are asked to compile their stories in a note book. This provides an opportunity for parents and teachers to review the child's stories and address the progress made so that creativity and imagination is encouraged.

(c) Play Activities

Play is an important part of childhood, having not only the effect of enjoyment but also learning. Through goal-directed play activities, change in the thoughts, feelings and behaviours of children can be brought about. Play is thus used as an instrument to teach more effective coping skills by addressing inaccurate cognitions. Concrete and visual depictions promote children's' involvement, and become essential in the intellectual development (Christina Suboh, 2008).

(d) Workbooks

There is a variety of workbooks that can be successfully employed as part of behaviour therapies for children and adolescents. Workbooks often include a range of exercises that match the children's developmental level, including crafts and stories.

(e) Craft Activities

Craft-oriented activities can also provide cognitive-behavioural components. The students are generally asked to prepare modules of simple nature on science, arts and the like. This exercise brings teachers and a student intimate and thus creates a bond between the teacher and students which is essential when addressing maladaptive cognitions (Friedberg and McClure, 2007).

Guiding Child Disaster Victim as recommended by John H. Ehrenreich (2001):

- Understand the feelings of your child without passing any judgment. Allow the child to cry or be sad. Don't expect him or her to "be tough." Talk about your own feelings, as well. Encourage your child to draw pictures about the disaster or write stories or poems about the disaster. This will help you understand how he or she views what happened.
- Provide your child with factual information about what happened and what is (or will happen). Use simple, direct language your child can understand. Shielding a child from unpleasant information usually leads to more difficulty in the future. Correct any misunderstandings your child may have (such as that the disaster was, in some way, his or her fault).
- Reassure your child that he or she and you are safe. Hold and touch and be affectionate with your child. Spend extra time with your child, especially at bedtime. Many children are calmed by gentle back and neck massages.

- If your child returns to babyish behaviours, such as bedwetting or thumb sucking, initially try to be accepting. These are signs the child needs comforting and reassurance. Do not shame the child (e.g., by calling him or her a "baby"). Resume normal expectations only gradually.
- Children are especially vulnerable to feeling abandoned when they are separated from their parents. Avoid "protecting" your children by sending them away from the scene of the disaster if this will separate them from their loved ones.
- Children benefit from routine and structure. Initially, you may want to relax the usual rules, but maintain family structure and responsibilities. Return the child to school as soon as feasible after the disaster and expect regular attendance.

Role of Teacher

It is essential for Teachers to use familiar psycho-educational strategies in a systematic and goal-oriented way, so that the students' psycho-social needs can easily be met. As a consequence, teachers, through their daily interaction with children, can be able to identify those, who despite their psychosocial efforts, still experience distress, and can thus able to refer them to a mental healthcare professional (Raundalen and Schultz, 2006).

It was observed that teachers blind to group assignment rated participating children significantly higher than the control group in terms of adaptive functioning. Early post-disaster intervention addressing children and their educational milieu provides children with significant symptomatic reduction, allowing the mobilisation of adaptive coping, thereby enhancing their overall functioning as observed in school. Hence it was that teachers could play an effective role in providing better intervention programmes (Leo Wolmer *et. al.*, 2006).

Role of School Psychologists

School psychologists should gain trauma mental health training through the American Psychological Association, the National Association of School Psychologists, and the International School Psychology Association. They can also be involved in school and community prevention, mitigation and educational programming. Play therapy interventions such as art therapy, guided imagery and journaling and their ability to provide a sanctuary for children working through trauma were suggested by Gaffney (2006).

Role of Volunteers

Vijayakumar L, and M. Suresh Kumar (2006) researched the effectiveness of trained volunteer-delivered mental health support for the bereaved persons observed that participants receiving interventions on a regular basis from trained volunteers were less likely to report depressive symptoms and general psychological distress compared with participants who did not receive the above intervention. Added to these suicidal attempts were reported to be significantly less among the intervention group. In settings where mental health professionals are limited in number, trained lay volunteers can offer empathetic listening, support and referrals that can be potentially beneficial.

Parents who are concerned about their children can ask their pediatrician or family doctor to refer them to a child and adolescent psychiatrist for an evaluation. 'Although the response to the 2004 tsunami has been the focus of numerous evaluations, which at least in theory may represent a shift towards greater accountability' (Bennett J, 2006), 'evaluations of the response to and recovery from later disasters indicate that there has not been sufficient progress since then' (Comfort LK, 2007; Nolte IM, *et. al.,* 2012; Groupe URD, 2011 and Grunewald F, 2010).

Role of Community

Supportive interventions include fostering a sense of safety and efficacy, connecting patients with communities and services, and helping parents talk about the trauma with their children could be better approach (Fetter JC, 2005). Relatively little evaluation of disaster-related interventions with children has been published, and recommendations for research are presented (U.S. Children's Bureau, 1995). Math S.B., *et. al.,* (2006) suggested that the disaster mental health team must be able to understand the local culture, traditions, language, belief systems and local livelihood patterns. They also need to integrate with the network of various governmental and non-governmental organisations to cater to the needs of the survivors. Hence the presence of a disaster mental health team is definitely required during the early phase of the disaster in developing countries.

Bringing people especially the survivors to normalcy is considered as a significant step and to be done immediately after the occurrence (Vijaykumar, L., *et. al.,* 2006). To make the programme effective the guiding principles for school counselling need to be following with strict adherence so that school children could be helped to cope up successfully. More over child-centred play therapy can also be used in school settings for better results (Shen, Y.J. and C.A. Sink, 2002). Leo Wolmer, *et. al.,* (2003) strongly advocated that school reactivation programmes after disaster could be beneficial.

It is advisable and most preferable that the majority of the post-disaster mental health interventions must be provided in the community itself by the local disaster workers. Supportive counselling, cognitive behaviour therapy, brief trauma/grief-focused psychotherapy, and play therapy are the commonly utilised methods of psychological intervention, which can be given in groups.

Information about the efficacy of medications is still emerging, while many are being used and found useful (Nilamadhab Kar, 2009).

Shen, Y.J. and C.A. Sink (2002) recommended for the employment of Professional School Counselling to cope up with the disaster as one of the best intervention strategies. Taking into account the emotional distress of elementary school going children to disasters and their needs for mental health assistance specifically warrants for school counselling interventions. Using a number of training materials, volunteers were trained to deal with the mental health needs of the survivors (Vijaykumar, L., *et. al.,* 2006). To make rejuvenation effective; where appropriate, families should be involved in the treatment of PTSD in children and young people (NICE, 2005). Hospital disaster response poses pediatric-specific challenges regarding care of those who present to the hospital, as well as those who must be discharged or transferred from a hospital that has been compromised by disaster (Debra L., 2009).

Children require caregivers and/or community providers including emergency medical services, fire, police, or military to get them to the hospital. Caregivers often seek care for children before themselves but understandably do not want to leave their children to obtain care elsewhere (Debra L., 2009). All children were studied in terms of post-traumatic, grief and dissociative symptomatology, as well as academic performance, social behaviour and general conduct. It was also compared the two groups in terms of severity of post-traumatic, grief and dissociative symptoms.

Role of Government

No one who experiences a disaster is untouched by it. Children and their families' are often among the most affected (Flynn, B.W. and M.E. Nelson, 1998). Mental health and medical professionals need to assist families and communities in dealing with common disaster-related stress reactions in children (Flynn, B.W. and M.E. Nelson, 1998). This may also affect coordination as these various mandates and goals may be unknown to other actors or even conflicting, while high equality between actors has been shown to have a strong impact on coordination (Nolte I M., *et. al.,* 2012).

Some measures should be taken by government and scientists to prevent maximum destruction from any other natural calamity. Human life is important and it is the responsibility of every single person to save it. During the disaster situation cooperation is very important thing. If one is able to prevent the after-effects of disaster then at least can give a helping hand to share the sorrows of the people. The psycho-social impact of disasters has attracted increasing attention. There is little consensus, however, about what priorities should be pursued in relation to mental health interventions, with most controversy surrounding the relevance of traumatic stress to mental health

(Silove D, Steel Z, Psychol M., 2008). Role of local, state, federal governments, as well as other organisations is vital and significant (Flynn, B.W. and M.E. Nelson, 1998). It is however not the different roles and responsibilities themselves that cause problems, but actors neither having sufficient understanding of their roles and responsibilities, nor of the roles and responsibilities of others that they need to coordinate (Gryszkiewicz A, Chen F., 2010).

The massive support from the public and governments around the world the government, UNICEF and other organisations were able to accelerate measures to save children's lives, return them to normalcy quicker, and protect them better from abuse and trafficking (Yin Yin New, 2005). The present overview suggests that acute traumatic stress may be a normative response to life threat which tends to subside once conditions of safety are established. At the same time, there is a residual minority of survivors who will continue to experience chronic post-traumatic stress disorder (PTSD) and their needs can be easily overlooked (Silove D, Steel Z, Psychol M., 2008).

The theoretical review below highlights three main areas of thinking about response coordination that may have applicability for coordination of disaster recovery as well. These are (Emmanuel Raju N and Per Becker, 2013):

- The roles and responsibilities of different actors,
- The functioning of coordination structures, and
- Factors affecting the effectiveness of coordination.

The ADAPT model offers an expanded perspective on the psycho-social systems undermined by disasters, encompassing threats to safety and security; interpersonal bonds; systems of justice; roles and identities; and institutions that promote meaning and coherence (Silove D, Steel Z, Psychol M., 2008).

Social reconstruction programmes that are effective in repairing these systems maximise the capacity of communities and individuals to recover spontaneously from various forms of stress. Within that broad recovery context, clinical mental health services can focus specifically on those psychologically disturbed persons who are at greatest survival risk (Silove D, Steel Z, Psychol M., 2008). Only a minority of persons with acute traumatic stress fall into that category, the remainder comprising those with severe behavioural disturbances arising from psychosis, organic brain disorders, severe mood disorders, and epilepsy (Silove D, Steel Z, Psychol M., 2008).

Disaster preparedness plans are necessary for all children and should be personalised for those with special needs and/or chronic medical problems (Debra L., 2009). A framework need to be established with the objective to combine efforts from different UN agencies into one programme. Further, the aim should be to create a system of common operational services (Emmanuel Raju N and Per Becker, 2013).

Establishing mental health services that are community-based, family-focused, and culturally sensitive in the post-emergency phase can create a model that helps shape future mental health policy for countries recovering from disaster (Silove D, Steel Z, Psychol M., 2008). Highlighting the amount and diversity of players involved, as well as the lack of accurate common goals and mutually understood mandates, roles and responsibilities, it may be appropriate to approach coordination as a governance problem (Emmanuel Raju N and Per Becker, 2013).

Taghi Doostgharin (2009) found that emotional need of children who were victims of disaster having experienced the loss of family members, their homes, and communities; lack of access to information about what had happened to their immediate family members and uncertainties concerning the future were the most important expressed difficulties. This has been suggested for addressing risk issues in general (Van Asselt M, and Renn O, 2011; Renn O, 2008 and Renn O, Schweizer PJ, 2009) and fits the context of recovery well.

Both the lifestyle of a community prior to the disaster and the quality of leadership are crucial for the successful implementation of a recovery programme (Abhay Joshi and Aoki Misa, 2013). The various factors such as social capital, trust, leadership, and networks, are said to be vital for initial recovery from disasters like tsunami (Abhay Joshi and Aoki Misa, 2013).

In practical in the state of Tamil Nadu, India the TNTRC was established to bring the variety of stakeholders to coordinate efforts and facilitate recovery at the state level. In addition to the TNTRC, the United Nations (UN) established the United Nations Team for Recovery Support (UNTRS). This structure was funded by six UN agencies (UNDP, ILO, FAO, WHO, UNICEF and UNFPA), with the mandate to coordinate all UN activities in the post-tsunami recovery, in an attempt to bring the various UN agencies under one umbrella for disaster recovery (Emmanuel Raju N and Per Becker, 2013).

Role of Social Capital

Social capital has an important role for successful policy implementation, which will lead people to utilise government resources to the optimum level for disaster recovery (Abhay Joshi and Aoki Misa, 2013). It was Hanifan (1961), who developed social capital as goodwill, fellowship, mutual sympathy, and social intercourse among a group of individuals and families who make up a social unit. He concluded that "The more the people do for themselves, the larger will community social capital become, and the greater will be the dividends upon the social investment," which implies that apart from various other resources; social capital becomes a major player in maintaining community life (Hanifan,1961).

Coleman (1988) observed that social capital, such as obligation, information, norms, and social networks, are central for even educational performance. Putnam *et. al.,* (1993) affirmed that the social capital, together with norms and civic engagement, accumulated in a region are the core influential criterion for the economic performance and excellent governance. Woolcock and Narayan (2000) gave an elaborate meaning by applying the social capital concept to development studies and defining the term social capital as the norms and networks that enable collective action in the community.

Social capital is classified normally as three types: bonding, bridging, and linking social capital. Bonding social capital is described as "undergirding specific reciprocity and mobilising solidarity" (Putnam, 2000) and defined in terms of relations between communities, such as family, friends, or business associates (Woolcock, 2002). Bridging social capital connects members of the group or network to extra-local networks, crossing ethnic, racial, religious groups (Aldrich, 2011).

Linking social capital is considered as "networks of trusting relationships between people who are interacting across explicit, formal or institutionalised power or authority gradients in society" (Szreter and Woolcock, 2004). Woolcock and Narayan (2000) suggested that different combinations of these types of social capital could be made in order to bring a range of crucial development and environmental outcomes.

Uphoff (2000) divided social capital into two groups: structural and cognitive. Structural social capital facilitates information sharing, collective action, and decision-making through established social networks and other social structures and cognitive social capital revolved around the intellectual properties of the community members. Studies (Babu, 2007; Chamlee-Wright, 2009; Nakagawa and Show, 2004; Aldrich, 2012; 2010) have confirmed that building social capital is fundamental for rehabilitation from disasters.

Kilby (2008) concluded that the trust and social capacity developed through previous community network activities facilitated local NGOs to initiate an effective response to disasters with specific reference to tsunami. Nakagawa and Shaw (2004) envisaged that a community with social capital can pro-actively participate in reconstruction activities, which shows the way to a thriving and timely recovery from disasters.

Aldrich (2011) pointed out both strong internal relationships and trans-local institutions are crucial for an effective recovery outcome in coastal villages of India. Babu (2007) identified the importance of social capital by studying an agrarian village which employed social capital as a strategy to recover themselves by participating in a reconstruction programme. It was also affirmed that for a long-term recovery; social capital, is a key factor in building trust between people (Aldrich, 2010).

Practically speaking in India, the possibility of development opportunities rests strongly on the following prominent factors (Abhay Joshi and Aoki Misa, 2013) such as:

- Size and duration of the reconstruction programme
- Demographics of the population
- Number of local political representatives of the ruling party in the central government
- Local, national, and bureaucratic leadership
- Availability of funds
- Demanding capacity of local people
- Strong political will
- Popular awareness (number of potential voters), and
- International and local pressure through mass media.

Role of Co-ordination

Coordination during disaster recovery is one of the most neglected areas of disaster risk management, as the majority of literature on coordination focuses on disaster response. In long-term recovery; there are five crucial factors that affect coordination were identified by Emmanuel Raju N and Per Becker, (2013):

(1) Need to coordinate
(2) Role of the government
(3) Knowledge networking
(4) Mandates and goals, and
(5) Coordination at the donor level.

Poor coordination between shelter reconstruction and water supply and sanitation efforts led to poor living conditions for children in many temporary housing units. As a result, there have been difficulties in retrofitting water and sanitation facilities to buildings not designed with these in mind. Poor coordination has also led to contamination of water sources and problems with the disposal of faecal matter. Agencies are now working to improve the situation, but the importance of coordination is a key lesson learned–not just within the sector, but with other sectors (Yin Yin New, 2005).

Follow-Up

Follow up is an important phase any programme so as to make the programme a complete one. As after any disaster, many feel the need to share their experiences and feelings with one another, trying to make sense of what has happened and comfort one another as they grief. The teachers articulate their concerns to mental health professionals and/or school counsellors, so that the children in need can receive more individualised attention (Raundalen and Schultz, 2006).

Key findings of follow up as identified by Yin Yin New (2005):

- Governments, assisted by UNICEF and other partners, are putting in place systems and policies to protect children affected by the tsunami.
- There are no substantiated cases of trafficking of tsunami-affected children, but all partners must continue to be vigilant, and continue with current prevention efforts.
- Most of the children who lost parents have now been placed with community or family members. Visits – of varying frequency across the region – suggest that they are being well looked after. Such visits will need to continue and formal systems for monitoring children's wellbeing will need to be put in place soon.
- Governments are developing mechanisms to support the host families looking after children who have lost their parents to the tsunami.
- Efforts need to continue in seeking better and more appropriate solutions for children who have been put in institutions and orphanages.
- UNICEF's monitoring of psychosocial activities shows that these activities are playing a crucial role in helping children recover from their trauma. Progress is revealed in children's drawings and their behaviour.

Coping Mechanisms

It is important to examine children's coping following a natural disaster because coping responses appear to influence the process of adapting to traumatic events. Research suggests that the use of blame and anger as a way of coping may create more distress for children following disasters (Lazarus P. J., *et. al.,* 2003). Most children respond sensibly and appropriately to disaster, especially if they experience the protection, support, and stability of their parents and other trusted adults. However, like adults, they may respond to disaster with a wide range of symptoms. Their responses are generally similar to those of adults, although they may appear in more direct, less disguised form (John H. Ehrenreich, 2001).

Children of all ages are strongly affected by the responses of their parents or other caretakers to disaster. Children are especially vulnerable to feeling abandoned when they are separated from or lose their parents. "Protecting" children by sending them away from the scene of the disaster, thus separating them from their loved ones, adds the trauma of separation to the trauma of disaster (John H. Ehrenreich, 2001). Anto P. *et. al.,* (2008) made an observation that qualitative changes in their social structure, processes, and attitudes towards different aspects of life were revealed. Survivors valued their unique individual, social and spiritual coping strategies more than formal mental health services.

The child may show separation anxiety with primary caretakers, "magical" explanations to fill in gaps in understanding, and other behaviours usually characteristic of much younger children. Other changes in behaviour, mood, and personality, obvious anxiety and fearfulness, withdrawal, loss of interest in activities, and "spacey" or distractible behaviour may appear (John H. Ehrenreich, 2001). In developing countries like India, limited availability of mental health professionals and poor knowledge about disaster mental health among the medical and para-medical staff, may lead to poor psycho-social rehabilitation of the survivors (Math S.B., *et. al.,* 2006). Many families have yet to regain their livelihoods or move into permanent houses. Rebuilding of basic services for children and infrastructure has only just begun and will take some time. But it is important not to rush in rebuilding, especially if a "Building Back Better" approach is taken, as promoted by President Clinton, the United Nations Special Envoy for Tsunami Recovery (Yin Yin New, 2005).

It is suggested that interventions after disaster should be grounded in ethno-cultural beliefs and practices and should be aimed at strengthening prevailing community coping strategies (Anto P. *et. al.,* 2008). As children grow as adolescence; their responses become increasingly like adult responses. Greater levels of aggressive behaviours, defiance of parents, delinquency, substance abuse, and risk-taking behaviours may be evident. School performance may decline. Wishes for revenge may be expressed. Adolescents are especially unlikely to seek out counselling (John H. Ehrenreich, 2001).

Two **myths** or **potential barriers** in recognising children's responses to disaster and must summarily are rejected:

- Children are innately resilient and will recover rapidly even from severe trauma.
- Children are not affected by disaster unless they are disturbed by their parents.

A wealth of evidence indicates that children experience the effects of disaster doubly. Even very young children are directly affected by experiences of death, destruction, terror, personal physical assault, and by experiencing the absence of powerlessness of their parents. They are also indirectly affected through identification with the effects of the disaster on their parents and other trusted adults (such as teachers) and by their parents' reactions to the disaster. Another barrier to recognising children's responses to disaster is the tendency of parents to misinterpret their children's reactions (John H. Ehrenreich, 2001).

Influencing Factors on Coping

Relocation

Relocation is a factor which influence coping as the frequent need for disaster survivors to relocate creates unique crisis problems and may contribute to the social, environmental, and psychological stress experienced by disaster survivors. Research suggests that relocation is associated with higher levels of ecological stress, crowding, isolation, and social disruption (Lazarus P. J., *et. al.,* 2002).

Parental Adjustment and Family Support

Parents' adjustment is an important factor in children's adjustment, and the adjustment of the child in turn contributes to the overall adjustment of the family. Altered family functions, separation from parents after natural disaster, and ongoing maternal preoccupation with the trauma are more predictive of trauma symptomatology in children than is the level of exposure. Thus, parents' reactions and family support following a natural disaster are important considerations in helping children's cope (Lazarus P. J., *et. al.,* 2002).

Emotional Reactivity

Preliminary findings suggest that children who tend to be anxious are those most likely to develop post-trauma symptomatology following a natural disaster (Lazarus P. J., *et. al.,* 2002).

Long-term Consequences of Disaster

Research suggests that long-term difficulties following a natural disaster are most likely to be seem among children who experienced any of the following (Lazarus P. J., *et. al.,* 2003):

- Threats to their physical safety.
- Thought they might die during the disaster.
- Report that they were very upset during the disaster.
- Lost their belongings or house as a result of the disaster.
- Had to relocate in the aftermath.
- Attended new schools that had multiple schedule changes.
- Disruptions and deviations in all walks of life.

Consequently crisis response team members need to identify students who experience these risk factors and closely monitor their status. These students may require long-term coping assistance. Prinstein, M. J., *et. al.,* (1996) proclaimed that the assistance of parents, teachers and friends to children to cope after a natural disaster is highly essential. Further it was reported that coping assistance from parents and friends was reported more frequently. It is suggested that coping assistance is an important construct for understanding children's reactions to natural disasters.

Newman, M. (2004) suggested that child centred play therapy proved effective in coping children of disaster victims. Pfefferbaum, B. (1998) recommended that the child and adolescent psychiatrist must play an essential role in the wake of disaster. The focus of the community and the world understandably turns to the physical devastation wrought, and emergency and medical efforts take centre stage. Christina Suboh, (2008) wanted to emphasise the importance of supporting the victims and survivors by providing opportunities to strengthen their coping skills, whether it is through cultural rituals and traditions, religious ceremonies or other socially acceptable activities.

Wrap up

Natural disasters; most of the time have a devastating consequences on children and often an entire community is affected. Poor academic achievements, mental health problems, social withdrawal and self-blaming were found among child survivors of disasters. Anxiety disorders are the most common psychiatric illnesses in children and adolescents. They are associated with significant distress and impairment. Moreover both physical injury and psychological perturbation-notably post-traumatic stress disorder are associated with disasters. It is common that children articulate their distress through their behaviour, as they are often less able to do so verbally. Withdrawal, nightmares, avoiding communication, poor concentration, and aggression were common. It is evident that frequency and intensity of disaster events increase around the globe, children are among those most at risk for the negative effects of disaster. Social vulnerability is another unavoidable phenomenon found among disaster victims.

It is eminent that the role of the teachers' is crucial and significant in the formation process of children. The teachers adopt various techniques such as demonstration, doing by learning, cognitive-behavioural modification, etc., to completely mould the students for a total personality. Added to it the school environment also make the students to related with the teachers, fellow students and others so that they could develop interrelationships, adjustments and understand the social realities. In particular the students are supported morally and socially during distress and disaster and thus make the school environment to play a supportive role in the life of children and hence the role of a teacher is essential in any one's life.

With this backdrop an empirical study is mooted with the following objectives so as to understand the unique issues of child survivors of Tsumani that attacked the Indian soil during 2004 on their psychosocial well being and on their school life and try to suggest coping measures in social work perspectives.

Objectives

- To describe the socio-demographic characteristics of the respondents.
- To study the mental health status of the tsunami affected children.
- To study the study habit and study involvement among the tsunami affected children.
- To analyse the level of anxiety and depression experienced by the respondents.
- To analyse the adjustment pattern among the children.
- To suggest suitable measures for the respondents to cope and deal with her/his emotional reactions.

Chapter - 9

Methods and Assessment Tools for Disaster Children

A disaster is a natural or man-made event that negatively affects life, property and livelihood; often resulting in permanent changes to human societies, eco system, and environment.

A natural phenomenon can easily turn into a natural disaster. Natural disasters may become more severe because of human actions prior, during, or after the disaster itself. A specific disaster may spawn different type of events and may reduce the survivability of the initial event. A classical example is an earthquake that collapses homes, and traps people inside gas mines that get ignited and burn people alive. Human activity in risk areas may cause natural disasters; volcano eruption gives rise to other events like fires, lashes, mudflows, landslides, earthquakes and tsunamis.

Among all the disasters Tsunami is one of the worst disasters that India faced in the post-independent era. The killer waves snatched away the lives of thousands in India, and all over the Southern Hemisphere; the count raised up to 2.5 million. Along with many other countries in South East Asia, India also is one of the worst affected countries, by Tsunami in the Indian Ocean on 26th December 2004. The states of Tamil Nadu, Andhra Pradesh, Kerala, and the Union Territories of Pondicherry, Andaman, and Nicobar Islands were severely affected in India. Children are the worst victims of this disaster as they lost their natural nurturing environment. Efforts have been put forward from the different human services agencies; still the scar in their mind will take years to heal.

The Pressing Issue

Disasters are abnormal experiences; they cause distress and emotional reactions in almost all people. But exposure to natural disaster has a devastating impact on the psychological and social well being of the children. A disaster like Tsunami disrupts the process of interaction the child has with his/her environment. It leads to displacement wherein the child loses his familiar environment (home, school, peers, etc).There is also a scene of panic and confusion in the family and the caregivers are unable to care for the child or stay around them for sometime or the other; and thus the regular life pattern is disrupted. There can be instances of losing either the parents, or one of the parents, siblings or even a pet, leaving the child with a sense of loss.

The tragedy of the disaster means the tragedy of children lost, children who have become orphans, children who have lost one parent, displaced children, children who have lost familiar environment (peers, school, neighbourhood.). Out of total deaths; it was informed that about 37-39 per cent is children below the age of 14 years. Of 1.5 million children who lost their parents in tsunami, a large number are from southern part of India. The number of children who lost their parents in Chennai, Cuddalore, Nagapattinam and Kanyakumari alone amounts to four thousand seven hundred and thirty (4730).

Disasters hamper the process of health; emotional and psychological development. The devastation not only washes the lives and livelihood, but also leaves other consequences like trauma, physical, psychological, and social impact among all type of individuals. Mental health and well being is integral to the health and functioning of individuals. The mental health of the victim children by tsunami, had a negative impact on study habit and study involvement of children, in turn increases the anxiety, depression, and adjustment problem of the children.

When there is low level of anxiety, depression and high level of adjustment there will be positive psycho-social well being of children. When there is high level of anxiety, depression, and low level of adjustment there will be negative outcome of psycho-social well being of the children, wherein all the children are the most affected group who really needs the attention of the social scientists. More over studies are seldom done on these aspects. This empirical study focused on the psycho-social impact of Tsunami as perceived by the high school students at Kanyakumari district; this is the place where tsunami had claimed not only many lives but also rendered them homeless, orphans and destitute. The following chart shows the outcome of psycho-social well being of the children.

Conceptual Frame Work

Positive Outcome

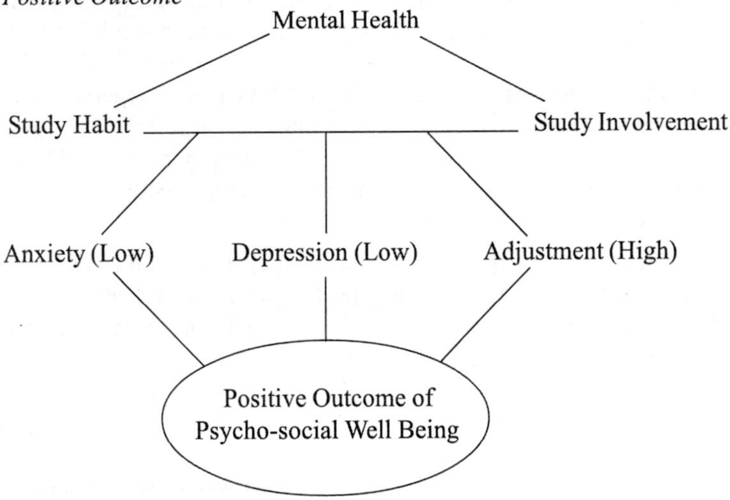

Negative Outcome

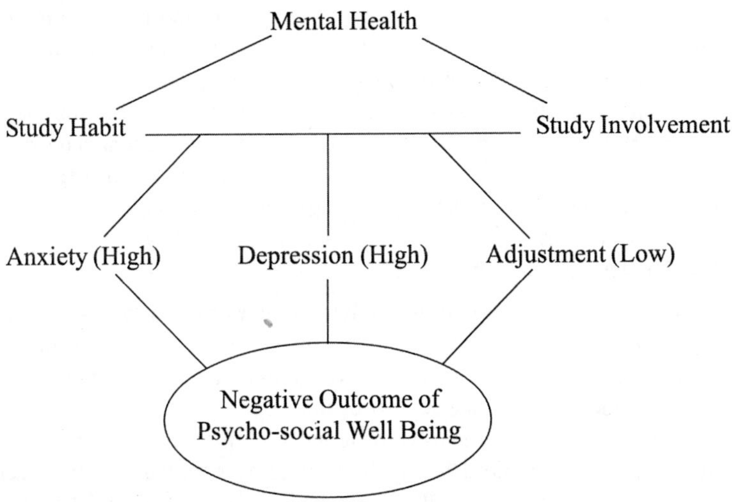

Chart - 12: Conceptual Frame Work.

Postulates of Children Well-Being

Children are the most important assets of a country, because they are the future nation, who could provide their potentials, for the country's development in the future. Childhood is very important, because it shapes their future. While, all the periods in a life span are important, some are more important than the others because of their immediate effects on the attitudes and behaviour, whereas others are significant because of their long-term effects. Childhood is one of the periods when both the immediate effects and long-term effects are important. Some periods are important for their physical and some for their psychological effects. Childhood is important for both. Accompanying these rapid and important physical developments, especially during late childhood period, rapid mental developments occur. These give rise to the need for mental adjustments and the necessity for establishing new attitudes values and interests.

When children experience a traumatic event, which they are unable to comprehend or cope up with, they tend to behave in a manner that is not always pleasant. For instance, children become disruptive in class, and start performing badly in school. At home they might wet the bed, use bad language, misbehave with visitors or scream and shout at family members. All these can actually make those around the child angry and that is not the solution. One needs to understand why the child is behaving in such a way. The child unknowingly resorts to such behaviour in order to deal with pain and sufferings being experienced within him.

After a horrifying disaster like the Tsunami, children react, emotionally and there can be behavioural changes. These are normal reactions to an abnormal event in their life. Children of different age groups react differently as they perceive the event differently. Often children are unable to identify the emotions that they are experiencing. To all appearances they may seem to be all right but there might be a lot of turmoil and conflicts which needs to be set aright.. Children process events around them according to their development ages. It is important to understand how the children of different groups feel and react to a disastrous situation, so that they can be helped out to feel better and lead a happy life.

Tsunami by its devastation, had left its footprints, not only on the shore side but also in people's mind especially the children. They are the ones who bore the brunt in large and were affected psychologically. Their mental health is affected due to anxiety and depression that might lead to adjustment problem which affects their study involvement and studying habit in turn. Hence an attempt is made to explore the psycho-social impact of tsunami as perceived by high school students so that intervention strategies could be planned accordingly.

Objectives Formulated

- To describe the socio-demographic characteristics of the respondents.
- To study the mental health status of the tsunami affected children.

- To study the study habit and study involvement among the tsunami affected children.
- To analyse the level of anxiety and depression experienced by the respondents.
- To analyse the adjustment pattern among the children.
- To suggest suitable measures for the respondents to cope and deal with her/his emotional reactions.

Hypothesis Enumerated

- Based on the objectives few hypotheses have been constructed.
- As anxiety increases depression also increases.
- When anxiety is high, the respondents' adjustment will be low.
- When anxiety is high the respondents study habits will be low.
- As anxiety increases the study involvement decreases.
- Higher the depression the lower will be their adjustment.
- As depression increases, the respondents' study habits decreases.
- As depression increases lower will be the mental health.
- Higher the adjustment, higher will be their mental health.
- Higher the mental health higher will be the study habit.
- As the study habit is higher study involvement will be higher.
- Higher the mental health higher will be their study involvement.
- Higher the anxiety level lower the mental health.

Design Drawn

The main aim of the present study is to portray the different characteristics of high school students with regards to their mental health, study habit, study involvement, anxiety, depression, and adjustment. It also attempts to test the relationships and associations of variables upon which hypotheses were formed (Royce Singleton, Bruce C. Straits, Margaret M. Straits and Ronald J Mc Allister, 1988). To make estimates of precision and generality of the findings descriptive design has been empowered.

Coverage Children

The universe of the present study consists of 400 students studying eighth, ninth, and tenth standard from the schools in Kanyakumari district during the year 2006-2007 and were affected by tsunami. The four local schools were covered and census method was used to study all the high school students in the universe.

Pilot Study

A visit was made to all the four schools (St. Mary's Higher Secondary

School, Colachel, St. Little Flower Higher Secondary School Melamanakudi, St. Alex High School Kottilpadu, Orient Matriculation Higher Secondary School, Kottilpadu); in order to find out the feasibility of conducting the study. Further discussion with the school administration on the purpose, significance and ethical concerns and need for future intervention were done. After obtained necessary permission and assured cooperation the students were met and rapport established.

Asserting Tools for Data Collection

The researcher used questionnaire as the tool for collecting the necessary data. The respondents were made aware of the purpose of the investigation and found competent enough to respond to the questionnaire. They answered the queries at a convenient time, without affecting their daily schedule. Before finalising the tools of data collection to be used, the researcher had discussions with the Principal, teachers, and high school students and decided on the relevant questions and the areas to be explored were done. A survey of existing literature on psycho-social impact of tsunami among high school students also helped to finalise the relevant tools of data collection.

The first part of the questionnaire covered the question pertaining to personal and socio-economic background of the respondents. In addition to that the following tools were also used.

I. Mental Health Inventory

Mental health inventory developed by V.D. Augustine (1978) was used. The reliability and validity of the tool was established by the aforesaid author (1978) and the reliability coefficient is found to be 0.8567.

The scoring procedure as instructed in the scale was followed. The scores are assigned depending upon the positive and negative question and the agreement with the scoring keys as mentioned below.

1 mark is assigned for the following questions, if the respondents' mode is "YES."

1, 5, 7, 8, 9, 10, 14, 16, 17, 22, 27, 31, 33, 34, 35, 37, 38, 40, 44, 45, 49, 50, 53, 54, 58 and 60.

1 mark is assigned for the following questions, if the respondent is "NO"

2, 3, 4, 6, 11, 12, 13, 15, 18, 19, 20, 21, 23, 24, 26, 28, 29, 30, 32, 36, 39, 41, 42, 43, 46, 47, 48, 51, 52, 55, 56, 57, 59.

S.No.	*Dimensions*	*Low Level*	*High Level*
1.	Mental Health	Up to 36	37 and above

II. Study Habit Inventory

Study habit inventory developed by B.V. Patel (1983) was used. The inventory consists of 45 statements grouped into seven dimensions namely, home environment and planning of work, reading and note taking, planning of subjects, habit of concentration, preparation for examination, general habits and attitudes and school environment. The reliability and validity of the tool was established by the same author (1983) and the reliability coefficient is found to be 0.9104.

Scoring for the Study Habit Inventory

It consists of 45 items under the dimensions namely,

1. Home environment and planning: 7 items–1, 2, 3, 4, 5, 6, 7
2. Reading and Note Taking: 5 items-8, 13, 14, 15, 16.
3. Planning of subjects: 4 items–17, 18, 21, 29.
4. Habits of Concentration: 5 items–22, 23, 24, 25, 32
5. Preparation for examinations–8 items–12, 19, 26, 27, 28, 30, 31
6. General Habits and Attitudes: 10 items–9, 10, 11, 33, 34, 35, 36, 37, 38, 39.
7. School Environment: 6 items-40, 41, 42, 43, 44, 45.

The scoring is done in a two point response which include 'Yes' and 'No' statements

Scoring will be

	Positive	*Negative*
Yes	2 Marks	1 Mark
No	1 Mark	2 Mark

The positive questions include 1, 2, 3, 4, 5, 6, 9, 10, 11, 12, 13, 14, 16, 17, 18, 19, 20, 23 and 27, 28, 29, 30, 33, 34, 35, 36, 37, 38, 39, 40, 41, 42, 43, 44.

The negative questions include 7, 8, 15, 21, 22, 24, 25, 26, 31, 32, 45. High score indicates good study habits among the students.

S. No.	*Dimensions*	*Low level*	*High Level*
1.	Home environment and planning	Upto 11	12 and above
2.	Reading and note taking	Upto 7	8 and above
3.	Planning of subjects	Upto 6	7 and above
4.	Habits of concentration	Upto 6	7 and above
5.	Preparation for examinations	Upto 12	13 and above
6.	General habits and attitudes	Upto 16	17 and above
7.	School environment	Upto 9	10 and above
8.	Overall	Upto 72	73 and above

III. Study Involvement Inventory

Study involvement inventory developed by Jayalakshmi (1978) was used in this study. The inventory consists of 25 items representing the dimensions of study instruments as school environment, self-confidence, involvement, feedback, and peer relations. The items are in the Likert format. The reliability and validity of the tool was established by the aforesaid author and reliability coefficient is found to be 0.7002.

The study involvement consists of 25 items under the 5 items as follows:

School Environment : 6 items 1, 2, 13, 14, 20, 23.

Self Confidence : 5 items 4, 9, 10, 15, 22.

Involvement : 6 items 3, 5, 16, 17, 21, 25.

Feedback : 5 items 7, 8, 11, 19, 24

Peer Relations : 3 items 6, 12 and 18.

The scoring is done in three point's mode response for the study involvement inventory. The choices are strongly agree, moderately agree, and not at all agree.

S.No.	*Choices*	*Scores*	
		Positive	*Negative*
1.	Strongly Agree	3 marks	1 mark
2.	Moderately Agree	2 marks	2 marks
3.	Not at all Agree	1 mark	3 marks

The positive questions include 12, 3, 4, and 5, 6, 7, 9, 10, 11, 12, 13, 14, 15, 16, 17, 18, 19, 22, 23. The negative questions includes 8, 20, 21, 24, 25. High scores indicates high involvement of the students.

S.No	*Dimensions*	*Low Level*	*High Level*
1.	School Environment	Upto 13	14 and above
2.	Self confidence	Upto 12	13 and above
3.	Involvement	Upto 13	14 and above
4.	Feedback	Upto 11	12 and above
5.	Peer relations	Upto 7	8 and above
6.	Over all	Upto 59	60 and above

IV. Anxiety Inventory

Anxiety inventory was developed by Taylor (1935 revised edition) was used. The subjects answered "True or False" to the item given. There are 27 items scored in terms of the number answered in the level items. If the response coincided with key, score one was calculated.

- **Scoring Key:**

  Items : 1, 3, 5, 6, 7, 10, 11, 12, 13, 14, 15, 16, 17, 18, 19, 20, 21, 22, 23, 24, 25, 26, 27, are True.

  Items: 2, 4, 8, and 9 are False.

  The reliability of the scale is 0.7398

  The researcher used median test to find out the low level anxiety and high level anxiety.

  Low level anxiety-Upto 12

  High level anxiety-13 and above

V. Depression Inventory

The questionnier was developed by Becks (1988) and consists of 21 categories of symptoms and attitudes towards depression. Namely, sadness, pessimist, sense of failure, dissatisfaction, guild, expection, self-dislike, self-accustations, suicidal ideas, crying, irritability, social withdrawl, indecisiveness, body image change, work participation, insomnia, fatigability, anorenia, weight loss, somatic preoccupation, loss of libido. Each category being a specific behaviour manifestation of depression. The statements are ranked according to the severity of the symptoms score ranges from 0-3 higher score indicates the higher level of depression. The reliability of the scale is 0.821.

The researcher used median test to find out the level of depression

Not Depressed 0-9

Depressed 10-20

Severely Depressed 2-63.

VI. Adjustment Inventory

Adjustment problem inventory developed by Ramamurthy (1968) has been used to find out the extent of adjustment problems in the dimensions of health, emotional, self, home, and social. The same tool has been also administered to find out the overall adjustment problems. The variability of the scale is found to be 0.8555.

Scoring Key

	Positive	*Negative*
Yes	2	1
No	1	2

The negative questions are 5, 12, 20, 33, 35, 40, 43 and 50. All the other questions are positive.

S. No.	*Dimensions*	*Item Numbers*
1.	Health	3, 6, 10, 14, 19, 22, 26, 31, 37, 48
2.	Emotional	1, 7, 11, 23, 27, 29, 32, 38, 42, 45
3.	Self	2, 16, 20, 24, 33, 39, 40, 43, 46, 49
4.	Home	4, 8, 12, 15, 17, 28, 30, 34, 36, 47
5.	Social	5, 9, 13, 18, 21, 25, 35, 41, 44, 50

The score indicates the degree of maladjustment (adjustment problems).The higher the score, the higher the maladjustment. The researcher used median test to categorise the various dimensions scores into two categories namely, low adjustmental problems and high adjustmental problems.

S. No.	*Dimensions*	*Low*	*High*
1.	Health	Upto 7	8 and above
2.	Emotional	Upto 11	12 and above
3.	Self	Upto 9	10 and above
4.	Home	Upto 9	10 and above
5.	Social	Upto 9	10 and above
6.	Overall	Upto 49	50 and above

Though for all the above mentioned tools of data collection, the reliability and validity have been established for Indian population by the concerned authors as mentioned above, for the purpose of the present study. The investigator has applied split half co-efficient test to establish the reliability for the above-mentioned tools of data collection as an additional measure. The results of such tests to establish reliability in the descriptive study are given below.

Sl. No.	*Name of the tool*	*Standardized for Indian population*	*Year*
1.	Mental Health	V.D. Augustine	1978
2.	Study Habit Inventory	Jayalakshmi	1978
3.	Study Involvement Inventroy	B.V. Patel	1983
4.	Anxiety Scale	Taylor	1935
5.	Depression Inventory	Becks	1988
6.	Adjustment Inventory	Ramamurthy	1968

Statistical Analysis

Statistical tests such as mean standard deviation, chi-square, one way analysis of variance, Karl Pearson's co-efficient of correlation and Z-test were applied to interpret the data to draw meaningful inferences. The mean and standard deviation were used for numerical data. The one-way analysis of the variance was used to find out the significant difference among three groups. The chi-square was used to find out the association between two variables.

The Karl Pearson's co-efficient of co-relation was used to find out the degree of relationship between two variables and it also shows the direction or nature of relationship between two variables. The above-mentioned tests were used to find out the relationship between the variables namely, socio-economic status, mental health, study habit study involvement, and anxiety, depression, and adjustment among the tsunami affected children. The same test were used to find out relationship between the personal data (age, class, religion, caste, area of residence, birth order, type of family and size of family) socio-economic status and above-mentioned variables.

Defining Terms

Tsunami

A **tsunami is** a Japanese word, which translates as "**harbor wave,**" now used internationally to refer to a series of waves travelling across the ocean with extremely long wavelengths.

Psycho-social Analysis

It means analyse on psycho-social impact among high school students due to tsunami. Psychological status (Mental health, Anxiety, Depression, and adjustment) and sociological status (Study Habit, Study Involvement) in the context of post-tsunami situation according to the study.

Area of Residence

The area of residence refers to students residing in worst affected area among 33 coastal villages in Kanyakumari district.

Mental Health Inventory

In this study, mental health is a state of emotional well being of the children to function comfortably within his a state of emotional well being of the children to function comfortably within his society and in which his personal achievements and characteristics are satisfactory to him.

Low Level of Mental Health Status

In the present study, the individual scores upto 36 in the mental health inventory of V.D. Augustine (1978) is termed as low level of mental health.

High Level of Mental Health Status

The individuals whose score reach 37 and above in the mental health inventory of; V.D. Augustine (1978) is termed as high level of mental health status in this study.

Study Habit

This refers to the patterns of the study, planning for homework, reading, notes taking, habit of concentration, planning for learning difficult subjects, preparation for examination, general habits, attitude towards education and school environment and home environment.

Low Level of Study Habit

In the present study, the individual scores upto 72 in the study habit inventory of B.V. Patel (1983) is termed as low level of study habit in this study.

High Level of Study Habit

The individual whose score reaches 73 and above in the study habit inventory of; B.V. Patel (1983) is termed as high level of study habit in this study.

Study Involvement

This refers to the study instrument in the areas of school environment, self-confidence, involvement, feedback and peer relations.

Low Level of Study Involvement

In the present study, the individual scores upto 59 in the study involvement inventory of Jayalakshmi (1978) are termed as low level of study involvement.

High Level of Study Involvement

In the present study, the individual scores reaches 60 and above in the study involvement inventory of Jayalakshmi (1978) is termed as high level of study involvement.

Anxiety

Anxiety as a diffuse fear which is not restricted to definite situations or objects and is subjectively experienced as dread, apprehension or tension and may arise in any situation in which the integrity of the personality is threatened.

Low Level of Anxiety

In the present study, the individual scores up to 12 in the Anxiety inventory of Taylor's (1935) is termed as low level of Anxiety.

High Level of Anxiety

In the present study, the individual scores reaches 13 and above in the Anxiety inventory of Taylor's (1935) is termed as High level of Anxiety.

Depression

Depression refers to the feeling of hopelessness, despair, low self-esteem, worthlessness, guilt and withdrawal from others.

Low Level of Depression

In the present study, the individual scores upto10-20 in the Depression inventory of Becks (1988) is termed as Low Level of Depression.

High Level of Depression

In the present study, the individual scores reaches 21-63 in the Depression inventory of Becks (1988) is termed as High Level of Depression i.e. Severely Depressed.

Low Level of Adjustment

In the present study, the individual scores upto 12 in the Adjustment Inventory of Ramamurthy (1968) is termed as Low Level of Adjustment.

High Level of Adjustment

In the present study, the individual scores reaches 13 and above in the Adjustment inventory of Ramamurthy (1968) is termed as High Level of Adjustment.

Rationale for Area Selection

Republic of India, is the seventh-largest country by geographical area, the second-most populous country, and the most populous democracy in the world. Bounded by the Indian Ocean on the south, the Arabian Sea on the west, and the Bay of Bengal on the east, India has a coastline of 7,517 kilometers (4,671 mi). It is bordered by Pakistan to the west; China, Nepal, and Bhutan to the north-east; and Bangladesh and Myanmar to the east.

In the southern part of India, Kanyakumari is the southernmost district of Tamil Nadu and India as well. The district is bounded by Tirunelveli District on the North and East. The South Eastern boundary is the Gulf of Mannar. On the South and South West the boundaries are the Indian Ocean and the Arabian Sea. On the West and North West it is bounded by Kerala.

It has 68 km long coastline studded with 44 coastal fishing villages. The coastline begins at Vatakottai (circular fort) at the east ends at Neerodi at the west. The confluence of the Indian Ocean, Bay of Bengal, and the Arabian

Sea at Kanyakumari makes the place strategically important and lures the attention of tourists. Nearly 33 coastal villages were affected due to the disaster–Tsunami 2004.

More than 2000 people were injured and nearly 1000 people including children were dead due to Tsunami. The Government of Tamil Nadu took immediate relief action through District Health Services in the affected coastal villages immediately after the Tsunami by involving the local people and private agencies.

For the purpose of relief and rehabilitation the State health officials divided the Tsunami affected coastal villages into five Zones for Tsunami relief works iz., Kanniyakumari, Rajakkaniangalam, Muttom, Colachel and Enayam.

According to an estimate, 2,17,440 fisher-folks are distributed in the 44 villages of Kanyakumari coast and constitute about 26 per cent of the total fisherman of Tamil Nadu. On 26.12.2004, a massive earthquake which occurred off the Indonesian coast by 6.30 AM (IST), triggered huge tidal waves, which hit the Indian coast between 8.15 AM to 11.15 AM resulted in the loss of thousands of lives and damages to properties. In Kanyakumari district, 33 coastal villages were affected by Tsunami, which resulted in loss of 798 lives. Among 33 coastal villages, 3 villages were affected worst (KRRC, 2005).

With this backdrop a study was initiated among children to measure the psycho-social impact in these area. The following four schools have been selected randomly for the purpose of this empirical study such as; St. Mary's Higher Secondary School, Colachel, St. Little Flower Higher Secondary School Melamanakudi and St. Alex High School, Kottilpadu, Orient Matriculation Higher Secondary School, Kottilpadu at Kanyakumari district.

Chapter - 10

Psycho-social Impact - An Empirical Discussion

The present chapter intends to explain the socio-economic profile of the respondents and their perception towards; Mental health, Study habits, Study involvement, Anxiety, Depression, and Adjustment in various aspects. As found that the relationship between the socio-demographic characteristics of the respondents and factors influencing their perception and behaviours among different groups.

The socio-demographic characteristics of the respondents include age, standard in which they are studying, religion, caste, nativity, birth order, parents' education and occupation, type and size of family. The standard of living of a person is also determined by the socio-demographic factors. The data on field is also determined by the respondent's situation and their opinion about the field before tsunami.

A systematic statistical analysis of the collected data and that are presented in a detailed manner in the following pages.

With regards to school, more than half of the respondents (51.0 per cent) are studying in St. Mary's Higher Secondary School at Colachel, Kanyakumari district and less than one-third of the respondents (30.8 per cent) are studying in Little Flower Higher Secondary School at Melamanakudi while small percentages of the respondents are studying (10.0 per cent, 8.3 per cent) at St. Alex High School, Kottilpadu and Orient Matriculation School, Kottilpadu respectively.

Table 1: Socio-Demographic Profile

Sl.No.	*Personal Profile*	*No. of Respondents (n = 400)*	*Percentage*
1.	**Age**		
	12 years	11	2.8
	13 years	102	25.2
	14 years	142	35.5
	15 years	126	31.5
	16 years	17	4.3
	17 years	2	0.5
2.	**Sex**		
	Male	199	49.8
	Female	201	50.3
3.	**Religion**		
	Christian	364	91.0
	Non-Christian	36	9.0
4.	**Community**		
	BC	32	8.0
	MBC	365	91.2
	SC	3	0.8
5.	**Class**		
	8th Std.	150	37.5
	9th Std	117	29.3
	10th Std	133	33.3
6.	**Type of family**		
	Joint	108	27.0
	Nuclear	292	73.0
7.	**Native background**		
	Rural	365	91.2
	Urban	35	8.8
8.	**No. of Siblings**		
	upto 2	2	0.6
	3	6	1.5
	4	76	19.0
	5	108	27.0
	6	63	15.8
	7	49	12.3
	8	45	11.3
	9	15	3.8
	10	15	3.8
	more than 10	21	5.3

Conti...

9.	**Birth Order**		
	First born	121	30.3
	2nd born	85	21.3
	3rd born	101	25.3
	4th born	42	10.5
	5th born	19	4.8
	Beyond 5	32	8.2
10.	**Present Living Place**		
	Near Seashore	365	89.0
	Far away from Seashore	44	11.0

With regards to age, more than one-third of the respondents (35.5 per cent) are 14 years old. Nearly one-third of them (31.5 per cent) are 15 years. While, nearly one-fourth of the respondents (25.2 per cent) are 13 years old and few of them (2.8 per cent, 4.3 per cent and 0.5 per cent) are 12 years, 16 years and 17 years respectively.

Looking into the sex of the respondents, half of the respondents (50.3 per cent) are females and very nearly half of the respondents (49.8 per cent) are males.

Regarding the religion followed by the respondents, it reveals that absolutely a majority of the respondents (91.0 per cent) belongs to Christianity and very meager percentage (9.0 per cent) belongs to other religions. Hence this study was conducted in the coastal area many of the respondents are belongs to Christian religion.

Caste is another variable which also has its influence upon the area of domicile. While observing the community, vast majority of the respondents (91.2 per cent) belongs to most backward while the other backward class and scheduled caste respectively share a small percentage (8.0 to 0.8 per cent) only.

When looking into the standard in which the respondents are studying. More than one-third of the respondents (37.5 per cent) are studying 8th standard. While, one-third of the respondents (33.3) are studying 10th standard and more than one-fourth of them (29.3 per cent) are studying 9th standard.

With respect to the type of family of the respondents it is evident that vast majority of the respondents (73.0 per cent) belongs to nuclear family system. While, less than one-third of the respondents (27.0 per cent) belongs to joint family system. Since majority of the respondents live under nuclear family system, the inferences one could derive is the traditional joint family system is fast disintegrating due to diverse socio-economic factors.

While analysing the number of siblings in the respondents' family, five sibling forms the maximum percentage (27 per cent). One and three becomes least minority (0.3 and 1.5 per cent) four, six and seven siblings group constitute (19 per cent, 15.8 per cent and 12.3 per cent). The birth order of the respondents has its influence over their relationship with their family members. Less than one-fourth of the respondents (30.3 per cent, 25.3 per cent and 21.3 per cent) are first, second and third born respectively. While less percentage of the respondents (10.5 per cent, 4.8 per cent, 3.5 per cent and 1.8 per cent, 1.5 per cent) are fourth born, fifth born, sixth born and seventh born and eighth born respectively and 1.1 per cent of the respondents are tenth born.

Since this study was conducted in the coastal villages, vast majority of the respondents (89.0 per cent) are living near sea shore and small per cent (11.0) are living faraway from sea shore.

Table 2: Parents' Education and Occupational Status

Sl. No.	*Education and occupational status of the respondents parents*	*No. of respondents (n=400)*	*Percentage*
1.	**Father's Education**		
	Illiterate	82	20.5
	Primary	183	45.8
	Middle	167	16.8
	SSLC	36	9.0
	Higher Secondary	27	6.8
	Under Graduation	5	1.3
2.	**Mother's Education**		
	Illiterate	71	17.8
	Primary	142	35.5
	Middle	99	24.8
	SSLC	60	15.0
	Higher Secondary	24	6.0
	Under Graduation	4	1.0
3	**Occupation of the Father**		
	Fishing	364	91.0
	Coolie	6	1.5
	Business	28	7.0
	None	2	0.5
4	**Occupation of the Mother**		
	Nurse	2	0.5
	Teacher	1	0.3
	Tailor	2	0.5
	None	395	98.7

The above table portrays the respondent's parent's occupational and educational status. It is found that vast majority of the respondent's fathers (91.0 per cent) occupation is fishing, hence this study was contacted among fisher folk community maximum number of the respondent's fathers are doing business like selling fishes in export and import, company. While remaining per cent of the respondent's fathers (1.5 per cent and 0.5 per cent) are working as coolies and they are not doing any other occupation respectively.

With regard to the respondents Father's education, more than one-third of the respondents fathers (35.5 per cent) have studied upto primary level and one-fourth of the respondents fathers (24.8 per cent) are illiterates, while few of the respondent's fathers (12.8 per cent) have studied upto middle school level and few per cent of the respondents fathers (9.0 per cent and 6.8 per cent) have been studied upto High School, and Higher Secondary level respectively and least number of the respondents' fathers (1.3 per cent) have been studied upto under graduation.

Regarding the occupational status of the respondents' mothers. It is very heartening to note that majority of the mothers of the respondents (98.7 per cent) are not working and few per cent of the mothers of the respondents (0.5 per cent, 0.5 per cent and 0.3 per cent) are working as a nurse, tailor and teacher respectively.

The fourth part of the table makes a study in contrast with the first part of table when looking into the respondents mothers educational status, it is clear that more than one-third of the respondents mothers have studied upto primary level and nearly one-fourth of the respondents mothers (24.8 per cent) have completed upto middle level. While small numbers of the respondent's mothers are illiterates and few percentages of the respondents mothers have studied upto SSLC and Higher Secondary. The paradox is professionally qualified mothers occupy the least percentage is (1.0 per cent).

With regards to the type of house, vast majority of the respondents (90.0 per cent) lives in their own house and few per cent of the respondents (7.3 per cent) live in rented house and remaining percentage of the respondents (2.8 per cent) lives in lease house.

When looking into the nature of housing conditions nearly half of the respondents (4.9.0 per cent and 41.3 per cent) lives in concrete and tiled houses respectively. While, few per cent of the respondent's live in huts. It has been found from other part of the table a sizable proportion of the respondents (56.5 per cent) are not satisfied with the facilities in their home.

Table 3: Socio-economic Status

Sl. No.	*Socio-economic Status*	*No. of respondents (n=400)*	*Percentage*
1.	**Type of house the respondents lives in**		
	Owned	360	90.0
	Rented	29	7.2
	Lease	11	2.8
2.	**Nature of housing conditions**		
	Hut	39	9.8
	Tiled	165	41.2
	Concrete	196	49.0
3.	**Satisfaction about the facilities in the house**		
	Yes	174	43.5
	No	226	56.5
4.	**Monthly family income**		
	Below 1000	364	45.8
	1001-7000	118	29.5
	Above 7001	99	24.8
5.	**Property possession**		
	Yes	106	26.5
	No	294	73.5
6.	**Debts**		
	Yes	378	94.5
	No	22	5.5

On the basis of the monthly family income of the respondents, the above table shows that the respondents belonging to families with a monthly income below ₹ 1000 (45.8 per cents) and more than one-fourth of the respondents (29.5 per cent) monthly family income ₹ 1001 to 7000 and one-fourth of the respondents (24.88 per cent) families' monthly income above ₹ 7001.

It is also observed that a majority of the respondents (73.5 per cent) families do not possess any property and vast majority of the respondent's family (94.5 per cent) have debts.

Geological feature such as bays reefs, river entrances, and undersea formation may dissipate the energy of a Tsunami. In some places a Tsunami may cause the sea to rise vertically only few inches feet. Sometimes an approaching Tsunami is preceded by a noticeable fall or rise in the water level.

Table 4: Details on Living Entitlements

Sl. No.	*Details on living entitlements*	*No. of Respondents (n=400)*	*Percentage*
1.	**Change the house after Tsunami**		
	Changed	147	36.8
	Not Changed	253	63.3
2.	**Residence at the time of tsunami**		
	Near the seashore	138	34.5
	Far away from the seashore	63	15.8
	3 km from seashore	461	11.5
	4 km from seashore	46	36.5
	5 km from seashore	7	1.8
3.	**Nature of the place at the time of Tsunami**		
	Flat Slightly	346	86.5
	Sloping	54	13.5
4.	**Sea position before tsunami**		
	Calm	314	78.5
	Normal	86	21.5
5.	**Sea position after Tsunami**		
	Colour changed	267	66.8
	High Tide	90	22.5
	Raise in the water level	43	10.8
6.	**Protection against tsunami**		
	Protected	342	85.5
	Not protected	58	14.5

Regarding data about the field majority of the respondents (63.3 per cent) has not been changed their houses after Tsunami, while more than one-third respondents (36.8 per cent) has changed their houses after tsunami and their residence is near the seashore at the time of Tsunami (34.5 per cent) and vast majority of the respondents says (86.5 per cent) their place was flat at the time of tsunami.

With regards to sea position before and after Tsunami majority of the respondents (18.5 per cent) said the sea position was calm before Tsunami, while after tsunami majority of the respondents (66.8 per cent) says the colour was changed after Tsunami and vast majority of the respondents (85.5 per cent) informed protection is taken by the government against tsunami.

The above table reveals that all the respondents (100 per cent) perceive high level of anxiety and depression respectively. Even though this study was conducted among children after one year, and many NGO's are concentrating to reduce the psychological impact, this study shows their level of impact due to tsunami.

Table 5: Overall Dimensions of Psycho-social Impact

Sl. No.	*Dimensions*	*No. of Respondents (n=400)*	*Percentage*
1.	**Mental Health-Overall**		
	Low Level	229	57.3
	High level	171	42.8
2.	**Study Habits-Overall**		
	Low Level	213	53.2
	High Level	187	46.8
3.	**Overall Study involvement**		
	Low Level	237	59.3
	High Level	163	40.8
4.	**Overall Anxiety**		
	High Level	400	100.0
5.	**Beck's Depression**		
	Severely Depressed	400	100.0
6.	**Adjustment-Overall**		
	Low Level	208	52.0
	High Level	192	48.0

While more than half of the respondents perceive low level of psycho-social impact in the variables such as Mental health (57.3 per cent), Study habit (53.3 per cent), Study involvement (59.3 per cent) and Adjustment (52 per cent) respectively. The finding of the present study correlates to the findings of the CDC (U.S. Centre for Disease Control and Prevention) Mental Health Study in Tsunami Affected Thailand (2006), (Ratnin Dewaraja, Hideyuki Sato and Toshiki Ogawa, 2005).

The above table depicts that majority of the respondents (79.0 per cent, 78.0 per cent,) have low level of study habit in the dimension of Reading and notes taking, habit of concentration and more than one-fourth of the respondents have low level of study habit in the dimensions namely, planning of subjects (73.8 per cent) and preparation for examination (72.8 per cent).

While, more than half of the respondents have low level of study habit in the various dimensions namely, home environment and planning (54.5 per cent), General habits and attitude (51.0 per cent) and school environment (60.8 per cent).

The overall score indicates that more than half of the respondents (53.3 per cent) have low level of study habit and 46.8 per cent have high level of study habit.

Table 6: Psycho-social Impact with Dimensions of Study Habits

Sl.No.	*Dimensions of Study Habits*	*No. of Respondents (n=400)*	*Percentage*
1.	**Home Environment and Planning**		
	Low Level	218	54.5
	High Level	182	45.5
2.	**Reading and Notes Taking**		
	Low Level	316	79.0
	High Level	84	21.0
3.	**Planning of Subject**		
	Low Level	294	73.5
	High Level	106	26.5
4.	**Habit of Concentration**		
	Low level	312	78.0
	High Level	88	22.0
5.	**Preparation for Examination**		
	Low level	291	72.8
	High Level	109	27.2
6.	**General Habits and Attitude**		
	Low level	204	51.0
	High Level	196	49.0
7.	**School Environment**		
	Low level	243	60.8
	High Level	157	39.2

Table 7: Psycho-social Impact with Dimensions of Study Involvement

Sl. No.	*Dimensions of Study Involvement*	*No. of Respondents (n=400)*	*Percentage*
1.	**School Environment**		
	Low Level	251	62.8
	High Level	149	37.3
2.	**Self Confidence**		
	Low Level	291	72.8
	High Level	109	27.3

(Contd...)

3.	**Involvement** Low Level High Level	 319 81	 79.8 20.3
4. 5.	**Feedback** Low Level High Level **Peer relations** Low Level High Level	 267 133 218 182	 66.8 33.3 54.5 45.5
6.	**Overall** Low Level High Level	 237 163	 59.2 40.8

The above table indicates that majority of the respondents have low level of study involvement in the various dimensions namely, school environment (62.8 per cent), self confidence (72.8 per cent), involvement (79.8 per cent), feedback (66.8 per cent) and peer relations (54.5 per cent).

The overall score reveals that 59.3 per cent of the respondents have low level of study involvement due to impact of Tsunami and 40.8 per cent have high level of study involvement. This table shows how much the respondents are affected psychologically and socially due to tsunami.

Table 8: Psycho-social Impact with Dimension of Adjustment

Sl. No.	***Dimension of Adjustment***	***No. of Respondents (n=400)***	***Percentage***
1.	**Health Adjustment** Low Level High Level	206194	51.548.5
2.	**Emotional Adjustment** Low Level High Level	255145	63.836.3
3.	**Self Adjustment** Low Level High Level	289111	72.327.8
4.	**Home Adjustment** Low Level High Level	231169	57.842.3

(Contd...)

5.	**Social Adjustment** Low Level High Level	270130	67.532.5
6.	**Overall Adjustment** Low Level High Level	208192	52.048.0

It is evident from the above table that majority of the respondents perceive low level of adjustment in various dimensions namely, self-adjustment (72.3 per cent), Emotional adjustment (63.8 per cent) and social adjustment (67.5 per cent). Further, more than half of the respondents perceive Low level of adjustment in the dimensions of Health (51.5 per cent) and home (57.8 per cent) respectively.

The overall score reveals that more than half of the respondents perceive low level of adjustment and 48 per cent of the respondents perceive high level of adjustment in the level of psycho-social impact.

Table 9: Karl Pearson's Correlation between Age and Overall Psycho-social Impact

Sl.No.	*Variables*	*Correlation Value*	*Statistical Inference*
1.	Mental Health-Overall	0.104*	P<0.05 Significant
2.	Study Habits-Overall	-0.099*	P<0.05 Significant
3.	Overall-Study involvement	-0.125*	P<0.05 Significant
4.	Anxiety	-0.136**	P<0.01 Significant
5.	Beck's Overall	-0.112*	P<0.05 Significant
6.	Adjustment Overall	-0.175**	P<0.01 Significant

It is evident from the above table that there is a significant association between the age of the respondents and various psycho-social impact in the dimensions of Mental Health, Study Habit, Overall Study Involvement, Anxiety, Depression and Adjustment. The findings of the present study correlate with the findings of Bolton, D., D.O' Ryan, *et. al.,* (2000). McDermott, B. M. C., and L. J. Palmer (1999); Claude M. Chemtob, Joanne P. Nakashima, Roger S. Hamada (2002) and Ratnin Dewaraja, Hideyuki Sato and Toshiki Ogawa (2005).

Table 10: Karl Pearson's Correlation between Age and Study Habits

Sl. No.	*Variables*	*Correlation Value*	*Statistical Inference*
1.	Reading and notes taking	-0.007	P>0.05 Not Significant
2.	Planning of Subject	-0.105*	P<0.05 Significant
3.	Habit of concentration	-0.156**	P<0.01 Significant
4	Preparation for examination	-0.107*	P<0.05 Significant
5.	General habits and attitude	-1.333**	P<0.01 Significant
6.	School Environment	-0.064	P>0.05 Not Significant
7.	Overall	-0.099*	P<0.05 Significant

It is observed that the means the age of respondents is highly influence the impact level among the respondents. This study shows when age advances the impacts also not wash out in their life and increased psychological impact among the children.

It is evident from the above table that there is a significant association between age of the respondents and their study habit in the dimensions of planning of subject, habit of concentration, preparation for examination. General habits and attitudes and over all study habit. (Lien L, Tambs K, Oppedal B, Heyerdahl S, Bjertness E., 2005).

However, there is no significant association between age of the respondents and their study habit in the dimensions of reading and notes taking and school environment. Which means the advance age influence the reading and notes taking and school environment among the respondents.

Table 11: Karl Pearson's Correlation between Age and Study Involvement

Sl.No.	*Variable*	*Correlation Value*	*Statistical Inference*
1.	School Environment	-0.019	P>0.05 Not significant
2.	Self confidence	-0.109*	P<0.05 Significant
3.	Involvement	-0.137**	P<0.01 Significant
4.	Feedback	-0.109*	P<0.05 Significant
5.	Peer relations	-0.030	P>0.05 Not significant
6.	Overall	-0.125*	P<0.05 Significant

The above table depicts that there is a significant association between the age of the respondents and their study involvement in the dimensions of self-confidence, involvement, feedback, and overall study involvement.

However, there is no significant association between the age of the respondents and their study involvement in the dimensions namely, school environment and peer relations.

Which means as the age of the respondents advances the study involvement in school environment as well as peer relation in the school decreased. Hence, relative age within a school year significantly influenced academic performances (Lien L, Tambs K, Oppedal B, Heyerdahl S, Bjertness E. 2005).

Table 12: Karl Pearson's Correlation between Age and Adjustment

Sl. No.	*Variable*	*Correlation Value*	*Statistical Inference*
1.	Health Adjustment	-0.134**	P<0.01 Significant
2.	Emotional Adjustment	-0.127*	P<0.05 Significant
3.	Self Adjustment	-0.136**	P<0.01 Significant
4.	Home Adjustment	0.180**	P<0.01 Significant
5.	Social Adjustment	-0.065	P>0.05 Not Significant
6.	Overall Adjustment	-0.175**	P<0.01 Significant

The above table describes that there is a significant association between the respondent's age and their adjustment in the dimensions such as health, emotional, self, home adjustment and over all adjustment. This shows that how the age influence their adjustment, emotional, health, self and home adjustment level.

However, there is no significant association between the respondent's Age and their adjustment in the dimension of social adjustment.

Table 13: Overall Psycho-social Impact–One Way Analysis of Variance

Sl. No.	*Source*	*DF*	*SS*	*MS*	*Mean*	*Statistical Inference*
1.	**Mental Health Overall**					
	Between Groups	3	154.679	51.560	G1=88.46 G2=87.08	F=1.602 P>0.05
	Within Groups	396	12742.511	32.178	G3=87.61 G4=89.12	Not Significant
2.	**Study Habits Overall**					
	Between Groups	3	297.826	99.275	G1=71.76 G2=73.80	F=4.013 P<0.05
	Within Groups	396	9796.484	24.739	G3=69.76 G4=71.80	Significant

(Contd...)

3.	**Over-all Study involvement** Between Groups Within Groups	3 396	79.048 5088.952	26.349 12.851	G1=42.19 G2=43.45 G4=41.96 G3=41.67	F=2.05 P>0.05 Not Significant
4.	**Overall Anxiety** Between Groups Within Groups	3 396	40.918 3829.579	13.639 9.671	G1=43.71 G2=44.40 G3=44.36 G4=43.45	F=1.41 P>0.05 Not Significant
5.	**Beck's Depression** Between Groups Within Groups	3 396	450.157 25652.04	150.052 64.778	G1=43.46 G2=46.63 G3=42.24 G4=43.20	F=2.316 P>0.05 Not Significant
6.	**Adjustment Overall** Between Groups Within Groups	3 396	205.556 19006.881	68.519 47.997	G1=76.95 G2=79.00 G3=77.45 G4=76.44	F=1.428 P>0.05 Not Significant

G1: St. Mary's Higher Secondary School, G2: St. Alex High School, G3: Orient Matriculation Higher Secondary School, G4: St. Little Flower Higher Secondary School.

The above table depicts that there is a significant difference among the various schools studying by the respondents with regard to the dimensions of psycho-social impact such as overall study habit exists.

Further the mean score reveals that the respondent in the Alex Middle School perceive high level of study habit in the above said dimension because of the involvement of their teacher and NGO's towards the progress of their students because their school was fully washed out (now they rebuilded) and many students died in the Tsunami.

However, there is no significant difference among the various schools studying by the respondents with regard to the dimension of psycho-social impact such as mental health, overall study involvement, anxiety, depression and overall adjustment.

Table 14: Dimensions of Study Habits–One Way Analysis of Variance

Sl. No.	*Source*	*DF*	*SS*	*MS*	*Mean*	*Statistical Inference*
1.	**Home Environment and Planning**					
	Between Groups	3	25.320	8.440	G1=11.06 G2=11.50	F=3.200 P<0.05
	Within Groups	396	1044.430	2.637	G3=10.64 G4=11.00	Significant
2.	**Reading and Notes Taking**					
	Between Groups	3	2.843	0.948	G1=7.76 G2=7.78	F=1.000 P>0.05
	Within Groups	396	375.147	0.947	G3=7.78 G4=7.81	Not Significant
3.	**Planning of Subject**					
	Between Groups	3	7.723	2.574	G1=6.72 G2=6.88	F=2.343 P>0.05
	Within Groups	396	435.117	1.099	G3=6.30 G4=6.81	Not Significant
4.	**Habit of Concentration**					
	Between Groups	3	5.995	1.998	G1=6.75 G2=6.48	F=1.954 P>0.05
	Within Groups	396	405.005	1.023	G3=6.61 G4=6.89	Not Significant
5.	**Preparation for Examination**					
	Between Groups	3	1.159	0.386	G1=12.70 G2=12.68	F=0.221 P>0.05
	Within Groups	396	691.618	1.747	G3=12.58 G4=12.77	Not Significant
6.	**General Habits and Attitude**					
	Between Groups	3	40.698	13.566	G1=17.03 G2=17.98	F=3.092 P<0.05
	Within Groups	396	1737.612	4.388	G3=16.67 G4=16.93	Significant
7.	**School Environment**					
	Between Groups	3	16.561	5.520	G1=9.75 G2=10.28	F=2.259 P>0.05
	Within Groups	396	967.816	2.444	G3=9.48 G4=9.59	Not Significant

(Contd...)

8.	**Overall** Between Groups Within Groups	3 396	297.826 9796.484	99.275 24.739	G1=71.76 G2=73.80 G3=69.76 G4=71.80	F=4.013 P<0.05 Significant

G1: St. Mary's Higher Secondary School, G2: St. Alex High School, G3: Orient Matriculation Higher Secondary School, G4: St. Little Flower Higher Secondary School.

It is inferred from the above table that there exist a significant difference among the various schools of the respondents with regard to study habit in the dimensions of home environment and planning, General habits and altitude, school environment and overall study habits. (Kreuger, L. and J. Stretch, 2003).

However there is no significant difference among the various schools of the respondents with regard to study habit in the dimensions namely, reading and notes taking, planning of subjects, habit of concentration, preparation for examination and school environment.

Further the mean score reveals that the respondents studying St. Alex High School have low level of study habits in the dimensions namely, reading and notes taking, planning of subjects, habit of concentration, preparation for examination and school environment. This school was fully wash out in the Tsunami. Now the children are studying in rebuilded school. Hence, this events associated with their study habits and their mental health (Janiee De Socio, R.N., 2004).

Table 15: Dimensions of Study Involvement–One Way Analysis of Variance

Sl. No.	*Source*	*DF*	*SS*	*MS*	*Mean*	*Statistical Inference*
1.	**School Environment** Between Groups Within Groups	3 396	5.994 561.516	1.998 1.418	G1=9.97 G2=10.28 G3=10.03 G4=9.84	F=1.409 P>0.05 Not Significant
2.	**Self Confidence** Between Groups Within Groups	3 396	0.546 370.164	0.182 0.935	G1=8.86 G2=8.90 G3=8.76 G4=8.89	F=.0.195 P>0.05 Not Significant

(Contd...)

3.	**Involvement** Between Groups Within Groups	3 396	1.301 425.139	0.434 1.074	G1=9.66 G2=9.78 G3=9.52 G4=9.69	F=0.404 P>0.05 Not Significant
4.	**Feedback** Between Groups Within Groups	3 396	14.053 776.125	4.684 1.960	G1=8.56 G2=9.10 G3=8.42 G4=8.44	F=2.39 P>0.05 Not Significant
5.	**Peer relation** Between Groups Within Groups	3 396	4.243 351.735	1.414 0.888	G1=5.13 G2=5.40 G3=4.94 G4=5.10	F=1.592 P>0.05 Not Significant
6.	**Overall** Between Groups Within Groups	3 396	79.048 5088.952	26.349 12.851	G1=42.19 G2=43.45 G3=41.67 G4-41.96	F=2.05 P>0.05 Not Significant

G1: St. Mary's Higher Secondary School, G2: St. Alex High School, G3: Orient Matriculation Higher Secondary School, G4: St. Little Flower Higher Secondary School.

The above table highlights that there is no significant difference among various schools studying by the respondents with regard to various dimensions of study involvement such as school environment, self-confidence, involvement, feedback, peer relations, and overall study involvement. This shows the socio-demographic characteristics (school) may not influencing their study involvement.

Further the mean score reveals that children those who are studying rebuilded schools due to Tsunami devastation, they are perceived low level of study involvement.

Table 16: Dimensions of Study Adjustment–One Way Analysis of Variance

Sl. No.	***Source***	***DF***	***SS***	***MS***	***Mean***	***Statistical Inference***
1.	**Health Adjustment** Between Groups Within Groups	3 396	23.361 2101.749	7.787 5.307	G1=15.32 G2=15.80 G3=15.79 G4=15.08	F=1.467 P>0.05 Not Significant

(Contd...)

2.	**Emotional Adjustment** Between Groups Within Groups	3 396	27.221 1869.716	9.074 4.722	G1=16.38 G2=16.98 G3=15.76 G4=16.46	F=1.922 P>0.05 Not Significant
3.	**Self Adjustment** Between Groups Within Groups	3 396	8.018 1100.079	2.673 2.778	G1=14.63 G2=15.03 G3=14.88 G4=14.57	F=0.962 P>0.05 Not Significant
4.	**Home Adjustment** Between Groups Within Groups	3 396	11.165 941.933	3.722 2.379	G1=16.16 G2=16.55 G3=16.42 G4=16.01	F=1.565 P>0.05 Not Significant
5.	**Social Adjustment** Between Groups Within Groups	3 396	4.310 1392.480	1.437 3.516	G1=14.45 G2=14.65 G3=14.61 G4=14.33	F=0.409 P>0.05 Not Significant
6.	**Overall Adjustment** Between Groups Within Groups	3 396	205.556 19006.881	68.519 47.997	G1=76.95 G2=79.00 G3=77.45 G4=76.44	F=1.428 P>0.05 Not Significant

G1: St. Mary's Higher Secondary School, G2: St. Alex High School, G3: Orient Matriculation Higher Secondary School, G4: St. Little Flower Higher Secondary School.

It is obvious from the above table that there is no significant difference among various schools studying by the respondents with regard to adjustment in the dimensions namely, health emotional, self-home, social and overall adjustment, it means that the respondents schools has a very little influence on the above mentioned dimensions of adjustment.

Table-17: Sex and Overall Psycho-social Impact

Sl. No.	*Various Dimension of Psycho-social Impact*	*Mean*	*SD*	*SE*	*Statistical Inference*
1.	**Mental Health Overall** Male (n:199) Female (n:201)	 71.27 72.36	 5.191 4.812	 0.366 0.341	Z=2.181 P<0.05 Significant
2.	**Study Habits Overall** Male (n:199) Female (n:201)	 88.69 88.22	 5.494 5.873	 0.389 0.414	Z=0.834 P>0.05 Not Significant

(Contd...)

3	**Over-all Study involvement** Male (n:199) Female (n:201)	42.09 42.31	3.375 3.813	0.239 0.269	Z=0.633 P>0.05 Not Significant
4	**Overall Anxiety** Male (n:199) Female (n:201)	43.53 43.98	3.120 3.101	0.221 0.219	Z=1.439 P>0.05 Not Significant
5	**Beck's Depression** Male (n:199) Female (n:201)	42.43 44.75	7.831 8.192	0.555 0.578	Z=2.894 P<0.05 Significant
6	**Adjustment Overall** Male (n:199) Female (n:201)	76.07 78.00	6.619 7.129	0.469 0.503	Z=2.812 P<0.05 Significant

The above table portrays that there is a significant difference between the male and female respondents with regard to psycho-social impact in the dimensions of overall study habits, depression and overall adjustment.

Further, the mean score reveals that the female respondents perceive high level of depression and low level of Adjustment at all level. Since they have no much diversion and due to cultural traits, they are not able to reduce their depression and adjustment.

However, there is no significant difference between the sex of the respondents with regard to psycho-social impact in the dimensions namely, mental health, study involvement and overall anxiety.

It is inferred from the above table that there exist a significant difference between the male and female respondents with regard to study habit in the dimensions of planning of subject, habit of concentration general habits and attitude.

Table 18: Sex and Dimensions of Study Habits

Sl. No.	*Various Dimension of Study Habits*	*Mean*	*SD*	*SE*	*Statistical Inference*
1.	**Home Environment and Planning** Male (n:199) Female (n:201)	10.95 11.20	1.483 1.772	0.105 0.125	Z=1.525 P>0.05 Not significant
2.	**Reading and Notes taking** Male (n:199) Female (n:201)	7.68 7.83	0.95 70.986	0.068 0.070	Z=1.569 P.>0.05 Not Significant
3.	**Planning of Subject** Male (n:199) Female (n:201)	6.59 6.87	1.054 1.038	0.075 0.073	Z=2.607 P<0.05 Significant

(Contd...)

4.	**Habit of Concentration** Male (n:199) Female (n: 201)	6.89 6.61	1.042 0.969	0.074 0.068	Z=2.858 P<0.05 Significant
5.	**Preparation for Examination** Male (n:199) Female (n:201)	12.60 12.81	1.325 1.305	0.094 0.092	Z=1.581 P>0.05 Not Significant
6.	**General Habits and Attitude** Male (n: 199) Female (n: 201)	16.77 17.36	2.027 2.157	0.144 0.152	Z=2.816 P<0.05 Significant
7.	**School Environment** Male (n:199) Female (n:201)	9.78 9.69	1.481 1.657	0.105 0.117	Z=0.587 P>0.05 Not significant

Further, the mean score reveals that the female respondents are found to perceive higher level of planning of subject and general habits and attitudes towards studies. Since they have no much diversion and generally they are more inclined to strive hard but the male respondents are found to perceive high level of habit of concentration.

However, there is no significant difference between the sex (male, female) of the respondents with regard to study habit in the dimensions namely, home environment and planning, reading and notes taking, preparation for examinations and school environment.

It is evident from the above table there is no significant difference between the male and female respondents with regard to their study involvement in all the dimensions namely, school environment self confidence, involvement, feedback, peer relations and overall study involvement. This means that male and female respondents do not differ in their study involvement towards the above mentioned dimensions.

Table 19: Sex and Dimensions of Study Involvement

Sl. No.	*Various Dimension of Study Involvement*	*Mean*	*S.D.*	*S.E.*	*Statistical Inference*
1.	**School Environment** Male (n: 199) Female (n: 201)	9.95 9.98	1.062 1.311	0.075 0.092	Z=0.254 P>0.05 Not significant
2.	**Self Confidence** Male (n: 199) Female (n: 201)	8.83 8.90	1.035 0.889	0.073 0.063	Z=0.740 P>0.05 NotSignificant
3.	**Involvement** Male (n: 199) Female (n: 201)	9.61 9.73	1.071 0.995	0.076 0.070	Z=1.096 P>0.05 Not Significant

(Contd...)

4.	**Feedback** Male (n: 199) Female (n: 201)	 8.52 8.62	 1.337 1.476	 0.095 0.104	Z=0.705 P>0.05 Not Significant
5.	**Peer Relations** Male (n: 199) Female (n: 201)	 5.18 5.09	 0.934 0.955	 0.066 0.067	Z=0.914 P>0.05 Not Significant
6.	**Overall** Male (n: 199) Female (n: 201)	 42.09 42.31	 3.375 3.813	 0.239 0.269	Z=0.633 P>0.05 Not Significant

Table 20: Sex and Dimensions of Adjustment

Sl. No.	*Various Dimension of Adjustment*	*Mean*	*S.D.*	*S.E.*	*Statistical Inference*
1.	**Health Adjustment** Male (n: 199) Female (n: 201)	 15.19 15.48	 2.427 2.180	 0.172 0.154	Z=1.243 P>0.05 Not significant
2.	**Emotional Adjustment** Male (n: 199) Female (n: 201)	 16.11 16.71	 2.117 2.206	 0.150 0.156	Z=2.779 P<0.05 Significant
3.	**Self Adjustment** Male (n: 199) Female (n: 201)	 14.45 14.89	 1.690 1.618	 0.120 0.114	Z=2.650 P<0.05 Significant
4.	**Home Adjustment** Male (n: 199) Female (n: 201)	 16.05 16.30	 1.587 1.497	 0.112 0.106	Z=1.642 P>0.05 Not significant
5.	**Social Adjustment** Male (n: 199) Female (n: 201)	 14.27 14.62	 1.849 1.881	 0.131 0.133	Z=1.907 P<0.05 Significant
6.	**Overall Adjustment** Male (n: 199) Female (n: 201)	 76.07 78.00	 6.619 7.129	 0.469 0.503	Z=2.812 P<0.05 Significant

Further the mean score reveals that the male respondents are found to perceive higher level of self-confidence with regard to their studies. However, in the dimension of feedback from their teacher, thermal respondents are found to perceive higher because their level of reception of knowledge is slightly higher than male.

It is evident from the above table that there exists a significant difference between the male and female respondents with regard to adjustment in the dimensions of emotional self, social, and overall adjustment. Further the mean score reveals that the female respondents are found to perceive high level of emotional and self adjustment (Singh, R.K., Singh, P., and Singh, R.K., 1989).

It means though the respondents born indifferent background they are highly adjust the entire situation than the male respondents.

However, there is no significant difference between the sex of the respondents with regard to adjustment in the dimensions namely, Health and home adjustment.

Table 21: Religion and Dimensions of Psycho-social Impact

Sl. No.	*Various Dimension of Psycho-social Impact*	*Religion*		*Statistical Inference*
		Non-Christian (n:36)	*Christian (n:364)*	
1.	**Mental Health–Overall**			χ^2 =0.046
	Low Level	20	209	df=1 P>0.05
	High Level	16	155	Not Significant
2.	**Study habits-Overall**			χ^2 =4.168
	Low Level	25	188	df=1 P>0.05
	High Level	11	176	Significant
3.	**Overall–Study Involvement**			χ^2 =5.625
	Low Level	28	209	df=1 P<0.05
	High Level	8	155	Significant
4.	**Adjustment Overall**			χ^2 =0.362
	Low Level	17	191	df=1 P>0.05
	High Level	19	173	Not Significant

It is inferred from the above that there is a significant association between the various religions followed by the respondents with regard to psycho-social impact in the dimension of study habit and overall study involvement.

It means that the respondents belonging to Christian religion perceive low level of study habit and study involvement than the other religions.

Table 22: Religion and Dimensions of Study Habits

Sl. No.	*Various Dimension of Study Habits*	*Religion*		*Statistical Inference*
		Non-Christian (n:36)	*Christian (n:364)*	
1.	**Home Environment and Planning**			χ^2 =2.362
	Low Level	24	194	df=1 P>0.05
	High Level	12	170	Not Significant

(Contd...)

2.	**Reading and Notes taking** Low Level High Level	 33 3	 283 81	χ^2 =3.826 df=1 $P<0.05$ Significant
3.	**Planning of Subject** Low Level High Level	 33 3	 261 103	χ^2 =6.703d f=1 $P<0.05$ Significant
4.	**Habit of Concentration** Low Level High Level	 31 5	 281 83	χ^2 =1.517 df=1 $P>0.05$ Not Significant
5.	**Preparation for Examination** Low Level High Level	 30 6	 261 103	χ^2 =0.068 df=1 $P>0.05$ Not Significant
6.	**General Habits and Attitude** Low Level High Level	 22 14	 182 182	χ^2 =1.618 df=1 $P>0.05$ Not Significant
7.	**School Environment** Low Level High Level	 25 11	 218 146	χ^2 =1.254 df=1 $P>0.05$ Not significant

However, there is no significant association between the various religions followed by the respondents with regard to psycho-social impact in the dimension of adjustment and overall mental health.

Table 23: Religion and Dimensions of Study Involvement

Sl. No.	*Various Dimension of Study involvement*	*Religion*		*Statistical Inference*
		Non-Christian (36)	*Christian (364)*	
1.	**School Environmental** Low Level High Level	 22 14	 229 135	χ^2 = 0.045 df=1 $P>0.05$ Not Significant
2.	**Self confidence** Low Level High Level	 27 9	 264 100	χ^2 = 0.101 df=1 $P>0.05$ Not Significant

(Contd...)

3.	**Involvement**			$\chi^2=0.991$
	Low Level	31	288	df=1 P>0.05
	High Level	5	76	Not Significant
4.	**Feedback**			$\chi^2=8.736$
	Low Level	32	235	df=1 P<0.05
	High Level	4	129	Significant
5.	**Peer Relations**			$\chi^2=1.406$
	Low Level	23	195	df=1 P>0.05
	High Level	13	169	Not Significant
6.	**Overall**			$\chi^2=5.625$
	Low Level	28	209	df=1 P<0.05
	High Level	8	155	Significant

The above table portrays that there is a significant association between the various religions followed by the respondents with regard to study habit in the dimension of reading and notes taking and planning of subject.

It means that the respondent's belongings to majority religion perceive low level of study habits in the dimension of reading and notes taking and planning of subject than the other religions followed by the respondents.

However, there is no significant association between the various religions followed by the respondents with regard to study habit in the dimension of home environment, and planning, habit of concentration, preparation for examination, general habits, and attitude and school environment.

The above table indicates that there is a significant association between the religion of the respondents and their study involvement in the dimension of feedback and overall study involvement. It means that the respondents belonging to majority religion has an influence in the dimension of feedback and overall study involvement than the other religions.

Table 24: Religion and Dimensions of Adjustment

Sl. No.	*Various Dimensions of Adjustment*	*Religion*		*Statistical Inference*
		Non-Christian	*Christian*	
1.	**Health Adjustment**			$\chi^2=0.026$
	Low Level	19	187	df=1 P>0.05
	High Level	17	177	Not Significant

(Contd...)

2.	**Emotional Adjustment**			χ^2=3.369
	Low Level	28	227	df=1 P>0.05
	High Level	8	137	Not Significant
3.	**Self Adjustment**			χ^2=0.000
	Low Level	26	263	df=1 P>0.05
	High Level	10	101	Not Significant
4.	**Home Adjustment**			χ^2=0.401
	Low Level	19	212	df=1 P>0.05
	High Level	17	152	Not Significant
5.	**Social Adjustment**			χ^2=0.068
	Low Level	25	245	df=1 P>0.05
	High Level	11	119	Not Significant
6.	**Overall Adjustment**			χ^2=0.362
	Low Level	17	191	df=1 P>0.05
	High Level	19	173	Not Significant

However, there is no significant association between the religions of the respondents and the dimensions of study involvement namely, school environment, self-confidence, involvement, peer relations, and overall study involvement.

When analysing whether the respondents' religion influences their perception towards adjustment, it is found from the above table that there is no significant association between the respondent's religion and adjustment in the dimension of health, emotional, self, home, social, and overall adjustment.

Table 25: One-way Analysis of Variance Among Various Classes and Psycho-social Impact

Sl. No.	*Source*	*DF*	*SS*	*MS*	*Mean*	*Statistical Inference*
1.	**Mental Health Overall**					
	Between Groups	3	419.793	209.896	G1=87.56 G2=88.28	F=4.777 P<0.05
	Within Groups	397	9674.517	24.369	G3=89.62	Significant

(Contd...)

2.	**Study Habits Overall** Between Groups Within Groups	3 397	303.094 12594.096	151.547 31.723	G1=72.87 G2=72.01 G3=70.45	F=8.613 P<0.05 Significant
3.	**Overall Study Involvement** Between Groups Within Groups	3 397	144.336 5023.664	72.168 12.654	G1=42.84 G2=42.27 G3=41.41	F=5.703 P<0.05 Significant
4.	**Overall Anxiety** Between Groups Within Groups	3 397	165.223 3705.274	82.612 9.333	G1=44.40 G2=43.91 G3=42.89	F=8.851 P<0.05 Significant
5.	**Beck's Depression** Between Groups Within Groups	3 397	660.315 25441.883	330.157 64.085	G1=44.90 G2=43.89 G3=41.89	F=5.152 P<0.05 Significant
6.	**Adjustment Overall** Between Groups Within Groups	3 397	686.267 18526.171	343.133 46.665	G1=78.29 G2=77.48 G3=75.24	F=7.353 P<0.05 Significant

Note: G1 = VIII STD, G2 = IX STD, G3 = X STD

It means that the respondent's religion has very little influence on the above-mentioned dimensions of adjustment.

It is found from the above table that there is a significant difference among the various classes studying by the respondents with regard to various dimensions of psycho-social impact such as overall mental health study habit overall study involvement, anxiety, depression and adjustment. (Lien L, Tambs K, Oppedal B, Heyerdahl S and Bjertness E., 2005).

Further, the mean score reveals that the respondents studying 9th standard perceive higher level of psycho-social impact. They have seen the impact at young age, it may increased their anxiety, Depression and Adjustment level.

Table 26: One Way Analysis of Variance Among Various Classes and Study Habits

Sl. No.	*Source*	*DF*	*SS*	*MS*	*Mean*	*Statistical Inference*
1.	**Home Environment and Planning** Between Groups Within Groups	3 397	28.824 1040.926	14.412 2.622	G1=11.35 G2=10.69 G3=11.10	F=5.497 P<0.05 Significant

(Contd...)

2.	**Reading and Notes Taking** Between Groups Within Groups	3 397	2.776 375.214	1.388 0.945	G1=7.77 G2=7.85 G3=7.65	F=1.468 P>0.05 Not Significant
3.	**Planning of Subject** Between Groups Within Groups	3 397	23.204 419.636	11.602 1.057	G1=6.83 G2=6.97 G3=6.40	F=10.976 P<0.05 Significant
4.	**Habit of Concentration** Between Groups Within Groups	3 397	14.069 396.931	7.034 1.000	G1=6.53 G2=6.79 G3=6.97	F=7.036 P<0.05 Significant
5.	**Preparation for Examination** Between Groups Within Groups	3 397	26.927 665.850	13.464 1.677	G1=12.79 G2=13.00 G3=12.36	F=8.027 P<0.05 Significant
6.	**General Habits and Attitude** Between Groups Within Groups	3 397	87.221 1691.089	43.611 4.260	G1=17.59 G2=17.05 G3=16.48	F=10.238 P<0.05 Significant
7.	**School Environment** Between Groups Within Groups	3 397	19.504 964.874	9.752 2.430	G1=10.01 G2=9.65 G3=9.50	F=4.012 P<0.05 Significant
8.	**Overall** Between Groups Within Groups	3 397	419.793 9674.517	209.896 24.369	G1=72.87 G2=72.01 G3=70.45	F=8.613 P<0.05 Significant

Note: G1 = VIII STD, G2 = IX STD, G3 = X STD

The above table highlights that there exists a significant difference among the various classes studying by the respondents with regard to various dimensions of study habit such as home environment, planning of subject, habit of concentration, general habits and attitudes, school environment and overall study habit.

Further the mean score reveals that the respondents with 9th standard perceive higher level of study habit in the above said dimensions because of the involvement of their teachers, counsellors and parents, towards the progress of their children.

However, there is no significant difference among the various classes studying by the respondents with regard to the dimensions of study habit such as reading and notes taking.

Table 27: One Way Analysis of Variance Among Various Classes and Study Involvement

Sl. No.	*Source*	*DF*	*SS*	*MS*	*Mean*	*Statistical Inference*
1.	**School Environment**					
	Between Groups	3	8.298	4.149	G1=10.15	F=2.946
					G2=9.90	P>0.05
	Within Groups	397	559.212	1.409	G3=9.82	Not Significant
2.	**Self Confidence**					
	Between Groups	3	7.413	3.706	G1=8.89	F=4.05
					G2=9.03	P<0.05
	Within Groups	397	363.297	0.915	G3=8.69	Significant
3.	**Involvement**					
	Between Groups	3	5.022	2.511	G1=9.75	F=2.365
					G2=9.75	P>0.05
	Within Groups	397	421.418	1.062	G3=9.51	Not Significant
4.	**Feedback**					
	Between Groups	3	16.399	8.199	G1=8.81	F=4.207
					G2=8.51	P<0.05
	Within Groups	397	773.779	1.949	G3=8.34	Significant
5.	**Peer Relations**					
	Between Groups	3	3.165	1.582	G1=5.25	F=1.781
					G2=5.08	P>0.05
	Within Groups	397	352.813	0.889	G3=5.05	Not Significant
6.	**Overall**					
	Between Groups	3	144.336	72.168	G1=42.84	F=5.703
					G2=42.27	P<0.05
	Within Groups	397	5023.664	12.654	G3=41.41	Significant

Note: G1 = VIII Std, G2 = IX Std, G3 = X Std

It is inferred from the above table that there is a significant difference among the various classes studying by the respondents with regard to study involvement in the dimensions such as self-confidence, feedback and overall study involvement.

Further, the mean score reveals that the respondents studying 9th standard perceive higher level of self-confidence with regard to their studies. However, in the dimension of feedback from the teachers, the 8th standard respondents found to perceive higher because their level of reception of knowledge is slightly lower than other class students.

However, there is no significant difference among the various class studying by the respondents with regard to study involvement in the dimensions namely, school environment and peer relations.

Table 28: One Way Analysis of Variance Among Various Classes and Adjustment

Sl. No.	*Source*	*DF*	*SS*	*MS*	*Mean*	*Statistical Inference*
1.	**Health Adjustment**					
	Between Groups	3	68.025	34.013	G1=15.74	F=6.564
					G2=15.45	P<0.05
	Within Groups	397	2057.085	5.182	G3=14.77	Significant
2.	**Emotional Adjustment**					
	Between Groups	3	58.589	29.295	G1=16.65	F=6.326
					G2=16.73	P<0.05
	Within Groups	397	1838.348	4.631	G3=15.87	Significant
3.	**Self Adjustment**					
	Between Groups	3	24.758	12.379	G1=14.96	F=4.536
					G2=14.65	P<0.05
	Within Groups	397	1083.340	2.729	G3=14.37	Significant
4.	**Home Adjustment**					
	Between Groups	3	31.575	15.787	G1=16.37	F=6.801
					G2=16.37	P<0.05
	Within Groups	397	921.523	2.321	G3=15.77	Significant
5.	**Social Adjustment**					
	Between Groups	3	5.332	2.666	G1=14.57	F=0.761
					G2=14.28	P>0.05
	Within Groups	397	1391.458	3.505	G3=14.45	Not Significant
6.	**Overall Adjustment**					
	Between Groups	3	686.267	343.133	G1=78.29	F=7.353
					G2=77.48	P<0.05
	Within Groups	397	18526.171	46.665	G3=75.24	Significant

Note: G1 = VIII Std, G2 = IX Std, G3 = X Std

The above table depicts that there exists a significant difference among the various class studying by the respondents with regard to various dimensions of adjustment such as health, emotional, self home, and overall adjustment.

Further, the mean score reveals that the respondents with 8th standard qualification perceive higher-level of Study involvement in the above-mentioned dimensions except social adjustment.

It means the lower the age group less will be their adjustment and commitment towards above said dimensions may be at an younger age had chances to see the such a traumatic event. However, there is no significant difference among the various class studying by the respondents and adjustment in the dimension namely, social adjustment.

Table 29: Type of Family and Dimensions of Psycho-social Impact

Sl. No.	*Various Dimensions of Psycho-social Impact*	*Mean*	*SD*	*SE*	*Statistical Inference*
1.	**Mental Health Overall**				
	Joint (n:108)	88.16	6.117	0.589	Z=0.636 P>0.05
	Nuclear (n:292)	88.57	5.524	0.323	Not Significant
2.	**Study Habits Overall**				
	Joint (n: 108)	71.12	5.171	0.498	Z=1.684 P>0.05
	Nuclear (n:292)	72.07	4.961	0.290	Not Significant
3.	**Overall Study Involvement**				
	Joint (n:108)	41.96	3.794	0.365	Z=0.801 P>0.05
	Nuclear (n:292)	42.29	3.527	0.206	Not Significant
4.	**Overall Anxiety**				
	Joint (n:108)	43.50	3.128	0.301	Z=0.986 P>0.05
	Nuclear (n:292)	43.85	3.110	0.182	Not Significant
5.	**Beck's Depression**				
	Joint (n:108)	43.54	8.469	0.815	Z=0.091 P>0.05
	Nuclear (n:292)	43.62	7.958	0.466	Not Significant
6.	**Adjustment Overall**				
	Joint (n:108)	77.05	7.045	0.678	Z=0.015 P>0.05
	Nuclear (n:292)	77.03	6.912	0.404	Not Significant

Note: DF = 398

The above table depicts that there is no significant difference between the respondents who are in joint and nuclear family system with regard to psycho-social impact in the dimension of mental health, study habit, study involvement, anxiety, depression and overall adjustment. It means the respondents who are in joint and nuclear family system do not differ in their perception with regard to the psycho-social impact towards the above mentioned dimensions.

The findings of the present study is also contract with the studies carried out by Suneeta, B. and Mayuri, K. (1999).

Table 30: Type of Family and Dimensions of Study Habits

Sl. No.	*Various Dimensions of Study Habits*	*Mean*	*SD*	*SE*	*Statistical Inference*
1.	**Home Environment and Planning**				
	Joint (n:108)	11.01	1.699	0.164	Z=0.488 P>0.05
	Nuclear (n:292)	11.10	1.616	0.095	Not Significant
2.	**Reading and Notes Taking**				
	Joint (n:108)	7.69	1.054	0.101	Z=0.756 P>0.05
	Nuclear (n:292)	7.78	0.943	0.055	Not Significant
3.	**Planning of Subject**				
	Joint (n:108)	6.53	1.072	0.103	Z=2.348 P<0.05
	Nuclear (n:292)	6.80	1.039	0.061	Significant
4.	**Habit of Concentration**				
	Joint (n:108)	6.93	1.011	0.097	Z=2.118 P<0.05
	Nuclear (n:292)	6.68	1.010	0.059	Significant
5.	**Preparation of Examination**				
	Joint (n:108)	12.52	1.364	0.131	Z=1.749 P>0.05
	Nuclear (n:292)	12.78	1.296	0.076	Not Significant
6.	**General Habits and Attitude**				
	Joint (n:108)	16.81	2.132	0.205	Z=1.443 P>0.05
	Nuclear (n:292)	17.16	2.100	0.123	Not Significant
7.	**School environment**				
	Joint (n:108)	9.63	1.598	0.154	Z=0.796 P>0.05
	Nuclear (n:202)	9.77	1.562	0.091	Not Significant

The above table describes that there is a significant difference between the respondents who are in joint and nuclear family system with regard to the dimension of study habit namely, planning of subject and habit of concentration. (Suneeta, B. and Mayuri, K., 1999).

However, there is no significant difference between the respondents from nuclear and joint family with regard to the dimensions of study habit namely, home environment and planning, reading and notes taking, planning.

Table 31: Type of Family and Dimensions of Study Involvement

Sl. No.	*Various Dimensions of Study Involvement*	*Mean*	*SD*	*SE*	*Statistical Inference*
1.	**School Environment**				
	Joint (n:108)	9.89	1.122	0.108	Z=0.776 P>0.05
	Nuclear (n:292)	9.99	1.218	0.071	Not Significant
2.	**Self Confidence**				
	Joint (n:108)	8.80	0.964	0.093	Z=0.867 P>0.05
	Nuclear (n:292)	8.89	0.964	0.056	Not Significant
3.	**Involvement**				
	Joint (n:108)	9.45	1.054	0.101	Z=2.563 P<0.05
	Nuclear (n:292)	9.75	1.017	0.059	Significant
4.	**Feedback**				
	Joint (n:108)	8.69	1.293	0.124	Z=1.097 P>0.05
	Nuclear (n:292)	8.52	1.446	0.085	Not Significant
5.	**Peer Relation**				
	Joint (n:108)	5.13	1.006	0.097	Z=0.037 P>0.05
	Nuclear (n:292)	5.13	0.923	0.054	Not Significant
6.	**Overall**				
	Joint (n:108)	41.96	3.794	0.365	Z=0.801 P>0.05
	Nuclear (n:292)	42.29	3.527	0.206	Not Significant

It is inferred from the above, table that there is a significant difference between the respondents who are in joint and nuclear family system with regard to their study involvement in the dimension of involvement.

It means that the respondents who are in joint family get good involvement in their studies which in turn reflect their performance in the school.

However, there is no significant difference between the respondents from joint and nuclear family with regard to the dimension of study involvement namely, school environment, self-confidence, feedback, peer relation and overall study involvement.

Table 32: Type of Family and Dimensions of Adjustment

Sl. No.	*Various Dimensions of Adjustment*	*Mean*	*SD*	*SE*	*Statistical Inference*
1.	**Health Adjustment**				
	Joint (n:108)	15.25	2.349	0.226	Z=0.448 P>0.05
	Nuclear (n:202)	15.37	2.296	0.134	Not Significant
2.	**Emotional Adjustment**				
	Joint (n:108)	16.28	2.324	0.224	Z=0.751 P>0.05
	Nuclear (n:292)	16.46	2.127	0.124	Not Significant
3.	**Self Adjustment**				
	Joint (n:108)	14.74	1.602	0.154	Z=0.498 P>0.05
	Nuclear (n:292)	14.65	1.692	0.099	Not Significant
4.	**Home Adjustment**				
	Joint (n:108)	16.28	1.617	0.156	Z=0.828 P>0.05
	Nuclear (n:292)	16.13	1.519	0.089	Not Significant
5.	**Social Adjustment**				
	Joint (n:108)	14.50	1.857	0.179	Z=0.357 P>0.05
	Nuclear (n:292)	14.42	1.879	0.110	Not Significant
6.	**Overall Adjustment**				
	Joint (n:108)	77.05	7.045	0.678	Z=0.015 P>0.05
	Nuclear (n:292)	77.03	6.912	0.404	Not Significant

It is found from the above table that there is no significant difference between the respondents who belongs to joint and nuclear family system with regard to adjustment in all the dimensions such as health, emotional, self, home, social, and overall adjustment. This means the respondents who are in joint and nuclear family system do not differ in their adjustment towards the above mentioned dimensions.

Table 33: Nature of House and Dimensions of Psycho-social Impact

Sl. No.	*Various Dimensions of Psycho-social Impact*	*Nature of the House*			*Statistical Inference*
		Hut (n:39)	*Titled (165)*	*Concrete (196)*	
1.	**Mental Health-Overall**				χ^2=3.53
	Low Level	27	97	105	df=2 P>0.05
	High Level	12	68	91	Not Significant

(Contd...)

2.	**Study Habits-Overall**				χ^2=0.57
	Low Level	23	87	403	df=2 P>0.05
	High Level	16	78	93	Not Significant
3.	**Overall Study Involvement**				χ^2=0.993
	Low Level	26	96	115	df=2 P>0.05
	High Level	13	69	81	Not significant
4.	**Overall Adjustment**				χ^2=0.669
	Low Level	20	82	106	df=2 P>0.05
	High Level	19	83	90	Not Significant

When looking into the influence of the nature of house on their relationship with psycho-social impact, it is found that there is no significant association between the respondent's type of house and psycho-social impact in all the dimensions namely, overall mental health, study habit, overall study involvement and adjustment.

It means that the respondent's type of house has a very little influence on the above mentioned dimensions of psycho-social impact.

Table 34: Nature of House and Dimensions of Study Habits

Sl. No.	*Various Dimensions of Study Habits*	*Nature of the House*			*Statistical Inference*
		Hut (n:39)	*Tiled (165)*	*Concrete (196)*	
1.	**Home Environment and Planning**				χ^2=0.713
	Low Level	21	94	103	df=2 P>0.05
	High Level	18	71	93	Not Significant
2.	**Reading and Notes Taking**				χ^2=0.245
	Low Level	32	130	154	df=2 P>0.05
	High Level	7	35	42	Not Significant
3.	**Planning of Subject**				χ^2=2.916
	Low Level	32	115	147	df=2 P>0.05
	High Level	7	50	49	Not Significant
4.	**Habit of Concentration**				χ^2=1.283
	Low Level	28	132	152	df=2 P>0.05
	High Level	11	33	44	Not significant

(Contd...)

5.	**Preparation for Examination**				χ^2=1.965
	Low Level	31	123	137	df=2
					P>0.05
	High Level	8	42	59	Not Significant
6.	**General Habits and Attitude**				χ^2=0.569
	Low Level	22	82	100	df=2
					P>0.05
	High Level	17	83	96	Not Significant
7.	**School Environment**				χ^2=3.358
	Low Level	29	98	116	df=2
					P>0.05
	High Level	10	67	80	Not Significant

It is evident from the above table that there is no significant association between the respondents nature of house and all the dimensions of study habit namely, home environment and planning, reading and notes taking, planning of subject, habit of concentration, preparation for examination, general habits and attitude, school environment.

It means that the type of house has a very little influence on the study habit of the respondents.

Table 35: Nature of House and Dimensions of Study Involvement

Sl. No.	*Various Dimensions of Study Involvement*	*Nature of the House*			*Statistical Inference*
		Hut (n:39)	*Tiled (165)*	*Concrete (196)*	
1.	**School Environmental**				χ^2=1.373
	Low Level	25	98	229	df=2
					P>0.05
	High Level	14	67	135	Not Significant
2.	**Self-confidence**				χ^2=3.069
	Low Level	33	118	140	df=2
					P>0.05
	High Level	6	47	56	Not Significant
3.	**Involvement**				χ^2=4.188
	Low Level	34	124	161	df=2
					P>0.05
	High Level	5	41	68	Not Significant
4.	**Feedback**				χ^2=1.202
	Low Level	29	110	128	df=2
					P>0.05
	High Level	10	55	68	Not Significant

(Contd...)

5.	**Peer Relations**				χ^2=0.35
	Low Level	23	89	106	df=2 P>0.05
	High Level	16	76	90	Not Significant
6.	**Overall**				χ^2=0.993
	Low Level	26	96	115	df=2 P<0.05
	High Level	13	69	81	Not Significant

The above table highlights that there is no significant association between the respondents nature of house and in all the dimensions of study involvement namely, school environment, self-confidence, involvement, feedback, peer relations and overall study involvement. The findings of the present study is also consistent with the studies carried out by Singh, R.K., Singh, A.K. and Singh, P. (1989).

The below table depicts that there is no significant association between the respondents nature of house and in all the dimensions of adjustment namely, health, emotional, self, home, social and overall adjustment.

It means that the respondent's type of house has a very little influence on the above mentioned dimensions of adjustment.

Table 36: Nature of House and Dimensions of Adjustment

Sl. No.	*Various Dimensions of Adjustment*	*Nature of the House*			*Statistical Inference*
		Hut (n:39)	*Tiled (165)*	*Concrete (196)*	
1.	**Health Adjustment**				χ^2=0.42
	Low Level	19	88	99	df=2 P>0.05
	High Level	20	77	97	Not Significant
2.	**Emotional Adjustment**				χ^2=1.285
	Low Level	28	105	122	df=2 P>0.05
	High Level	11	60	74	Not Significant
3.	**Self Adjustment**				χ^2=0.2
	Low Level	27	120	142	df=2 P>0.05
	High Level	12	45	54	Not Significant
4.	**Home Adjustment**				χ^2=2.564
	Low Level	27	91	113	df=2 P>0.05
	High Level	12	74	83	Not Significant

(Contd...)

5.	**Social Adjustment**				χ^2=0.824
	Low Level	24	114	132	df=2 P>0.05
	High Level	15	51	64	Not Significant
6.	**Overall Adjustment**				χ^2=0.699
	Low Level	20	82	106	df=2 P>0.05
	High Level	19	83	90	Not Significant

The below table clearly states that there is a significant association between the respondents residing in different native background with regard to various dimensions of psycho-social impact namely, study habit and overall study involvement. It means that the respondents residing in rural areas have good study habit and study involvement than the other dimensions. However, there is no significant association between the respondents residing in different native background with regard to various dimensions of psycho-social impact namely, over all adjustment and mental health.

Table 37: Native Background and Dimensions of Psycho-social Impact

Sl. No.	*Various Dimensions of Psycho-social Impact*	*Native Background*		*Statistical Inference*
		Rural (n:365)	*Urban (n:35)*	
1.	**Mental Health-Overall**			χ^2=0.138
	Low Level	210	19	df=1 P>0.05
	High Level	155	16	Not Significant
2.	**Study Habits–Overall**			χ^2=5.092
	Low Level	188	25	df=1 P<0.05
	High Level	177	10	Significant
3.	**Overall–Study Involvement**			χ^2=6.84
	Low Level	209	28	df=1 P<0.05
	High Level	156	7	Significant
4.	**Overall Adjustment**			χ^2=0.607
	Low Level	192	16	df=1 P>0.05
	High Level	173	19	Not Significant

Table 38: Native Background and Dimensions of Study Habits

Sl. No.	*Various Dimensions of Study Habits*	*Native Background*		*Statistical Inference*
		Rural (n:365)	*Urban (n:35)*	
1.	**Home Environment and Planning**			χ^2=0.468
	Low Level	197	21	df=1
				P>0.05
	High Level	168	14	Not Significant
2.	**Reading and Notes taking**			χ^2=2.118
	Low Level	285	31	df=1
				P>0.05
	High Level	80	4	Not Significant
3.	**Planning of Subject**			χ^2=6.33
	Low Level	262	32	df=1
				P>0.05
	High Level	103	3	Not Significant
4.	**Habit of Concentration**			χ^2=1.33
	Low Level	282	30	df=1
				P>0.05
	High Level	83	5	Not Significant
5.	**Preparation for Examination**			χ^2=1.976
	Low Level	262	29	df=1
				P>0.05
	High Level	103	6	Not Significant
6.	**General Habits and Attitude**			χ^2=2.158
	Low Level	182	22	df=1
				P>0.05
	High Level	183	13	Not Significant
7.	**School Environment**			χ^2=5.961
	Low Level	215	28	df=1
				P>0.05
	High Level	150	7	Not Significant

It is evident from the above table that there exists a significant association between the respondent's native background and the dimension of study habit namely, planning of subject and school environment.

It means the respondents residing in rural background have lower level of planning of subject and school environment contributing less towards their study habit.

However, there is no significant association between the respondent's native background and their study habit in the dimensions namely, home environment and planning, reading and notes taking, habit of concentration, preparation for examination, general habits and attitudes.

It is inferred from the below table that there exist a significant association between the respondents residing in different native backgrounds with regard to their study involvement in the dimension of feedback, peer relation and overall study involvement.

It means the respondents residing in rural background get good feedback from the teachers which in turn reflect their influence among peer relations and overall study involvement.

However, there is no significant association between the respondents residing in different native background with regard to their study involvement in the dimensions namely, school environment, self-confidence, and involvement.

Table 39: Native Background and Dimensions of Study Involvement

Sl. No.	*Various Dimensions of Study Involvement*	*Native Background*		*Statistical Inference*
		Rural (n:365)	*Urban (n:35)*	
1.	**School Environment**			χ^2=0.144
	Low Level	228	23	df=1 P>0.05
	High Level	137	12	Not Significant
2.	**Self Confidence**			χ^2=0.338
	Low Level	267	24	df=1 P>0.05
	High Level	98	11	Not Significant
3.	**Involvement**			χ^2=3.239
	Low Level	287	32	df=1 P>0.05
	High Level	78	3	Not Significant
4.	**Feedback**			χ^2=13.103
	Low Level	234	33	df=1 P>0.05
	High Level	131	2	Not Significant
5.	**Peer Relations**			χ^2=6.055
	Low Level	192	26	df=1 P>0.05
	High Level	173	9	Not Significant

(Contd...)

6.	**Overall**			χ^2=6.84
	Low Level	209	28	df=1
				P>0.05
	High Level	156	7	Not Significant

It is found from the below table there is no significant association between native background of the respondents and all the dimensions of adjustment namely, health adjustment, emotional adjustment self-adjustment home adjustment social adjustment and overall adjustment. It means the native background of the respondents has a very little influence on the above mentioned dimensions of adjustment.

Table 40: Native Background and Dimensions of Adjustment

Sl. No.	*Various Dimension of Adjustment*	*Native Background*		*Statistical Inference*
		Rural (n:365)	*Urban (n:35)*	
1.	**Health Adjustment**			χ^2=0.132
	Low Level	189	17	df=1
				P>0.05
	High Level	176	18	Not Significant
2.	**Emotional Adjustment**			χ^2=1.842
	Low Level	229	26	df=1
				P>0.05
	High Level	136	9	Not Significant
3.	**Self Adjustment**			χ^2=0.817
	Low Level	266	23	df=1
				P>0.05
	High Level	99	12	Not Significant
4.	**Home Adjustment**			χ^2=2.277
	Low Level	215	16	df=1
				P>0.05
	High Level	150	19	Not Significant
5.	**Social Adjustment**			χ^2=0.377
	Low Level	248	22	df=1
				P>0.05
	High Level	117	13	Not Significant
6.	**Overall Adjustment**			χ^2=0.607
	Low Level	192	16	df=1
				P>0.05
	High Level	173	19	Not Significant

Table 41: Karl Pearson's Correlation between Number of Siblings and Dimensions of Psycho-social Impact

Sl. No.	*Variables*	*Correlation Value*	*Statistical Inference*
1.	Mental Health-Overall	-0.029	P>0.05 Not Significant
2.	Study Habits-Overall	-0.089	P>0.05 Not Significant
3.	Overall-Study involvement	-0.093	P>0.05 Not Significant
4.	Overall-Anxiety	-0.068	P>0.05 Not Significant
5.	Beck's Depression-Overall	-0.035	P>0.05 Not Significant
6.	Overall Adjustment	0.011	P>0.05 Not Significant

It is evident from the above table that there is no significant association between the number of siblings and in all the dimensions of psycho-social impact namely, mental health, study habits, study involvement, anxiety, depression and overall adjustment.

This means the respondent's number of siblings does not differ in their perception with regard to psycho-social impact towards the above mentioned dimensions.

Table 42: Karl Pearson's Correlation between Number of Siblings and Dimensions of Study Habits

Sl. No.	*Variables*	*Correlation Value*	*Statistical Inference*
1.	Reading and Notes taking	-0.020	P>0.05 Not Significant
2.	Planning of Subject	-0.058	P>0.05 Not Significant
3.	Habit of Concentration	0.098	P>0.05 Not Significant
4.	Preparation for Examination	-0.104*	P<0.05 Significant
5.	General Habits and Attitude	-0.101*	P<0.05 Significant
6.	School Environment	-0.081	P>0.05 Not Significant
7.	Overall	-0.089	P>0.05 Not Significant

The above table highlights that there exists a significant association between the number of siblings and the respondents study habit in the dimension of preparation for examination and general habits and attitude which means when the number of siblings increases in the family it affects their examinations preparation and their general habits and attitudes.

However, there is no significant association between the number of siblings and the respondents study habit in the dimensions namely, home environment and planning, reading and note taking, planning of subjects, habit of concentration, school environment, and overall study habit.

It is inferred from the below table that there exists a significant association between the number of siblings of the respondents and their study involvement in the dimension of involvement revealing that as the number of sibling of the respondent's increases the study involvement among the respondents will decrease.

However, there is no significant association between the number of siblings and the respondent's study involvement in the dimensions namely, school environment, self-confidence, feedback, peer relations, and overall study involvement.

Table 43: Karl Pearson's Correlation between Number of Siblings and Dimensions of Study Involvement

Sl. No.	*Variables*	*Correlation Value*	*Statistical Inference*
1.	School Environment	-0.051	P>0.05 Not Significant
2.	Self Confidence	-0.037	P>0.05 Not Significant
3.	Involvement	0.101*	P<0.05 Significant
4.	Feedback	-0.036	P>0.05 Not Significant
5.	Peer Relations	-0.089	P>0.05 Not Significant
6.	Overall	-0.093	P>0.05 Not Significant

Table 44: Karl Pearson's Correlation between Number of Siblings and Dimensions of Adjustments

Sl. No.	*Variable*	*Correlation Value*	*Statistical Inference*
1.	Health Adjustment	0.016	P>0.05 Not Significant
2.	Emotional Adjustment	0.016	P>0.05 Not Significant
3.	Self Adjustment	0.002	P>0.05 Not Significant
4.	Home Adjustment	0.015	P>0.05 Not Significant
5.	Social Adjustment	-0.010	P>0.05 Not Significant
6.	Overall Adjustment	0.011	P>0.05 Not Significant

It is obvious from the above table that there is no significant association between the number of siblings and in all the dimensions of adjustment namely, health, emotional, self, home, social and overall adjustment. It means one number of siblings has a very little influence in the adjustment of the respondents.

Table 45: Karl Pearson's Correlation between Birth Order and Dimensions of Psycho-social Impact

Sl. No.	*Variables*	*Correlation Value*	*Statistical Inference*
1.	Overall-Mental Health	-0.023	P>0.05 Not Significant
2.	Overall-Study Habits	0.032	P>0.05 Not Significant
3.	Overall-Study involvement	-0.012	P>0.05 Not Significant
4.	Overall-Anxiety	-0.008	P>0.05 Not Significant
5.	Overall-Beck's Depression	-0.011	P>0.05 Not Significant
6.	Overall Adjustment	-0.039	P>0.05 Not Significant

The above table clearly explains that there is no significant association between the birth order of the respondents and all the dimensions of psycho-social impact namely anxiety, depression, adjustment, study habit, mental health and overall study involvement. It means that the birth order of the respondents has a very little influence on the above mentioned dimensions of psycho-social impact.

Table 46: Karl Pearson's Correlation between Birth Order and Dimensions of Study Habits

Sl. No.	*Variables*	*Correlation Value*	*Statistical Inference*
1.	Reading and notes taking	0.054	P>0.05 Not Significant
2.	Planning of Subject	-0.034	P>0.05 Not Significant
3.	Habit of Concentration	0.032	P>0.05 Not Significant
4.	Preparation for Examination	-0.047	P<0.05 Significant
5.	General Habits and Attitude	-0.040	P<0.05 Significant
6.	School Environment	-0.089	P>0.05 Not Significant
7.	Overall	-0.023	P>0.05 Not Significant

The above table clearly explains that there is no significant association between the birth order of the respondents and all the dimensions of study habit namely, home environment and planning, reading and note taking, planning of subjects, habit of concentration, preparation for examinations, general habits and attitudes, school environment and overall study habit. It means that the birth order of the respondents has a very little influence on the above-mentioned dimensions of study habits.

Table 47: Karl Pearson's Correlation between Birth Order and Dimensions of Study Involvement

Sl. No.	*Variables*	*Correlation Value*	*Statistical Inference*
1.	School Environment	0.014	P>0.05 Not Significant
2.	Self Confidence	0.020	P>0.05 Not Significant
3.	Involvement	-0.003	P<0.05 Significant
4.	Feedback	-0.035	P>0.05 Not Significant
5.	Peer Relations	-0.028	P>0.05 Not Significant
6.	Overall	-0.012	P>0.05 Not Significant

It is evident from the above table that there is no significant association between the birth order of the respondent and in all the dimensions of study involvement namely, school environment, self-confidence, involvement, feedback, peer relations and overall study involvement. It means that the birth order of the respondents has a very little influence on the study involvement of the respondents.

Table 48: Karl Pearson's Correlation between Birth Order and Dimensions of Adjustment

Sl. No.	*Variables*	*Correlation Value*	*Statistical Inference*
1.	Health Adjustment	-0.060	P>0.05 Not Significant
2.	Emotional Adjustment	-0.012	P>0.05 Not Significant
3.	Self Adjustment	-0.042	P>0.05 Not Significant
4.	Home Adjustment	-0.030	P>0.05 Not Significant
5.	Social Adjustment	0.007	P>0.05 Not Significant
6.	Overall Adjustment	-0.039	P>0.05 Not Significant

The above table clearly explains that there is no significant association between the birth order of the respondents and all the dimensions of adjustment namely, health, emotional, self, home, social and overall adjustment. It means that the birth order of the respondents has a very little influence on the above mentioned dimensions of adjustment.

Table 49: Present Living Place and Dimensions of Psycho-social Impact

Sl. No.	*Various Dimensions of Psycho-social Impact*	*Present Living Place*		*Statistical Inference*
		Near Seashore (n:356)	*Away from Seashore (n:44)*	
1.	**Mental Health-Overall**			χ^2=0.068
	Low Level	203	26	df=1 P>0.05
	High Level	153	18	Not Significant
2.	**Study Habits-Overall**			χ^2=0.019
	Low Level	190	23	df=1 P<0.05
	High Level	166	21	Not Significant
3.	**Overall-Study Involvement**			χ^2=0.001
	Low Level	211	26	df=1 P>0.05
	High Level	145	18	Not Significant
4.	**Adjustment-Overall**			χ^2=3.537
	Low Level	191	17	df=1 P>0.05
	High Level	165	27	Not Significant

It is inferred from above table that there is no significant association between the respondent's present living place and various dimensions of psycho-social impact namely, overall adjustment, study habit, mental health, and overall study involvement. It means that the present living place has a very little influence on the above mentioned dimension of psycho-social impact. The findings of the present study contradicts to the findings of Singh, R.K., Singh, P. and Singh, R.K. (1989).

Table 50: Present Living Place and Dimensions of Study Habits

Sl. No.	*Various Dimensions of Study Habits*	*Present Living Place*		*Statistical Inference*
		Near Seashore (n:356)	*Away from Seashore (n:44)*	
1.	**Home Environment and Planning**			χ^2=0.404
	Low Level	196	22	df=1 P>0.05
	High Level	160	22	Not Significant

(Contd...)

2.	**Reading and Notes Taking**			χ^2=0.089
	Low Level	282	34	df=1
				P>0.05
	High Level	74	10	Not Significant
3.	**Planning of Subject**			χ^2= 4.200
	Low Level	256	38	df=1
				P<0.05
	High Level	100	6	Significant
4.	**Habit of Concentration**			χ^2=1.069
	Low Level	275	37	df=1
				P>0.05
	High Level	81	7	Not Significant
5.	**Preparation for Examination**			χ^2=0.51
	Low Level	257	34	df=1
				P>0.05
	High Level	99	10	Not Significant
6.	**General Habits and Attitude**			χ^2=0.608
	Low Level	184	20	df=1
				P>0.05
	High Level	172	24	Not Significant
7.	**School Environment**			χ^2=0.798
	Low Level	219	24	df=1
				P>0.05
	High Level	137	20	Not Significant

The above table reveals that there is a significant association between the respondent's present living place and study habit in the dimension of planning of subject.

However, there is no significant association between the respondents and their study habit in the dimensions of home environment and planning, reading and notes taking, habit of concentration, preparation for examination, general habit and attitude and school environment.

Table 51: Present Living Place and Dimensions of Study Involvement

Sl. No.	*Various Dimensions of Study Involvement*	*Present Living Place*		*Statistical Inference*
		Near Seashore (n:356)	*Away from Seashore (n:44)*	
1.	**School Environment**			χ^2=0.744
	Low Level	226	25	df=1
	High Level	130	19	P>0.05 Not Significant
2.	**Self Confidence**			χ^2=0.51
	Low Level	257	34	df=1
	High Level	99	10	P>0.05 Not Significant
3.	**Involvement**			χ^2= 2.417
	Low Level	280	39	df=1
	High Level	76	5	P>0.05 Not Significant
4.	**Feedback**			χ^2=0.646
	Low Level	240	27	df=1
	High Level	116	17	P>s0.05 Not Significant
5.	**Peer Relations**			χ^2=0.099
	Low Level	195	23	df=1
	High Level	161	21	P>0.05 Not Significant
6.	**Overall**			χ^2=0.001
	Low Level	211	26	df=1
	High Level	145	18	P>0.05 Not Significant

The above table indicates that there is no significant association between the respondents present living place and in all the dimensions of study involvement such as school environment self-confidence, involvement, feedback, peer relations and over all study involvement.

It means that the respondent's present living place has a very little influence on the above-mentioned dimensions of study involvement.

Table 52: Present Living Place and Dimensions of Adjustment

Sl. No.	*Various Dimensions of Adjustment*	*Present Living Place*		*Statistical Inference*
		Near Seashore (n:356)	*Away from Seashore (n:44)*	
1.	**Health Adjustment**			χ^2=7.667
	Low Level	192	14	df=1 P<0.05
	High Level	164	30	Significant
2.	**Emotional Adjustment**			χ^2=0.000
	Low Level	227	28	df=1 P>0.05
	High Level	129	16	Not Significant
3.	**Self Adjustment**			χ^2=2.922
	Low Level	262	27	df=1 P>0.05
	High Level	94	17	Not Significant
4.	**Home Adjustment**			χ^2=1.217
	Low Level	209	22	df=1 P>0.05
	High Level	147	22	Not Significant
5.	**Social Adjustment**			χ^2=1.594
	Low Level	244	26	df=1 P>0.05
	High Level	112	18	Not Significant
6.	**Overall Adjustment**			χ^2=3.537
	Low Level	191	17	df=1 P>0.05
	High Level	165	27	Not Significant

It is evident from the above table that there exists a significant association between the respondents present living place and the adjustment in the dimension namely, health adjustment. It means that the respondents who are living near seashore have perceived that health is affected less.

However, there is no significant association between the respondent's present living place and the adjustment in the dimensions such as emotional self, home, social, and overall adjustment.

The findings of the present study is also consistent with the studies carried out by Singh, R.K., Singh, P., and Singh, R.K. (1989) about a study of some social and familial variables in relation to school adjustment.

Table 53: Psycho-social Impact–Inter Correlations Matrix

Psycho-social Impact	*Mental Health Overall*	*Study Habits Overall*	*Study Involvement Overall*	*Anxiety*	*Overall Depression*	*Adjustment Overall*
Mental Health Overall	1					
Study Habits Overall	-0.248**	1				
Overall-Study Involvement	0.307**	0.598**	1			
Anxiety	0.092	-0.264**	-0.156**	1		
Overall Depression	0.298**	-0.127*	0.087	0.352**	1	
Adjustment Overall	0.297**	-0.006	-0.006	-0.340**	-0.601**	1

** Correlation is significant at the 0.01 level (2-tailed)

* Correlation is significant at the 0.05 level (2-tailed)

From the above table, it is inferred that there is a correlation between various dimensions. It is found that all the variables namely, mental health, study habit, study involvement, anxiety, depression, and adjustment have a significant relationship with each other.

Table 54: Study Habits and Inter Correlations Matrix

Study Habits	*Home environment and Planning*	*Reading and notes taking*	*Planning of subject*	*Habit of concentration*	*Preparation for examination*	*General habits and attitude*	*School Environment*	*Overall*
Home environment and Planning	1							
Reading and notes taking	0.013	1						
Planning of subject	0.079	0.001	1					
Habit of concentration	-0.078	- -0.159**	-0.255**	1				
Preparation for examination	0.078	0.141**	0.272**	-0.332**	1			
General habits and attitude	0.357**	0.021	0.463**	-0.309**	0.245**	1		
School Environment	0.417**	0.006	0.292**	-0.184**	0.191**	0.471**	1	
Overall	0.629**	0.214**	0.541**	-0.182**	0.467**	0.786**	0.721**	1

** Correlation is significant at the 0.01 level (2-tailed)

* Correlation is significant at the 0.05 level (2-tailed)

The above table revels that all the dimension of study habit influences each others. It is found that all the dimensions of study habit i.e. home environment and planning, reading and notes taking, planning of subject, habit of concentration, preparation for examination, general habits and attitudes, school environment and overall adjustment. Hence, there is a significant relationship among all the dimensions at 0.01 level of significance.

Table 55: Study Involvement and Inter Correlation Matrix

Study Involvement	*School environment*	*Self confidence*	*Involve-ment*	*Feed-back*	*Peer relations*	*Overall Study Involvement*
School environment	1					
Self-confidence	0.190**	1				
Involvement	0.074*	0.428**	1			
Feedback	0.508**	0.330**	0.303**	1		
Peer relations	0.195*	0.174**	0.114*	0.273**	1	
Over all Study Involvement	0.653**	0.628**	0.575**	0.806**	0.513**	1

**Correlation is significant at the 0.01level (2-tailed)

*Correlation is significant at the 0.05level (2-tailed)

The above table revels that all the dimension of study Involvement influences each others. It is found that all the dimensions of study Involvement i.e. School environment, Self-confidence, Involvement Feedback, Peer relations and Overall Study Involvement influence each other. Hence, there is a significant relationship among all the dimensions.

Table 56: Adjustment-Inter Correlations Matrix

Adjustment	*Health*	*Emotional*	*Self*	*Home*	*Social*	*Overall*
Health	1					
Emotional	0.540**	1				
Self	0.366**	0.481**	1			
Home	0.449**	0.423**	0.353**	1		
Social	0.209**	0.408**	0.485**	0.285**	1	
Overall	0.746**	0.813**	0.722**	0.666**	0.647**	1

**Correlation is significant at the 0.01 level (2-tailed)

The above table revels that all the dimension of Adjustment influences each others. It is found that all the dimensions of Adjustment i.e. Health, Emotional, Self, Home, Social, and Overall Adjustment influence each other. Hence, there is a significant relationship among all the dimensions of adjustment at 0.01 level.

Chapter - 11

Psycho-social Wellbeing–Hypothesis Testing and Findings

The data collected is processed and systematically analysed. A brief summary of the findings of the study are presented in the following passages starting with Hypothesis Testing, Major findings on Demographic and socio-economic status and psycho-social impact. Moreover, the implication of this present study, social work interventions, and suggestions for the future exploration of research are also discussed.

I. Hypothesis Testing

There are number of hypothesis formulated and treated statistically in order to have a deeper understanding and analysis so that a strong theoretical formulation could be possible in the future.

Null Hypothesis -1

There is no significant relationship between anxiety and depression.

To test the above hypothesis Karl Pearson's coefficient of correlation test was applied and it is inferred that there is a significant relationship between anxiety and depression.

It has been proved that there is no significant relationship between anxiety and depression. Hence the null hypothesis is rejected (Table 53).

Null Hypothesis - 2

There is no significant relationship between anxiety and adjustment.

To test the above hypothesis Karl Pearson's coefficient of correlation test was applied and it is inferred that there is a significant relationship between anxiety and adjustment.

The result showed that there is no significant relationship between anxiety and adjustment. Hence, the null hypothesis is rejected (Table 53).

Null Hypothesis - 3

There is no significant relationship between anxiety and study habits.

To test the above hypothesis Karl Pearson's coefficient of correlation test was applied and it is inferred that there is a significant relationship between anxiety and study habits.

As there is no significant relationship between anxiety and study habits; the null hypothesis is rejected (Table 53).

Null Hypothesis - 4

There is no significant relationship between anxiety and study involvement.

To test the above hypothesis Karl Pearson's coefficient of correlation test was applied and it is inferred that there is a significant relationship between anxiety and study involvement.

It has been found that there is no significant relationship between anxiety and study involvement. Hence, null hypothesis is rejected (Table 53).

Null Hypothesis - 5

There is no significant relationship between depression and study involvement.

To test the above hypothesis, Karl Pearson's coefficient of correlation test was applied and it is inferred that there is a significant relationship between depression and study involvement.

It is proved that there is no significant relationship between depression and study involvement. Hence, null hypothesis is rejected (Table 53).

Null Hypothesis - 6

There is no significant relationship between depression and study habits.

To test the above hypothesis Karl Pearson's coefficient of correlation test was applied and it is inferred that there is a significant relationship between depression and study habit.

The result is that there is no significant relationship between depression and study habits. Hence, null hypothesis is rejected (Table 53).

Null Hypothesis - 7

There is no significant relationship between depression and mental health.

To test the above hypothesis Karl Pearson's coefficient of correlation test was applied and it is inferred that there is a significant relationship between depression and mental health.

The statistical analysis indicated that there is no significant relationship between depression and mental health. Hence, null hypothesis is rejected (Table 53).

Null Hypothesis - 8

There is no significant relationship between adjustment and mental health.

To test the above hypothesis Karl Pearson's coefficient of correlation test was applied and it is inferred that there is a significant relationship between adjustment and mental health

The null hypothesis is rejected (Table 53) as there is no significant relationship between adjustment and mental health.

Null Hypothesis - 9

There is no significant relationship between mental health and study habits.

To test the above hypothesis Karl Pearson's coefficient of correlation test was applied and it is inferred that there is a significant relationship between mental health and study habit.

It has been observed that there is no significant relationship between mental health and study habits. Hence, null hypothesis is rejected (Table 53).

Null Hypothesis - 10

There is no significant relationship between study habits and study involvement.

To test the above hypothesis Karl Pearson's coefficient of correlation test was applied and it is inferred that there is a significant relationship between study habit and study involvement.

It is true that there is no significant relationship between study habits and study involvement. Hence, null hypothesis is rejected (Table 53).

Null Hypothesis - 11

There is no significant relationship between mental health and study involvement.

To test the above hypothesis Karl Pearson's coefficient of correlation test was applied and it is inferred that there is a significant relationship between mental health and study involvement.

The hypothesis is proved as there is no significant relationship between mental health and study involvement. Hence, null hypothesis is rejected (Table 53).

Null Hypothesis - 12

There is no significant relationship between anxiety and mental health.

To test the above hypothesis Karl Pearson's coefficient of correlation test was applied and it is inferred that there no significant relationship between anxiety and mental health.

The null hypothesis is accepted as there is no significant relationship between anxiety and mental health (Table 53).

II. Prominent Findings

A. Demographic and Socio-economic Profile

- More than one-third of the students (36.5 per cent) are in the age group of 14 years.
- There is more or less equal representation of male and female as close to half of the respondents (50.3 per cent) are females and another half of the respondents (49.8 per cent) are males respectively.
- Absolutely majority of the respondents (91.0 per cent) belong to Christianity as the study area is dominated by Christians.
- More than one-third of the respondents (37.5 per cent) are studying 8th standard.
- Vast majority of the respondents (91.3 per cent) belongs to most backward class.
- A vast majority of the respondents (91.3 per cent) hail from the rural areas.
- Majority of the respondents (73.0 per cent) belong to nuclear family.
- It is unequivocal to understand that the study area is accounted for cent per cent literacy rate and the adoption of the concept of family planning is low as more than one-fourth of the respondents have five siblings in their family.
- More than one-fourth of the respondents (27 per cent) are fifth born and nearly one-third of the respondents (30.3 per cent) are first born.
- Nearly half of the respondents' fathers' (45.8 per cent) have studied up to primary level.
- More than one-third of the respondent's mothers' (35.5 per cent) have studied up to primary level.
- A vast majority of the respondents' fathers' (91 per cent) are fishermen.

- A vast majority of the respondent's mothers' (98.7 per cent) are homemakers.
- Nearly half of the respondents' monthly family income (45 per cent) is below Rs 1000.
- A vast majority of the respondents (90 per cent) live in own house.
- More than half of the respondents (49 per cent) are living in concrete house.
- More than half of the respondents (56.5 per cent) are not satisfied with the facilities in their home.
- Majority of the respondents (73.5 per cent) have not possessed any property.
- A vast majority of the respondents (94.5 per cent) have debts.
- Majority of the respondents (63.3 per cent) have not yet changed their houses even after Tsunami.
- More than one-third of the respondent's residences (36.5 per cent) are four kilometers away from seashore at the time of Tsunami.
- Vast majority of the respondents (86.5 per cent) said that their houses were flat at the time of Tsunami.
- Vast majority of the respondents (78.5 per cent) informed that the sea position is calm before Tsunami.
- Majority of the respondents (66.8 per cent) said that sea colour was changed in the sea after Tsunami.
- A vast majority of the respondents (85.5 per cent) felt that government initiated protection mechanisms against Tsunami.

B. Psycho-social Impact–Simple Observations

- Low level of mental health status has been observed among more than half (57.3 per cent) of the respondents.
- More than half of the students (53.3 per cent) have low level of study habit.
- It has been observed a low level of study involvement among (59.3 per cent) of the students
- There is a high level of anxiety perceived among all the respondents (100 per cent).
- Similarly almost all the respondents (100 per cent) perceive high level of depression.
- More than half of the respondents (52 per cent) have low level of adjustment.

C. Psycho-social Impact and Dimensions of Study Habit

- More than half of the respondents (54.5 per cent) perceive low level of study habits in the dimensions of home environment and planning.
- Vast majority of the respondents (79.0 per cent) perceive low level of study habits in the dimensions of reading and notes taking.
- Majority of the respondents (73.5 per cent) have low level of study habits in the dimension of planning of subject.
- Majority of the respondents (78 per cent) have habit of concentration at low level.
- Majority of the respondents (72.98 per cent) perceive low level of preparation for examination.
- More than half of the respondents (51 per cent) perceive low level of general habits and attitude.
- Majority of the respondents (72.3 per cent) have low-level impact in the dimension of school environment.

D. Psycho-social Impact and Dimensions of Study Involvement

- Majority of the respondents (62.8 per cent) have low level of study involvement in the dimension of school environment.
- There is a low level of self-confidence perceived among the majority of the respondents (79.8 per cent).
- Absolutely majority of the respondents (79.8 per cent) have low level of involvement.
- Low level of involvement in studies has been observed among majority of the respondents (66 per cent).
- More than half of the respondents (54.5 per cent) have low level of peer relation.
- When the overall dimensions of study involvement analysed it has been found that nearly 59.3 per cent of the respondents perceive low level of study involvement.

E. Psycho-social Impact and Dimensions of Adjustment

- Low level of self-adjustment has been observed among the vast majority of the respondents (72.3 per cent).
- Majority of the respondents (67.5 per cent) perceive low level of social adjustment.
- Adjustment with home is a problem for more than half of the respondents (57.8 per cent).
- Low level of emotional adjustment is found among the majority of the respondents (63.8 per cent).

- More than half of the respondents (51 per cent) have low level of health adjustment.
- The overall adjustment is found to be low among more than half of the respondents (52.0 per cent).

F. Psycho-social Impact and Personal Variables

1. There is a significant association between age of the respondents and overall psycho-social impact in all the dimensions namely, mental health, study habit, study involvement, anxiety, depression and overall adjustment.
2. There is a significant difference among various schools studying by the respondents with regard to overall dimensions of study habit. However, there is no significant difference among the various school studying by the respondents with regard to the overall dimension of psycho-social impact such as mental health, study involvement, anxiety, depression, and overall adjustment.
3. There is a significant difference between the sex of the respondents with regard to various dimensions of psycho-social impact such as depression, adjustment, and overall study habits. However, there is no significant difference between the sex of the respondents with regard to various dimension of psycho-social impact such as mental health status, overall study involvement and anxiety.
4. There is a significant association between the various religions followed by the respondents with regard to the psycho-social impact in the dimension of overall study habit and study involvement. It means that the respondents belonging to Christian religion perceive high level of study involvement and study habit than the other religions. However, there is no significant association between the various religions followed by the respondents with regard to psycho-social impact in the variables of overall adjustment and overall mental health.
5. There is a significant difference among the various classes studying by the respondents with regard to various variables of psycho-social impact such as, mental health, overall study habits, overall study involvement, overall anxiety, overall depression and overall adjustment.
6. There is a significant difference between the respondents who are in joint and nuclear family system with regard to psycho-social impact in the variables of mental health, study habits, study involvement, anxiety, depression and overall adjustment. It means that the respondents who are in joint and nuclear family system do

not differ in their perception with regard to the psycho-social impact towards the above-mentioned variables.

7. There is no significant association between the respondents type of house and psycho-social impact in all the variables namely, mental health, study habits, study involvement and overall adjustment.
8. There is a significant association between the respondents residing in different native background with regard to various variables of psycho-social impact namely, overall study habits and overall study involvement. However, there is no significant association between the respondents residing in different native background with regard to other variables of psycho-social impact namely, overall adjustment and overall mental health status.
9. There is a significant association between the number of siblings and in all the variables of psycho-social impact namely, mental health, study habits, study involvement, anxiety, depression and overall adjustment.
10. There is a significant association between the birth order of respondents and in all the variables of psycho-social impact namely, mental health status, study habits, study involvement, anxiety, depression and adjustment.
11. There is a significant association between the respondents present living place and in all the variables of psycho-social impact namely, mental health, study habits, study involvement, anxiety, depression and overall adjustment.

G. Study Habit and Personal Profile Matched

1. There is a significant association between the age of the respondents and their study habits in the dimensions of planning of subject, habit of concentration, preparation for examination, general habits, and attitudes and overall study habits. However, there is no significant association between age of the respondents and their study habit in the dimension of reading and notes taking and school environment.
2. There is a significant difference among the various schools of the respondents with regard to dimensions of study habit namely, home environment and planning general habits and attitude, school environment and overall study habits. However, there is no significant difference among the various schools studying by the respondents with regard to study habit namely, reading and notes taking, planning of subjects, habit of concentration, preparation for examination and school environment.
3. There is a significant difference between the male and female respondents with regard to study habit in the dimensions of planning

of subject, habit of concentration general habits and attitude. However, there is no significant difference between the sex of the respondents with regard to study habit in the dimensions of study habits namely, home environment and planning, reading and notes taking, preparation for examinations and school environment.

4. There is a significant association between various religions followed by the respondents with regard to study habit in the dimension of reading and notes taking and planning of subject. However, there is a significant association between various religion followed by the respondents with regard to study habit in the dimensions namely, home environment and planning habit of concentrations, general habits and attitudes and over all study habit.
5. There is a significant difference among the various classes studying by the respondents with regard to various dimensions of study habit such as home environment and planning, planning of subject, habit of concentration, preparation for examination, general habits and attitudes, school environment and overall study habits. However, there is no significant difference among various class studying by the respondents with regard to the dimensions of study habit such as reading and notes taking.
6. There is a significant difference between the respondents who are in joint and nuclear family system with regard to the dimensions of study habit namely, planning of subject and habit of concentration. However, there is no significant difference between the respondents from nuclear family and joint family with regard to the dimension of study habits namely, reading and notes taking, planning of subjects, habit of concentration, preparation for examination and school environment.
7. There is no significant association between the respondents type of house and all the dimension of study habits namely, home environment and planning, reading and notes taking, planning of subject, habit of concentration preparation for examination general habits and attitude and school environment.
8. There is a significant association between the respondent's native background and the dimension of study habit namely, planning of subject and school environment. However, there is no significant association between the respondent's native background and their study habit in the dimensions namely, home environment and planning, reading and notes taking, habit of concentration, preparation for examination and general habits and attitude.
9. There is a significant association between the number of siblings and their study habits in the dimension of preparation for examination

and general habits and attitudes. However, there is no significant association between the number of siblings and the respondents study habit in the various dimension namely, home environment and planning of subjects habit of concentration, school environment and overall study habits.

10. There is no significant association between the birth order of the respondents and all the dimensions of study habits namely, home environment and planning, reading and notes taking, planning of subjects, habit of concentration, preparation for examinations, general habits and attitudes school environment and overall study habits.
11. There is a significant association between the respondent's present living place and study habits in the dimension of planning of subjects. However, there is no significant association between the respondents present living place and their study habits in the dimensions of home environment and planning, reading and notes taking, habit of concentration, preparation for examination, general habits and attitude and school environment.

H. Study Involvement and Personal Profile Matched

1. There is a significant association between the age of the respondents and their study involvement in the dimensions of self-confidence, involvement, feedback, and overall study involvement. However, there is no significant association between the age of the respondents and their study involvement in the dimensions namely, school environment and peer relation.
2. There is no significant difference among various schools studying by the respondents with regard to various dimension of study involvement such as school environment, self-confidence, involvement, feedback, peer relations and overall study involvement.
3. There is no significant difference between the male and female respondents with regard to their study involvement in all the dimensions namely, school environment, self-confidence, involvement, feedback, peer relations and overall study involvement.
4. There is a significant association between the various religion followed by the respondents and their study involvement in the dimensions of feedback and overall study involvement. However, there is no significant association between the various religions followed by the respondents and their study involvement in the dimension of school environment, self confidence, involvement, peer relations and overall study involvement.

5. There is a significant difference among various class studying by the respondents with regard to study involvement in the dimensions of self-confidence, feedback and overall study involvement. However, in the dimensions of feedback from the teachers, the 8th standard respondents were found to perceive higher because their level of knowledge is slightly lower than other class students. However, there is no significant difference among the various class studying by the respondents with regard to study involvement in the dimensions of school environment and peer relation.
6. There is a significant difference between the respondents who are in joint and nuclear family system with regard to their study involvement in the dimension of involvement. However, there is no significant difference between the respondents from joint and nuclear family with regard to their study involvement namely, school environment, self-confidence, feedback, peer relations and overall study involvement.
7. There is no significant association between the respondents type of house and all the dimensions of study involvement namely, school environment, self confidence, involvement, feedback, peer relations and overall study involvement.
8. There is a significant association between the respondent's native background with regard to their study involvement in the dimensions of feedback, peer relations and overall study involvement.
9. There is a significant association between the number of siblings of the respondents and their study involvement in the dimension of involvement. However, there is no significant association between the number of siblings and the respondent's study involvement in the dimensions namely, school environment, self-confidence, feedback, peer relations and overall study involvement.
10. There is no significant association between the birth order of the respondent and in all the dimensions of study involvement namely, school environment, self-confidence, involvement, feedback, peer relations, and overall study involvement. It means that the birth order of the respondents has a very little influence on the study involvement of the respondents.
11. There is no significant association between the respondents present living place and in all the dimensions of study involvement such as school environment, self-confidence, involvement, feedback, peer relations and over all study involvement. It means that the respondent's present living place has a very little influence on the above-mentioned dimensions of study involvement.

I. Adjustment and Personal Profile Matched

1. There is a significant association between age of the respondents and their adjustment in the dimensions such as health, emotional, self home adjustment and overall adjustment. However, there is no significant association between the respondent's age and their adjustment in the dimension of social adjustment.
2. There is a significant difference among the various school, studying by the respondents with regard to various dimension of adjustment namely, health, emotional, self, home, social and overall adjustment. It means that the respondent's schools have a very little influence on the above mentioned dimensions of adjustment.
3. There is a significant difference between sex of the respondents with regard to adjustment in the dimensions of emotional, self, social and overall adjustment.
4. There is a significant association between the religion of the respondents and various dimension of adjustment namely, health adjustment, emotional adjustment, self adjustment, home adjustment, social adjustment and overall adjustment.
5. There is a significant difference among the various class studying by the respondents with regard to various dimension of adjustment such as health, emotional self home and overall adjustment. However there is no significant difference among the various classes studying by the respondents with regard to adjustment in the dimension of social adjustment.
6. There is no significant difference between the respondents who are in joint and nuclear family system with regard to adjustment in all the dimensions such as health adjustment, emotional adjustment, self adjustment, home adjustment, social adjustment, and overall adjustment.
7. There is no significant association between the respondents' type of house and adjustment in all the dimensions such as health adjustment, emotional adjustment, and self adjustment, home adjustment, social adjustment, and overall adjustment.
8. There is no significant association between the respondents with various native backgrounds and all the dimensions of adjustment such as health adjustment, emotional adjustment, and self adjustment, home adjustment, social adjustment, and overall adjustment.
9. There is significant association between the number of siblings and the adjustment of the respondents in all the dimensions such as, health adjustment, emotional adjustment, self adjustment, home adjustment social adjustment and overall adjustment.

10. There is no significant association between the birth order of the respondents' and their adjustment in all the dimensions such as, health adjustment, emotional adjustment, self adjustment, home adjustment, social adjustment and overall adjustment.
11. There is a significant association between the respondents' present living place and adjustment in the dimensions of health adjustment. However there is no significant association between the respondents living place and the various dimensions of adjustment such as emotional adjustment, self adjustment, home adjustment, social adjustment, and overall adjustment.

Chapter - 12

Implication, Social Work Intervention and Conclusion

A. Implications

This empirical and descriptive study has established that tsunami influenced the mental health of the high school students in a negative way. A careful examination of the data indicates that close to half of the children had poor mental health, all self-reported a high level of anxiety and depression, and more than half had a high level of depression according to a more objective measure. More than half had poor study habits and a majority had low levels of involvement in their studies. In short, the mental well-being of the children is highly correlated with their motivation to stay in school and learn. Although the Government of India had started implementing the District Mental Health Programme (DMHP) in Kanyakumari district; to enhance the mental care in the affected areas (Ramya Kannan, 2005). It is to be keenly noted by the social worker that these negative traits were present even after two full years after the tsunami hit.

The school authorities need to arrange for mental health programmes towards bringing about positive mental well-being in the children and providing them with experiences that strengthen their ability to cope up with and counter the environmental stressors and disadvantages they face in the yester years.

While observing their mental health, the present investigation reported that the tsunami had negatively influenced the mental health of the children. Even though number of NGO's initiated mental health programmes for various population in tsunami affected area especially in Colachel village; still they had unexplained worries and fear about event. Due to that, they were showing lack of interest in their academic achievements. The teachers also supported that they were showing poor performance in their studies. The present study also supported these observations as more than fifty per cent of the respondents had poor level in their studies after having gone through the traumatic event. The students regularly report frequent physical problems especially stomachache after fleeing from tsunami.

While looking at their study involvement, most of the high school students showed low level of involvement in their studies. In addition to that during investigation the respondents also reported that they had inability to sit in one place and they were not able to focus their attention towards studies. Many of the senior students had day dreaming about the traumatic event, due to which they are showing lack of interest in studies which lead them to not able to complete their academic task promptly. Hence life skill education programme and mental well being programme by the trained social worker in schools need to be arranged.

There is a negative outcome of psycho-social well being was observed as all the children had high level of anxiety and depression and low level of adjustment. The children had nightmares, worries and flashbacks about the traumatic event. Some children expressed that they would never go near the sea, especially on Sunday. The main thrust of the present investigation is to establish the influence of the traumatic event on the mental health status of the children in a predictable way. This could be treated by applying psychotherapy and behaviour therapy. The therapist can help the children to establish new ways of thinking by directing their attention to both right and wrong assumption about themselves. Through this therapy, they can understand their behaviours, emotions, and ideas that contribute to his / her depression and they can learn coping techniques and problem-solving skills.

It is significant to help these children recover from all these psycho-social implications so that the mental well being could be achieved. Schools provide convenient access to children and families in a developmentally appropriate environment. School personnel are a natural source of support for children and classrooms provide formal and informal opportunities for assessing and addressing psychological responses and for correcting misperceptions.

School-Based Programmes

School-based programmes can normalise the trauma experience and minimise the stigma associated with mental healthcare. The structure and routine of school are important aspects of the recovery environment for children. The various stakeholders such as parents, teachers, school authorities, social workers, health personnel, etc need to be coordinated for a concerted effort to build a very conducive environment for the children to grow in overall development.

School-based interventions must initiate efforts to identify, refer, and treat children in need of intensive treatment. They should be part of a network that provides not only outreach but also triage and referral to those with specialised training and expertise who can offer more comprehensive and intensive treatment. Following criteria need to be considered for a successful school intervention programme:

(1) A model or plan specific to the school or institution need to be developed to coordinate necessary services and interventions. It should include safety, security, mental health, and public information.

(2) The crisis response plan should outline roles and responsibilities of crisis team members, with generic response protocols as well as unique adaptations for these types of crisis events.

(3) Government - Community- School partnerships (GCS): Crisis teams should also incorporate the expertise of community professionals from a broad range of relevant disciplines (e.g., mental health, public health, medical, police, fire, safety, disaster management, youth groups, etc.).

(4) School crisis response plans should not be developed in isolation from the community; community-response plans must incorporate schools.

(5) Parents are the first and foremost stakeholders and they need to be involved in all the stages of the intervention programmes and their support need to be ascertained.

(6) Similarly, the needs of teachers and other school personnel must be addressed so that they could provide quality service.

(7) School personnel need to be trained about the trauma reactions and its management.

(8) Schools could support with outreach programme to provide services and to carry out research programmes. They must review them to determine their appropriateness for the setting and to balance the needs for supportive intervention and normalisation

(9) Crisis response plans should address the broad range of potential events and not be solely designed for a rare catastrophic events. Crisis response plans and teams should also be mobilised to respond to more common crisis events. This allows the teams to develop and maintain the necessary skills and emerge as a functioning team that recognises the often-profound impact these events may have on children and school staff.

(10) Integrated approach should be the basis of the programmes so that intervention of every aspect is possible.

Therefore, the school should play an important role to improve general academic environment through mental health programme. The school teachers would be equipped with the practical knowledge of psychology of working growing children. Counselling skills could be appropriately incorporated into the teacher training curricula at different levels. An intensive programme could be provided to teachers on disaster management especially to those who were affected by tsunami. The teachers should be given training in mental health so that it would reduce their anxiety and depression and may improve their study habit and study involvement. The teachers could form part of the Crisis Intervention programme to help the children to improve the study habits and ultimately attain the psycho-social well being.

B. Social Work Intervention

A school is an essential socialising agent for the child's life has profound impact on child's overall growth and development. Large number of children attends school at least in early childhood. Schools play very crucial role in building one's self-esteem and a sense of competence.

It is learnt that any disaster in general and Tsunami in particular has a devastating consequences on the psycho-social wellbeing of the children. The present study reveals that nearly majority of the high school students have low level of mental health status due to devastating impact of tsunami, it affected the study habit and study involvement of children. Mental well being of the children is directly correlated wherein the child is motivated to stay and learn in the school. Since the schools lack any School Social Workers in Tamil Nadu state; Policy decisions need to be taken to appoint School Social Workers so that the social worker can arrange for mental health programme to bringing about positive mental well being in children as well as providing experience that will strengthen children's coping abilities to address the environmental stressors and disadvantages in future.

The mental health programme could be both environment centred as well as child centred. This includes working with the schools to improve the general academic environment as well as working with children on individuals or group level.

However, some disaster survivors may develop psychiatric disorders. The psychological impact of disaster varies from transient reactions like tension, anxiety, panic, confusion, fear, repeated 'flashbacks' etc.; to lifelong emotional scars. Some of the psychological symptoms, which may disturb the disaster affected victims for several months after a disaster are sadness, pessimistic thoughts, inactivity, withdrawn behaviour, and anxiety manifested as physical symptoms. Majority of the people are able to cope well with these emotional reactions due to their innate coping mechanisms/resilience.

Since the mental health of the children were affected by tsunami, it leads to have influence on study habit and study involvement of children, which in turn increases the anxiety, depression, and adjustment problem of the children. In this study, the researcher found that all the respondent, perceived high level of anxiety and depression. More than half of the respondents have low level of adjustment. In this situation, the social worker helps the child to adopt healthy coping strategies.

When the child has anxiety and depression that will often be confused about what can help him/her. For this, the first task is to normalise their life routines by helping them to get involved in routine tasks. The social worker can help them to get involved in routine tasks like helping with household work, getting back to attend school, and so on. Moreover, the social worker needs to be available to play and talk where the child may want to talk or play out his/her experience. Both these will help the child regain his/ her original level of functioning. Some simple psychotherapeutic techniques like brief supportive psychotherapy and building trusting and confiding relationships between physician and patient are very helpful. Apart from this some specific psycho-social intervention techniques like psychological/emotional first aid, crisis counselling, crisis intervention and problem solving counselling can be given by the social worker to help the disaster affected individuals especially children.

The school social worker can identify the student with problem and interview individually and his/her problems need to be understood from biological and psycho-social point of view.

The social worker can organise group work service for the children having problems like anxiety and depression due to tsunami. Wherein, the counsellor acts as a therapeutic agent in enabling the group to have positive interactions in such a way that they understand each other and solve their problem mutually. The group support will help them effective solution to their problems especially the children.

The school social worker could introduce topics related to mental health of children and role of parents and teachers in parent teacher associations. In this session the social worker, can utilise other mental health professional like psychiatrists, psychiatric social worker, play therapists, and occupational therapists.

Life skills education programme can be organised by the social worker for adaption of positive behaviour among the tsunami affected children that enable the individuals to deal effectively with the demand and challenges of everyday life.

Trauma counselling should never be provided unless an appropriate and sustained follow-up mechanism is guaranteed. Defense mechanisms exist for a reason and breaking them down before, the child is ready that in a safe physical and emotional environment leave him/her open and vulnerable to a re-traumatisation. There are serious risks associated with trauma counselling carried out by non-professionals. Dramatic consequences for a child's life pathway can have more damaging consequences for the individual's well-being than the traumatic event itself (an example would be a child's loss of parents having to grow up as an orphan, or destruction of school system leaving children without education). The psycho-social well-being of adults, particularly parents and caregivers has a direct impact on that of children, should thus be addressed through concurrent parent-focused psycho-social interventions.

Children and adults participation in decisions, which affect their lives, has a positive effect on their mental health, empowers them and helps them to regain control over their own lives. Grounding all psycho-social interventions in the culture, unless it is not in the best interests of the child, is both ethical and more likely to produce a sustained recovery.

At the same time, schools should play a new, more complex, and comprehensive role in relief and rehabilitation, and provide continuous social and psychological support to their students. In administrative terms, an effort should be made to reduce or wave school fees, donate books, replace educational certificates, and provide transportation to school-going children from affected areas.

A school social worker can also function as a mental health consultant to the teaching members in the school in helping them to individualise education thereby to devise materials and teaching styles that meet the needs of all children. To accomplish these goals, the social worker can organise brainstorming sessions with all the teachers on curriculum development, with an overall emphasis on human relations.

A school social worker can be seen as both a specialist in the diagnosis of emotional difficulties in children as a support staff person with the most extensive psychiatric and medically based training where he could extend individual counselling and support services to children in need. An orientation programme towards the positive mental health could be extended to children to help them feel comfortable about themselves, to feel right towards others and to meet the demands of life.

In this study, the researcher found that nearly majority of the respondents have low level of study habit and low level of study involvement. Therefore, considering these multifarious problems pertaining to achievement, it is essential that they requires timely assistance, guidance and suggestions, specially from teachers in respect of various psychological and psychiatric problems and their early signs and symptoms, interpersonal relationship skills, principles of interviewing and listening, source of referrals, and ways and means of collaborating with mental health agencies. This knowledge could be applied in day-to-day interaction with the children in the class room/hostels and in times of crisis. Counselling skills training could be appropriately incorporated into the teacher-training curricula at different levels of teacher education. These mental health inputs would prepare the teacher-counsellors in better dealing with the children clients.

Many of the children are facing problem in developing health study habit, study involvement due to various crisis like disaster. In such situation school teachers can be involved in training in life skill education programme for children and adolescents. In the life skill education programme the teachers are trained in life skills issues so as to transfer these skills to the adolescents. Teachers can also be trained in student's enrichment programmes, which would cover developing health study habits, preparing for examination, and stress management. This could be incorporated in the school curriculum and could be conducted on regular basis.

Hence, it is very important that the parents spend most of the time with their children and participate in their activities and in keeping with the age and aspirations of the children, the parents must have trust in them and entrust them with responsibilities. This will create a friendly bond between the parents and the children and encourage the children to confide in their parents. Hence, Family Life Education plays a vital role.

Employing Social Work Methods

- Case work is an essential method to intervene with psychological problems of the tsunami affected children. Individual counselling should be to remove them from grief.
- Group work should be used for recreational purpose and educating them.
- Through community organisation problems awareness can be created about the precautionary measures they have taken at the time of disaster. Disaster management can also be another ingredient.
- Social workers should be appointed on full time basis to mould the personality of the tsunami affected children.
- A wide publicity of government schemes for the welfare of children in particular should be made through mass media.

Crisis Intervention

The Random House Crisis Intervention Handbook (2000) defines crisis as "a dramatic emotional or circumstantial upheaval in a person's life" and "a stage in a sequence of events at which the trend of all future events, especially for better or worse, is determined a turning point".

A wide range of human emotions and behaviours can accompany crisis, particularly when the crisis relates to victimisation. People react differently to stress and crises based on their own skills or behaviours, abilities to cope, maturation levels, and personalities. For some, a crisis may be coupled with changes in behaviour such as sleeplessness or over-eating. For others, a crisis may include denial, disbelief, and the inability to cope. Still others may experience physiological changes such as an increase in their heart rate, sweating, or fainting.

Crisis intervention for victims of disaster is of paramount importance. The goal of such intervention is to help victims confront the reality of what happened; begin to deal with the crisis, and to go beyond the pain and emotional trauma toward new strength and opportunities for growth and change. Victims may include those who were directly affected by the crisis, as well as significant others such as parents, spouses, friends, or witnesses. The challenge for crisis intervention programmes is to provide effective crisis support and assistance as soon as possible following victimisation, and to make available resources and services to meet the needs of victims by providing direct assistance or referrals to other agencies.

Crisis intervention for victims of disasters varies depending on the needs of the victim and the type of victimisation or the degree of trauma they underwent. However, there are some critical elements to crisis intervention services that are necessary for all victims including psychological first aid; survivor needs assessment and empathic support and recovery intervention.

Phases of Crisis Intervention

Both governmental agencies and non-governmental agencies have developed crisis intervention teams staffed by professional social workers to respond to crisis when they receive emergency calls. To be effective, crisis intervention must be provided in an orderly, structured, humanistic manner and must focus on the individuality of the victim and his or her needs.

The first phase of crisis intervention include Immediate crisis intervention or "psychological first aid". It involves establishing a rapport with the victim, gathering information for short-term assessment and service delivery, and averting a potential state of crisis.

Immediate crisis intervention also includes caring for the medical, physical, mental health and personal needs of the victim, and providing information to the victim about local resources or services. Referrals should be made to other agencies for other services, such as shelter facilities, home security or for disaster victim compensation. However, many victims may be resistant to crisis intervention due to fear or anxiety. Resistance is one form of the victim's response to a crisis. Additionally, the immediacy of the response is critical to ensure the safety of the victim and his or her family. Time may be extremely important because of impending danger to the victim or the family. Victims should not wait hours or days to see a crisis intervention counsellor to assist in their time of need.

The second phase of crisis intervention involves an assessment of needs to determine the services and resources required by the victim. The purpose of this phase is to determine how the crisis is affecting the victim's life so that a plan for recovery can be developed, allowing the victim to begin moving towards the future.

The third phase—recovery intervention—helps victims to re-stabilise their lives and become healthy again. It also involves helping the victim prevent further victimisation by the government or other agencies the victim may encounter in the aftermath of victimisation or trauma. This initial period of recovery for the victim may require considerable time, effort and resources before he or she resolves long-term issues associated with the victimisation.

Victim service providers also focus on reducing risk factors for victims, maximising their social support systems, maximising and improving their coping skills and helping victims gain greater self-esteem and self-worth. These service providers often work with other agencies to reduce added trauma imposed on victims who go through the complex and often-frustrating process of accessing the available resources.

Crisis intervention is an important element of the healing process for victims. Crisis intervention should not be to the responsibility of one specific agency or organisation, but rather should play an important role for each agency or organisation that deals with victims of disaster, including victim advocacy organisations (such as hospitals or schools), social services agencies, law enforcement, and corrections.

Avenues for Future Research

- The present study confines only to a reputed higher secondary school, which was worst affected during tsunami. Other studies may be conducted in other schools if their building have been demolished and rebuild after tsunami.
- This study is mainly concentrating on the mental health status of children those who are affected by tsunami. To gain better insight into mental health of children an attempt could be made to study the psychological effects of parent's mental health on children who experience disaster like tsunami.

- The high school students those who perceive high level of anxiety and depression can be selected separately as samples and an in-depth study may be conducted among these samples in order to find out the reasons for their high level of anxiety and depression due tsunami. This will help them how to overcome their mental health problem when they come across various crisis.
- Keeping these findings as base macro study at metropolis level could also be undertaken among the children those who became orphan children due to tsunami and other major disaster.
- The present study is limited to study habits and study involvement of children only. Thus, room is made for further study of levels of their achievements at later stages.
- This study mainly concentrated on tsunami-affected children. Other studies may be conducted among the children those who had seen the disaster in the media and find out how they were psychologically affected.

Conclusion

The present descriptive study is conducted with a view to understand the socio-demographic characteristics, their mental health status, study habit, study involvement, anxiety, depression and adjustment. To analyse the psycho-social impact among high school students; Standardised tools were used namely:

Mental health inventory	V.D. Augustine (1978)
Study habit inventory	B.V. Patel (1983)
Study involvement inventory	Jayalakshmi (1978)
Anxiety inventory	Taylor (1935 revised edition)
Depression inventory	Becks (1988)
Adjustment inventory	Ramamurthy (1968).

The literature was reviewed extensively and a systematic summary of relevant researches both national and international were presented. The study also portrayed the research methodology adopted as well as the layout of the study. The data collected were systematically processed, analysed, and presented in the form of tables and diagrams to draw meaningful inferences. In the present study, the researcher has also applied various statistical testes such as Chi-square test, student Z–test, one–way analysis of variance (F-Test) and Karl Pearson's coefficient of correlation test to arrive at meaningful conclusions.

As the major findings; nearly majority of the respondents (57.3 per cent) have low level of mental health status and more than half of the respondents (53.3 per cent) have low level of study habit. Nearly majority of the respondents (59.3 per cent) have low level of study involvement. It is important to note that: (i) All the respondents (100 per cent) perceive high level of anxiety; (ii) All the respondents (100 per cent) perceive high level of depression. And more than half of the respondents (52 per cent) have low level of adjustment. The high level of depression and anxiety on each child due to Tsunami led to psycho-social distress among children.

Based on these findings it is strongly recommended that school social work need to be given importance and in each and every school a professional social worker need to be appointed to enhance the psycho-social well being of the children, to provide crisis counselling, crisis intervention, and problem solving counselling; family life education, family counselling and mental health programmes. Thus, school mental health programme would promote mental wellbeing in children's coping abilities to counter the environmental stressors and disadvantages encountered in their growing years and hence the development of overall personality of the children is ensured.

References

Abramowitz, JS. (1996), Variants of exposure and response prevention in the treatment of obsessive-compulsive disorder: a meta-analysis, *Behavior Therapy*, 27:583–600.

Abhay Joshi and Aoki Misa, (2013), The Role of Social Capital and Public Policy in Disaster Recovery A Case Study of Tamil Nadu State, India, International Journal of Disaster Risk Reduction, http://dx.doi.org/10.1016/j. ijdrr.2013.09.004.

Abramowitz, JS. (2006), The psychological treatment of obsessive-compulsive disorder, *Canadian Journal of Psychiatry*, 51: 407–416.

Adler, DA, Irish J, McLaughlin TJ, Perissinotto C, Chang H, Hood M, (2004), The work impact of dysthymia in a primary care population. *Gen Hosp Psychiatry*. Jul-Aug; 26(4): 269-76.

Airaksinen, E, Larsson M, Lundberg I, Forsell Y. (2004), Cognitive functions in depressive disorders: evidence from a population-based study, *Psychological Medicine,* Jan; 34(1):83-91.

Albano, A. M., Chorpita, B. F., and Barlow, D. H. (2003), Childhood anxiety disorders, In E. J. Mash and R. A. Barkley (Eds.), Child psychopathology (2nd ed., pp. 279-329). New York: Guildford Press.

Alberts, DS, Huber RK, Moffat J. (2010), NATO NEC C2 maturity model overview, in NATO NEC C2 maturity model. Washington D.C, CCRP Publications.

Aldrich, DP (2011), The Externalities of Strong Social Capital: Post-Tsunami Recovery in Southeast India, Journal of Civil Society; 8(1): 81-99.

Aldrich, DP, Crook K. (2008), Strong Civil Society as a Double-Edged Sword: Siting Trailers in Post-Katrina New Orleans. Political Research Quarterly; 61(3): 379-389.

Aldrich, DP. (2010), Fixing Recovery: Social Capital in Post-Crisis Resilience, Journal of Homeland Security; 6: 1-10.

Aldrich, DP. (2011), Ties that Bond, Ties that Build: Social Capital and Governments in Post Disaster Recovery, Studies in emergent order; 4:58-68.

Aldrich, DP. (2012), Building Resilience: Social Capital in Post-Disaster Recovery, University of Chicago Press.

Altshuler, L.L, Hendrich V, Cohen LS. (1998), Course of mood and anxiety disorders during pregnancy and the postpartum period, Journal of Clinical Psychiatry, 59: 29.

Amaya-Jackson, L. (2000), Post-traumatic stress disorder in children and adolescents. In: Sadock B, Sadock V, eds. Kaplan and Sadock's Comprehensive textbook of psychiatry, 7th ed. Philadelphia: Lippincott Williams and Wilkins, 2763-2769.

American Academy of Child and Adolescent Psychiatry (AACAP) (1998), Practice parameters for the assessment and treatment of post-traumatic stress disorder in children and adolescents, Journal of American Academy for Child Adolescent Psychiatry; 37(10 Suppl):4S-26.

American Counseling Association (2005), Code of ethics and standards of practice, Alexandria.

American Psychiatric Association (2000), Diagnostic and Statistical Manual of Mental Disorders, Fourth Edition, Text Revision.

American Psychiatric Association (2010), Ethical principles of psychologist and code of conduct, Washington, DC.

American Psychiatric Association (1980), *Diagnostic and Statistical Manual of Mental Disorders*, 3rd ed. Washington, DC: American Psychiatric Association.

Anto, P. Rajkumar, Titus S. Premkumar, Prathap Tharyan (2008), Coping with the Asian tsunami: Perspectives from Tamil Nadu, India on the determinants of resilience in the faced adversity, Social Science and Medicine, Volume 67, Issue 5, pp. 844-853.

APA (American Psychiatric Association) (2000), Diagnostic and statistical manual of mental disorders, 4th ed. Text Revision, The American Psychiatric Association, Washington DC.

Aptekar, L. and J. A. Boore (1990), The emotional effects of disaster on children: A review of the literature, International Journal of Mental Health 19(2): 77-90.

Arunya Tuicomepee, John L. Romano Thai (2008), Adolescent Survivors 1 Year After the 2004 Tsunami: A Mixed Methods Study Journal of Counseling Psychology, Volume 55, Issue 3, pp. 308-320.

Asarnow, J., Glynn, S., Pynoos, R. S., Nahum, J., Gunthrie, D., Cantwell, D. P., and Franklin, B. (1999), When the earth stops shaking: Earthquake sequelae among children diagnosed for pre-earthquake psychopathology, Journal of the American Academy of Child and Adolescent Psychiatry, 38, 1016-1023.

Ashraf, H (2005), Tsunami wreaks mental health havoc, Bulletin of the World Health Organisation, Vol. 83, no. 6, pp. 405-406.

Axelson, DA, Birmaher B. (2001), Relation between anxiety and depressive disorders in childhood and adolescence published by Inter science Depress Anxiety14 (2):67-78.

Babu, P.G, (2007), Local community's support for post-tsunami recovery efforts in an agrarian village and a tourist destination: a comparative analysis. Oxford University Press and Community Development Journal.

Bahrick, L. E., J. F. Parker, R. Fivush, and M. Levit (1998), The effects of stress on young children's memory for a natural disaster, Jl of Experimental Psychology: Applied 4(4): 308-331.

Bakken, K, Vaglum P. (2007), Predictors of suicide attempters in substance-dependent patients: a six-year prospective follow-up, *Clin Pract Epidemol Ment Health,* 3:20.

Barbui, C, Motterlini N, Garattini L(2006), Health status, resource consumption, and costs of dysthymia. A multi-center two-year longitudinal study, *J Affect Disord*, Feb; 90(2-3):181-6.

Barlow, D. H. (2002), Anxiety and its disorders: The nature and treatment of anxiety and panic (2nd ed.). New York: Guildford Press Ball, J. and K. Allen (2000), Consensus recommendations for responding to children's emergencies in disasters, National Academies of Practice Forum: Issues in Interdisciplinary Care 2(4): 253-257.

Becker, SM (2007), Psycho-social care for adult and child survivors of the tsunami disaster in India, Journal of Child and Adolescent Psychiatric Nursing, Vol. 20, No. 3, pp. 148-155.

Beggs, JJ, Haines VA, Hurlbert JS. (1996), The Effects of Personal Network and Local Community Contexts on the Receipt of Formal Aid during Disaster Recovery, International Journal of Mass Emergencies and Disasters 14: 57–78.

Bendick, R, and R. Bilham, (1999), A Search for Buckling of the SW Indian Coast related to Himalayan Collision, in Macfarlane, A., Sorkhabi, R. B., and Quade, J., eds., Himalaya and Tibet: Mountain Roots to Mountain Tops: Geol Soc Amer. 328, 313-322.

Benight, C.C. and A. Bandura (2004), 'Social cognitive theory of post-traumatic recovery: The role of perceived self-efficacy', Behaviour Research and Therapy, 42, 1129-1148.

Bennett, J, Bertrand W, Harkin C, Samarasinghe S, Wickramatillake H. (2006), Coordination of international humanitarian assistance in tsunami-affected countries. London: Tsunami Evaluation Coalition.

Berke, PR, Kartez J, Wenger D (1993), Recovery after disaster: achieving sustainable development, mitigation and equity. Disasters; 17: 93–109.

Bernal, M, Haro JM, Bernert S, Brugha T, de Graaf R, Bruffaerts R, (2007), Risk factors for suicidality in Europe: results from the ESEMED study, *J Affect Disord*. Aug; 101 (1-3): 27-34.

Berninghausen, W. H., (1966), Tsunamis and Seismic Seiches reported from regions adjacent to the Indian Ocean, Bull. Seism. Soc. Am., 56 (1), 69-74.

Bhugra, Dinesh; van Ommeren, Mark (2006), Mental health, psycho-social support and the tsunami Information Healthcare Volume 18, Number 3, June.

Bhushan, B and Kumar, JS (2007), Emotional distress and post-traumatic stress in children surviving the 2004 tsunami, Journal of Loss and Trauma, Vol. 12, No. 3, pp. 245-257.

Bilham, R, R. Engdahl, N. Feld, and S.P. Sayabala (2005), Partial and complete rupture of the Indo-Andaman plate boundary 1847-2004, Seism. Res. Lett., 76 (3), 299-311.

Birkmann, J., Wisner, B. (2006), Measuring the un-measurable, The challenge of vulnerability, Bonn: UNUEHS. Bonn.

Blaikie, P., Cannon, T., Davis, I., and Wisner, B. (1994), At risk: Natural hazards, people's vulnerability, and disasters. Routledge: London.

Bolton, P, Bass J, Neugebauer R, Verdeli H, Clougherty KF, Wickramaratne P (2003), Group interpersonal psychotherapy for depression in rural Uganda: a randomized controlled trial. *JAMA*. Jun 18; 289(23): 3117-24.

Bolton, D., O'Ryan, D., Udwin, O., Boyle, S., and Yule, W., (2000), The long-term psychological effects of a disaster experienced in adolescence: II: General psychopathology, Journal of Child Psychology and Psychiatry and Allied Disciplines, 41, 513-523.

Bradburn, I. S. (1991), After the earth shook: Children's stress symptoms 6- 8 months after a disaster, Advances in Behaviour Research and Therapy 13(3): 173-179.

Brock, S. E., Lazarus, P. J., and Jimerson, S. R. (Eds.), (2003), Best practices in school crisis prevention and intervention, Bethesda, MD: National Association of School Psychologists.

Bulut, S. (2004), Factor Structure of Post-traumatic Stress Disorder in Children Experienced Natural Disaster, Psychological: An International Jl of Psychology in the Orient 47(3): 158-168.

Burke, J. D., P. Moccia, Borus, B.J., and Burns (1986), Emotional distress in fifth-grade children ten months after a natural disaster, Journal of the American Academy of Child Psychiatry 25(4): 536-541.

Carballo, Manuel; Heal, Bryan; Horbaty, Gabriela (2006), Impact of the tsunami on psycho-social health and well-being, Information health care, pp. 217-223(7).

Casement, MD, Shestyuk, AY, Best, JL, Casas, BR, Glezer, A, Segundo, MA (2008) Anticipation of affect in dysthymia: Behavioral and neurophysiological indicators. *Biol Psychol.* Feb; 77(2): 197-204.

Casey, P (2008), Diagnosing adjustment disorder with depressive features, Expert Review of Neurotherapeutics. 8 (8):1203-8, 2008 Aug.

Catani, C, Jacob, N, Schauer, E, Kohila, M, Neuner, F. (2008), Family violence, war, and natural disasters: a study of the effect of extreme stress on children's mental health in Sri Lanka. BMC Psychiatry, 8:33.

CDC (2006), Effects of the December 2004 tsunami on people in affected areas of Southern Thailand, Aug. 7, Vol. 2 No. 405.

Chamlee-Wrigh, EC., (2009), Club Goods and Post-Disaster Community Return, Rationality and Society; 21(4): 429-458.

Chamlee-Wright, E. (2010), The Cultural and Political Economy of Recovery: Social Learning in a post-disaster environment. London and New York: Routledge.

Chandra, Vijay, Pandav, Rajesh and Bhugra, Dinesh (2006), Mental health and psycho-social support after the tsunami: Observations across affected nations, Information Healthcare, Volume 18, Number 3, pp. 205-211(7).

Chesler, P. (1972), Women and Madness, New York: Palgrave Macmillan.

Christina Suboh (2008), The Aftermath of the Tsunami -Post-traumatic stress disorder in children - Teacher's role in psychosocial intervention A literature review, Uni.of Oslo, Norway.

Christoplos, I, Rodriguez, T, Schipper, L, Narvaez, EA, Meija, K, Buitrago, R, (2010), Learning from recovery after Hurricane Mitch. Disasters; 34: S202-19.

Christoplo, I. (2006), The elusive 'window of opportunity' for risk reduction in post disaster recovery, Bangkok: In ProVention Consortium Forum.

Coleman, J S., (1988), Social Capital in the Creation of Human Capital, American Journal of Sociology, 94: 95-120.

Comfort, LK. (2007), Crisis management in hindsight: cognition, communication, coordination, and control, public administration review. special issue. Hurricane Katrina; (S)188-196.

Covell, NH, Donahue SA, Allen G, Foster MJ, Felton CJ, Essock SM.(2006), Use of Project Liberty counseling services over time by individuals in various risk categories, Psychiatric Services, 57:1268-1270.

CRED (2005), Report, (*www.cred.be/publications*)

Crits-Christoph, P., Newman, M. G., Rickels, K., Gallop, R., Gibbons, M. B. C., Hamilton, J. L., Ring-Kurtz, S., and Pastva, A. M. (2011), Combined medication and cognitive therapy for generalised anxiety disorder, .*Journal of Anxiety Disorders, 25*(8), 1087-1094.

Cutter, S.L., Boruff, B.J. and Shirley, L.W. (2003), Social vulnerability to environmental hazards, Social Science Quarterly, 84 (2). 242-261.

Cutter, S. and Finch, C. (2008), Temporal and spatial changes in social vulnerability to natural hazards, In PNAS - USA, February 19, Vol. 105(7), S. 2301-2306.

Cutter, S.L., Barnes, L., Berry, M., Burton, C., Evans, E., Tate, E., Webb, J. (2008), A Place-based model for understanding community resilience to natural disasters, Global Environmental Change, 18, 598-606.

David Abramson, Tasha Stehling Ariza, Richard Garfield, RN and Irwin Redlener, (2008), Prevalence and Predictors of Mental Health Distress Post-Katrina: Gulf Coast, Child and Family Health Study.

David Abramson, Tasha Stehling-Ariza, Richard Garfield, RN, and Irwin Redlener, (2007), Prevalence and Predictors of Mental Health Distress Post-Katrina: Journal of traumatic stress, Jun; Vol. 20, No. 3, pp. 263-9.

Davidson, J, Smith R. (1990), Traumatic experiences in psychiatric outpatients, Journal of Trauma Stress, 3:459-475.

De Silva, Padmal (2006), The tsunami and its aftermath in Sri Lanka: Explorations of a Buddhist perspective, Information Healthcare, Vol. 18, No. 7, pp. 281-287.

Debra, L. (2009), Lessons Learned From Disasters Affecting Children, Weiner, Vol. 10, No. 3.

Dinesh Bhugra; Mark van Ommeren (2006), Mental health, psycho-social support and the tsunami International Review of Psychiatry, Volume 18, Issue 3, pp. 213-216.

Disaster Resource Centre (DRC), (2014), Annual Reports www.udel.edu/DRC/, retrieved on 20 Feb 2014.

Dollard, J, Miller NE. (1950), *Personality and Psychotherapy; an Analysis in Terms of Learning, Thinking and Culture*, New York, McGraw-Hill.

Dollinger, S. J. and P. Cramer (1990), Children's defensive responses and emotional upset following a disaster: A projective assessment, Jl. of Personality Assessment 54(1-2): 116-127.

Donnelly, CL, Amaya-Jackson, L. (2002), Post-traumatic stress disorder in children and adolescents: epidemiology, diagnosis and treatment options. Pediatric Drugs; 4:159-170.

Dunning, M.C. (2009), Social Vulnerability Analysis Methods for Corps Planning, Draft report 10/29/09.

Durkin, M. S., N. Khan, L L Davidson, S S Zaman, Z A Stein (1993), The effects of a natural disaster on child behaviour: Evidence for posttraumatic stress, American Journal of Public Health 83(11): 1549-1553.

Edna, B. Foa, (2010), Cognitive Behavioral therapy of obsessive compulsive disorder, Dialogues Clin Neurosci. Jun 2010; 12(2): 199-207.

Ell, Kathleen (1996), Crisis theory and social work treatment Social work treatment, F. Turner (Ed.), (4th ed.), New York: Free Press.

Emmanuel, Raju N and Per Becker (2013), Multi-organisational coordination for disaster recovery: The story of post-tsunami Tamil Nadu, India International Journal of Disaster Risk Reduction, Feb. 28.

Essex, MJ, Kraemer HC, Armstrong JM, Boyce WT, Goldsmith HH, Klein MH, Woodward H, Kupfer DJ (2006), Exploring risk factors for the emergence of children's mental health problems, Department of Psychiatry, University of Wisconsin-Madison 53719, Arch Gen Psychiatry. Nov; 63(11): 1246-56.

Feinberg, T. (1999), The midwest floods of 1993: Observations of a natural disaster. In A.S. Canter and S.A. Carroll (Eds.), Crisis prevention and response: A collection of NASP resources (pp. 223-239). Bethesda, MD: National Association of School Psychologists.

Fekadu, A, Kebede D, Alem A, Fekadu D, Mogga S, Negash A, Medhin G, Beyero T, Shibre T (2006), Clinical outcome in bipolar disorder in a community-based follow-up study in Butajira, Ethiopia. Acta Psychiatrica Scandinavica, 114, 426-434.

Fekete, A. (2008), The scale dependence of social and ecological vulnerability in context to river floods in Germany, EGU General Assembly 2008, Geophysical Research Abstracts, Vol. 10, Vol. 10, EGU2008- A-03903, SRef-ID: 1607-7962/gra/EGU2008-A-03903, Vienna.

Ferrara, F., (2009), State-of-art on vulnerability of socio-economic systems, Methodologies to assess vulnerability of structural territorial and economic systems, EC, Brussels.

Fetter, JC (2005), Psychosocial Response to Mass Casualty Terrorism: Guidelines for Physicians, Prim Care Companion Journal of Clinical Psychiatry; 7: 49-52.

Flannery-Schroeder, E. C. (2004), Generalised anxiety disorder, In T. L. Morris and J. S. March (Ed), Anxiety disorders in children and adolescents (II) pp. 125-140). New York: Guilford Press.

Flynn, B. W. and M. E. Nelson (1998), Understanding the needs of children following large-scale disasters and the role of government, Child & Adolescent Psychiatric Clinics of North America 7(1): 211-227.

Foa, EB, Goldstein AJ. (1978), Continuous exposure and complete response prevention in the treatment of obsessive-compulsive neurosis, *Behavior Therapy*, No. 9: 821–829.

Foa, EB, Kozak MJ. (1985), Treatment of anxiety disorders: implications for psychopathology, In: Tuma AH, Maser JD, eds. *Anxiety and the Anxiety Disorders*, Hillsdale, NJ: Lawrence Erlbaum Associates, 421-452.

Foa, EB, Liebowitz MR, Kozak, MJ, (2005), Randomized, placebo-controlled trial of exposure and ritual prevention, clomipramine and their combination in the treatment of obsessive-compulsive disorder, *Am J Psychiatry*. 162: 151-161.

Foa, EB, Steketee G, Grayson JB (1985), Imaginal and in vivo exposure: a comparison with obsessive-compulsive checkers. *Behavior Therapy* ;16: 292-302.

Foa, EB, Steketee G, Turner RM, Fischer SC. (1980); Effects of imaginal exposure to feared disasters in obsessive-compulsive checkers, *Behav Res Therapy* 18: 449-455.

Friedberg, RB and McClure, JM (2007), Clinical practice of cognitive therapy with children and adults, The Guildford Press, New York.

Galante, R. and D. Foa (1987), An epidemiological study of psychic trauma and treatment effectiveness for children after a natural disaster, Annual Progress in Child Psychiatry and Child Development: 349-364.

Galderisi, A., Ceudech, A., Ferrara, F. F., Profice, A. S. (2010), Integration of different vulnerabilities vs. Natural and Na-tech Hazards, ENSURE Project.

Ganesan, M (2006), Psycho-social response to disasters–some concerns, International Review of Psychiatry, Vol. 18, No. 3, pp. 241-247.

Ganesan, M (2006), Psycho-social response to disasters—some concerns Information Healthcare, Volume 18, No. 7, pp. 241-247.

George, P.C, (2004), Natural Disasters in Oceania, in International Perspectives on Natural Disasters: Occurrences, Mitigation, and Consequences -Book Series: Advances in Natural and Technological Hazards Research, Western Michigan University, Nov. Springer Publishing.

George, Pararas Carayannis (2003), Near and Far-Field Effects of Tsunamis Generated by the Paroxysmal Eruptions, Explosions, Caldera Collapses and Massive Slope Failures of The Krakatau Volcano in Indonesia on August 26-27, 1883, Science of Tsunami Hazards, 21 (4), 191-222.

Georges, Ramalanjaona (2011), Impact of 2004 Tsunami in the Islands of Indian Ocean: Lessons Learned, Emergency Medicine International, Volume 2011, (www.dx.doi.org/)

Ghodse, H and Galea, S (2006), Tsunami: Understanding mental health consequences and the unprecedented response, International Review of Psychiatry, Vol. 18, No. 3, pp. 289-297.

Ghodse, Hamid, Galea, Susanna (2006), Tsunami: Understanding mental health consequences and the unprecedented response, Information Healthcare, Vol. 18, No. 9.

Giannopoulou, I, Dikaiakou A, Yule W (2006), Cognitive-behavioural group intervention for PTSD symptoms in children following the Athens 1999 earthquake: a pilot study. Clinical Child Psychology and Psychiatry 11: 543-553.

Goenjian, A .K., Molina, L., Steinberg, A. M., and Fairbanks, L. A. (2001), Post-traumatic stress and depressive reactions among adolescents after Hurricane Mitch. American Journal of Psychiatry, 158, 788-794.

Gopalakrishnan, S., (2005), Disaster, Dept. of Community Medicine Publications, Stanley Medical College, Chennai.

Government of India (GOI), (2005), India Post-tsunami recovery program: preliminary damage and needs assessment. Report prepared by Asian Development Bank, United nations and World Bank for Government of India, New Delhi, India.

Govt. of India (2013), NCPCR, Report.

Govt. of Tamilnadu (2005), DRC Reports.

Green, B. L., Korol, M., Grace, M. C., & Vary, M. G. (1991), Children and disaster: Age, gender and parental effects on PTSD symptoms. Journal of the American Academy of Child and Adolescent Psychiatry, 30, 945-951.

Green, B. L., M. Korol, Grace, M. C., Vary, M. J., Leonard, A. C., Gleser, E. C (1991), Children and disaster: Age, gender, and parental effects on PTSD symptoms, Journal of the American Academy of Child & Adolescent Psychiatry 30(6): 945-951.

Greengard, Samuel, (1988), Crime After Crime, Barrister Magazine 15 (4): 23-27 Groupe URD (2011), Beyond emergency relief in Haiti. Grouoe URD, Paris.

Grunewald, F, Binder A, Georges Y.(2010), Inter-agency real-time evaluation in Haiti: 3 months after the earthquake. Paris and Berlin: Groupe URD and Global Public Policy Institute (GPPI);

Gryszkiewicz, A, Chen F. (2010), Design requirements for information sharing in a crisis management command and control centre. In: Proceedings of the 7th international ISCRAM conference. Seattle, USA; Guildford Press.

Gurwitch, R. H., J. F. Silovsky, Schultz, S, Kees, M, Burlingame, S (2002), Reactions and guidelines for children following trauma/disaster, Communication Disorders Qutly. 23(2): 93-99.

Gurwitch, R. H., M. A. Sullivan, and Long, P. J. (1998), The impact of trauma and disaster on young children, Child & Adolescent Psychiatric Clinics of North America 7(1): 19-32.

Hakeem, Irfan (2013), Uttarakhand disaster: Now, all eyes on unclaimed kids, Sunday, Jun 30.

Hamada, R. S., Kameoka, V., Yanagida, E., and Chemtob, C. M. (2003), Assessment of elementary school children for disaster-related posttraumatic stress disorder symptoms: The Kauai recovery index, Journal of Nervous & Mental Disease 191(4): 268-272.

Hamblen, J. (2006), PTSD in children and adolescents: A National Centre for PTSD fact sheet http://wps.ablongman.com/ab_myhelpinglab_resources_1/59/15297/3916266.cw

Hamid, Ghodse; Susanna Galea (2006), Tsunami: Understanding mental health consequences and the unprecedented response International Review of Psychiatry, Vol.18, No. 3, pp. 289-297.

Hammer, Mark B., Trauma and the Vietnam War Generation (1992), Report of Finding from the National Vietnam Veterans Readjustment Study, Jl. of Traumatic Stress, 5 (2): 321-322.

Hanifan, LJ. (1961), The Rural School Community Center, The Annals of the American Academy of Political and Social Science; 67: 130-138.

Hanns, Möhler, Dan J. Steinc, Thomas Mueggler, David S. Baldwina, (2009), Research in anxiety disorders: From the bench to the bedside, Eur. Neuropsychopharmacol. www.depression-understood.org

Hayden, EP, Klein DN. (2001), Outcome of dysthymic disorder at 5-year follow-up: the effect of familial psychopathology, early adversity, personality, comorbidity, and chronic stress, *Am J Psychiatry*, Nov;158(11):1864-70.

Heck, N.H. (1947), List of seismic sea waves, Bulletin of Seismological Society, 37, 269-286.

Hermens, ML, van Hout HP, Terluin B, van der Windt DA, Beekman AT,(2004), The prognosis of minor depression in the general population: a systematic review. *Gen Hosp Psychiatry*. Nov-Dec; 26(6): 453-62.

Hewitt, K. (1997), Regions of Risk: A Geographical Introduction to Disasters, London: Longman.

Hoare, P. (1993), Essential child psychiatry. Edinburgh: Churchill Livingstone.

Hoehn-Saric, R., Hazlett, R. L. and McLeod, D. R. (1993), Generalised anxiety disorder with early and late onset of anxiety symptoms. Comprehensive Psychiatry, 34, 291-297.

Hoffman, MA, Bizzman A. (1996), Attributions and responses to the Arab Israeli conflict: a developmental analysis. Child Development; 67:117-128.

IFRC (2009), Psychosocial interventions: A handbook, International Federation of Red Cross and Red Crescent Societies Reference Centre for Psychosocial Support, Denmark.

Ignacio Jarero, Lucina Artigas, María Montero y López Lena (2008), The EMDR Integrative Group Treatment Protocol: Application With Child Victims of a Mass Disaster, Journal of EMDR Practice and Research, Volume 2, Number 2.

James, R. and Gilliland, B. (2001), Crisis intervention strategies, (4 ed), Pacific Grove, CA.

Jeney-Gammon, P., T. K. Daugherty, Finch, A. J., Jr., Belter, R. W., and Foster, K. Y. (1993), Children's coping styles and report of depressive symptoms following a natural disaster, Journal of Genetic Psychology 154(2): 259-267.

Jenike, MA. (1983), Obsessive compulsive disorder, *Compr Psychiatry*, 24: 99-115.

Jennifer Baggerly, Dee Ray, and Sue Bratton (2010), Child-centered play therapy Research The Evidence Base for Effective Practice, *John Wiley and Sons Ltd, London.*

John, H. Ehrenreich, (2001), Coping with Disaster: A Guide Book to Psychosocial Intervention, Centre for Psychology and Society, State University of New York.

John Mahoney; Vijay Chandra; Harrischandra Gambheera; Terrence De Silva; T. Suveendran (2006), Responding to the mental health and psycho-social needs of the people of Sri Lanka in disasters, International Review of Psychiatry, Volume 18, Issue 6, pp. 593-597.

John Mahoney; Vijay Chandra; Harrischandra Gambheera; Terrence De Silva; T. Suveendran (2006), Responding to the mental health and psycho-social needs of the people of Sri Lanka in disasters International Review of Psychiatry, Volume 18, Issue 6, pp. 593-597.

Johnson, JE, Zlotnick C. (2008), A pilot study of group interpersonal psychotherapy for depression in substance-abusing female prisoners, *J Substance Abuse Treat*, Jun; 34 (4):371-7.

Johnson, JG, Cohen P, Kasen S, Brook JS.(2005), Personality disorder traits associated with risk for unipolar depression during middle adulthood. *Psychiatry Res*. Sep 15;136(2-3):113-21.

Johnson, K. (1998), Trauma in the Lives of Children: Crisis and Stress Management Techniques for Counselors, Teachers, and Other Professionals. 2nd Ed. Alameda, CA: Hunter House.

Johnson, K. (1998), Trauma in the Lives of Children: Crisis and Stress Management Techniques for Counselors, Teachers, and Other Professionals. 2nd Ed. Alameda, CA: Hunter House.

Jones, L. (2008), Responding to the needs of children in crisis International Review of Psychiatry; 20:291-303.

Jones, R.T; Ribbe D. P. and Cunningham P., (1994), Psycho-social correlates of fire disaster among children and adolescents, Journal of traumatic stress , Vol. 7, No 1, pp. 117-122.

Jones, R. T., D. P. Ribbe, Cunningham, P. B., Weddle, J. D., Langley, A. K. (2002), Psychological impact of fire disaster on children and their parents, Behavior Modification 26(2): 163-186.

Jones, R. T., Fray, R., Cunningham, J. D., and Kaiser, L. (2001), The psychological effects of hurricane Andrew on ethnic minority and Caucasian children and adolescents: A case study. Cultural Diversity and Ethnic Minority Psychology, 7, 103-108.

Jordan, Blair; Perryman, Kristi; Anderson, Leslie (2011), A case for child-centered play therapy with natural disaster and catastrophic event survivors, Int. Jl. of Play Therapy, Vol. 22(4), Oct.

Jyotsana Shukla (2013), Extreme Weather Events and Mental Health: Tackling the Psychosocial Challenge ISRN Public Health Volume 2013, www.researchgate.net

Kar, N, Bastia BK. (2006), Post-traumatic stress disorder, depression and generalised anxiety disorder in adolescents after a natural disaster: a study of comorbidity, Clinical Practical Epidemiological Mental Health; 2: 17.

Kar, N, Jagadisha, Murali N. (2001), Post-traumatic stress disorder in children following disaster, Kerala Journal of Psychiatry; 16: 7-14.

Kar, N, Mohapatra PM, Nayak KC, Pattanaik P, Swain SP, Kar HC (2007), Post-traumatic stress disorder in children and adolescents one year after a super-cyclone in Orissa, India: exploring cross-cultural validity and vulnerability factors. BMC Psychiatry 7: 8.

Kar, N. (2006), Psycho-social issues following a natural disaster in a developing country: a qualitative longitudinal observational study, Int. Journal of Disaster Medicine, 4: 169-176.

Kathleen, B. Lustyk . W. G. Gerrish (2010), Premenstrual Syndrome and Premenstrual Dysphoric Disorder: Issues of Quality of Life, Stress and Exercise Adjustment Disorder, Springer Science and Business Media, LLC (USA).

Keitner, GI, Ryan CE, Solomon DA. (2006), Realistic expectations and a disease management model for depressed patients with persistent symptoms, *J Clin Psychiatry*, Sep; 67(9):1412-21.

Keller, MB, Harrison W, Fawcett JA, Gelenberg A, Hirschfeld RM, Klein D, (1995), Treatment of chronic depression with sertraline or imipramine: preliminary blinded response rates and high rates of under treatment in the community, *Psychopharmacol Bull.*;31(2):205-12.

Kelly, O, Matheson K, Ravindran A, Merali Z, Anisman H (2007), Ruminative coping among patients with dysthymia before and after pharmacotherapy. *Depress Anxiety.*; 24(4): 233-43.

Kennedy, J, Ashmore J, Babister E, Kelman I. (2008), The meaning of 'build back better': evidence from post-tsunami Aceh and Sri Lanka. Journal of Contingencies and Crisis Management; 16: 24-36.

Kessing, LV (2007), Epidemiology of Subtypes of Depression, *Acta Psychiatr Scand.* 115 (Suppl 433): 85-89.

Kilby, P. (2008), The strength of networks: the local NGO response to the tsunami in India. Disasters 32 (1): 120-130.

Klein, DN, Schwartz JE, Rose S, Leader JB.(2000), Five-year course and outcome of dysthymic disorder: A prospective, naturalistic follow-up study. *Am Jl of Psychiatry.* Jun; 157(6): 931-9.

Klein, DN, Shankman SA, Lewinsohn PM, Rohde P, Seeley JR. (2004), Family study of chronic depression in a community sample of young adults, *Am J Psychiatry.* Apr; 161(4): 646-53.

Klein, DN, Shankman SA, Rose S.(2006), Ten-year prospective follow-up study of the naturalistic course of dysthymic disorder and double depression. *Am J Psychiatry.* May; 163 (5): 872-80.

Kodish, Carol Rockhill, Sheryl Ryan, Chris Varley (2011), Pharmacotherapy for Anxiety disorders for children and Adolescents, Pediatric clinics of North America, Vol. 58, Issue 1, Feb; www.sciencedaily.org

Kreuger, L. and J. Stretch (2003), Identifying and helping long term child and adolescent disaster victims: Model and method, Journal of Social Service Research 30(2): 93-108.

Kulatunga, U.(2011), Project management of disaster reconstruction. In: Amaratunga D, Haigh R, editors. Post-disaster reconstruction of the built environment: rebuilding for resilience. Chichester: Wiley- Blackwell; pp. 133-50.

Kumaraguru, A. K. Jayakumar, J. Jerald Wilson and C. M. Ramakritinan (2005), Impact of the tsunami of 26 December 2004 on the coral reef environment of Gulf of Mannar and Palk Bay in the southeast coast of India, Current Science, Vol. 89, No. 10, 25 November.

L. LeDe, J.C.Gaillard, and W.Friesen (2013), Remittances and disaster: A Review, International Journal of Disaster Risk Reduction, No. 4.

La Greca, A .M., Vernberg, E. M. Silverman, W. K., Vogel, A. L., and Prinstein, M. J. (1994). Helping children prepare for and cope with natural disasters: A manual for professionals working with elementary age children. Department of Psychology, University of Miami.

Lakshmi Vijayakumar; G. K. Kannan; B. Ganesh Kumar; P. Devarajan (2006), Do all children need intervention after exposure to tsunami International Review of Psychiatry, Volume 18, Issue 6, , pp. 559-562.

Lakshmi Vijaykumar; R. Thara; Sujit John; Shanti Chellappa (2006), Psycho-social interventions after tsunami in Tamil Nadu, India International Review of Psychiatry, Volume 18, Issue 3, pp. 225-231.

Lam, JN, Steketee GS., (2001), Reducing obsessions and compulsions through behaviour therapy, *Psycho-anal Inquiry.* ; 21: 157-182.

Landreth, G. L. (2002), Play therapy: The art relationship (IIed) New York: Brunner-Routledge.

Laor, N., L. Wolmer, Mayes, A. Golomb, R. Weizman, D. Silverberg, D.J. (2003), Facing war, terrorism, and disaster: Toward a child-oriented comprehensive emergency care system, Child & Adolescent Psychiatric Clinics of North America 12(2): 343-361.

Laptook, RS, Klein DN, Dougherty LR., (2006), Ten-year stability of depressive personality disorder in depressed outpatients, *Am J Psychiatry*. May;163(5): 865-71.

Lassa, J.A (2012), Post-disaster governance, complexity and network theory: evidence from Aceh, Indonesia after the Indian Ocean Tsunami 2004. Working paper1, IRGSC. Available from: /http://www.irgsc. org/pubs/wp.html

Lazarus P. J, Shane R. Jimerson, Santa Barbara and Stephen E. Brock (2003), Responding to Natural Disasters: Helping Children and Families: Information for School Crisis Teams, Retrieved from www.nasponline.org (National Association of School Psychologists) Feb 2013.

Lazarus, P. J., and Gillespie, B. (1996), Critical actions in the aftermath of natural disasters, The School Administrator, 53(2), 35-36.

Lazarus, P. J., and Jimerson, S. R., Brock, S. E. (2002), Natural disasters, In S. E. Brock, P. J. Lazarus, and S. R. Jimerson (Eds.), Best practices in school crisis prevention and intervention (pp. 435-450), Bethesda, MD: National Association of School Psychologists.

Lee, O. (1999), Science knowledge, world views, and information sources in social and cultural contexts: Making sense after a natural disaster, American Educational Research Journal 36(2): 187-219.

Leichsenring, F, Hiller W, Weissberg M, Leibing E (2006), Cognitive-behavioural therapy and psychodynamic psychotherapy: techniques, efficacy, and indications. *Am J Psychother.*; 60(3): 233-59.

Leichsenring, F, Leibing E. (2007), Psychodynamic psychotherapy: a systematic review of techniques, indications and empirical evidence. *Psychol Psychother*, Jun; 80: 217-28.

Lerner, D, Adler DA, Chang H, Lapitsky L, Hood MY, Perissinotto C. (2004), Unemployment, job retention, and productivity loss among employees with depression. *Psychiatr Serv*. Dec; 55(12): 1371-8.

Lieberman, A.F.; van Horn, P. (2004), Assessment and treatment of young children exposed to traumatic events, In: Osofsky, J.D., ed. Young Children and Trauma: Intervention and Treatment, New York: Guilford Press.

Lien, L, Tambs K, Oppedal B, Heyerdahl S, Bjertness E. (2005), Is relatively young age within a school year a risk factor for mental health problems and poor school performance? A population-based cross-sectional study of adolescents in Oslo, Norway, Institute of General Practice and Community Medicine, University of Oslo, BMC Public Health. Oct 5; 5: 102.

Linda, Evans Judy Oehler-Stinnett (2003), Children and Natural Disasters. The effect of a severe disaster on the mental health of adolescents: a controlled study, School Psychology International, Vol. 27, No. 1, 33-55 (2006) Aug 30; 362(9385): 691-6.

Lisitzin, E. (1974), Sea Level Changes, Elsevier Oceanographic Series, No. 8, p. 273 New York.

Lonigan, C. J., J. L. Anthony, *et. al.,* (1998), Diagnostic efficacy of posttraumatic symptoms in children exposed to disaster, Journal of Clinical Child Psychology 27(3): 255-267.

Lonigan, C. J., M. P. Shannon, *et. al.,* (1991), Children's reactions to a natural disaster: Symptom severity and degree of exposure, Advances in Behaviour Research and Therapy 13(3): 135-154.

Lonigan, C. J., M. P. Shannon, *et. al.,* (1994), Children exposed to disaster: II. Risk factors for the development of post-traumatic symptomatology, Journal of the American Academy of Child and Adolescent Psychiatry 33(1): 94-105.

Lonigan, C. J., Shannon, M. P., Finch, A. J. Jr., and Daugherty, T. K. (1991), Children's reaction to a natural disaster: Symptoms severity and degree of exposure, Advances in Behavioral Research and Therapy, 13, 135-154.

Lori, Peek (2008), Children and Disasters: Understanding Vulnerability, Developing Capacities, and Promoting Resilience, An Introduction, Children, Youth and Environments 18(1), 217-223.

Lori, Peek (2008), Children and Disasters: Understanding Vulnerability, Developing Capacities, and Promoting Resilience–An Introduction, Children, Youth and Environments 18(1): 1-29.

Lynne, Jones (2008), Responding to the needs of children in crisis International Review of Psychiatry, Volume 20, Issue 3, Pages 291-303.

Maia Szalavitz and Maiasz Time (2013), How Disasters and Trauma Can Affect Children's Empathy, Health and Family, Jan. 22.

Manuel Carballo; Bryan Heal; Gabriela Horbaty (2006), Impact of the tsunami on psycho-social health and well-being, International Review of Psychiatry, Volume 18, Issue-3.

Markowitz, JC, Bleiberg KL, Christos P, Levitan E (2006), Solving interpersonal problems correlates with symptom improvement in interpersonal psychotherapy: preliminary findings. *J Nerv Ment Dis*. Jan; 194(1): 15-20.

Markowitz, JC, Kocsis JH, Bleiberg KL, Christos PJ, Sacks M. (2005), A comparative trial of psychotherapy and pharmacotherapy for pure dysthymic patients. *J Affect Disord*. Dec; 89(1-3): 167-75.

Markowitz JC, Skodol AE, Petkova E, Xie H, Cheng J, Hellerstein DJ, (2005), Longitudinal comparison of depressive personality disorder and dysthymic disorder. *Compr Psychiatry*. Jul-Aug; 46(4): 239-45.

Mash and R. A. Barkley (Eds.), (2007), Child psychopathology (2nd ed., pp. 279-329). New York.

Masi, G, Millepiedi S, Mucci M, Pascale RR, Perugi G, Akiskal HS. (2003), Phenomenology and comorbidity of dysthymic disorder in 100 consecutively referred children and adolescents: beyond DSM-IV. *Can J Psychiatry*. Mar; 48(2): 99-105.

Mastellone, M. (1974), Aversion therapy: a new use for the old rubber band, *Journal of Behavior Therapy Experimental Psychiatry*. 5: 311-312.

Math, SB, Girimaji, Satish Chandra; Benegal, Vivek; Kumar, G. S. Uday; Hamza, Ameer; Nagaraja, D.(2006), Tsunami: Psycho-social aspects of Andaman and Nicobar islands, Assessments and intervention in the early phase, Information Healthcare Vol. 18, No.7, pp. 233-239.

Math, SB, Tandon S, Girimaji SC, Benegal V, Kumar U, Hamza A,(2008), Psychological impact of the tsunami on children and adolescents from the Andaman and Nicobar islands. Prime Care Companion, Journal of Clinical Psychiatry; 10: 31-37.

Mathur, S. M., (1998), Physical Geology of India, National Book Trust of India, New Delhi.

McCullough, JP Jr, Klein DN, Borian FE, Howland RH, Riso LP, Keller MB, (2003), Group comparisons of DSM-IV subtypes of chronic depression: validity of the distinctions, part 2. *Journal of Abnormal Psychology,* Nov; 112(4): 614-22.

McDermott, B.M., E.M. Lee, *et. al.,* (2005), Post traumatic Stress Disorder and General Psychopathology in Children and Adolescents Following a Wildfire Disaster, Canadian Journal of Psychiatry 50(3): 137-143.

McDougall, D (2005), Trauma of quake's shattered children, The Observer, http://www.guardian.co.uk/environment/2005/oct/23/naturaldisasters.kashmir.

McEntire, D. McDermott, B. M. C. and L. J. Palmer (1999), Post-disaster service provision following proactive identification of children with emotional distress and depression, Australian and New Zealand Journal of Psychiatry 33(6): 855-863.

McFarlane, AC (1987), Post-traumatic phenomena in a longitudinal study of children following a natural disaster, Journal of American Academy for Child Adolescent Psychiatry 26: 764-769.

McFarlane, A. C. (1987), Family functioning and overprotection following a natural disaster: The longitudinal effects of post-traumatic morbidity, Australian and New Zealand Journal of Psychiatry 21(2): 210-218.

McFarlane, A. C. (1987), Posttraumatic phenomena in a longitudinal study of children following a natural disaster, Jl of the American Academy of Child and Adolescent Psychiatry 26(5): 764-769.

McFarlane, AC., SK. Policansky, Irwin, CP., (1987), A longitudinal study of the psychological morbidity in children due to a natural disaster, Psychological Medicine 17(3): 727-738.

McIvor, David; Paton, Douglas, (2007), Preparing for natural hazards: normative and attitudinal influences, Disaster Prevention and Management: An International Journal, Volume 16, Number 1, pp. 79-88(10) Publisher: Emerald Group Publishing Limited.

Meyer, V (1966), Modification of expectations in cases with obsessional rituals, *Behavior Research Therapy,* 4:273-280.

Michael, E. (2006), Wells Psychotherapy for families in the aftermath of a disaster, Journal of Clinical Psychology, Volume 62, Issue 8, pp. 1017-1027, August.

Mitchell, G. Weiss, Benedetto Saraceno, Shekhar Saxena and Mark van Ommeren, (2001), Mental Health in the Aftermath of Disasters: Consensus and Controversy, published by WHO, Geneva, Switzerland.

Mitchell, J. T., and Everly, G. S. (1996), Critical incident stress debriefing: An operations manual for the prevention of traumatic stress among emergency services and disaster personnel (2nd ed), www.kellybear.com

Mowrer, OH. (1939), Stimulus response theory of anxiety, *Psychol Rev*. 46:553-565.

Mowrer, OH. (1960), *Learning Theory and the Symbolic Processes*, New York, NY: Wiley.

Murphy, JA, Byrne GJ. (2012), Prevalence and correlates of the proposed DSM-5 diagnosis of Chronic Depressive Disorder, *J Affect Disord,* Feb 29.

Murty, T. S., A. Bapat and Vinayak Prasad (1999), Tsunamis on the coastlines of India, Science of Tsunami Hazards, 17 (3), 167-172.

Murty, T.S., (1984), Storm surges-meteorological ocean tides, Bulletin of Fisheries Research Board of Canada, Ottawa.

Murty,T.S., Bapat and Vinayak Prasad (1999), Tsunamis on the coastlines of India, Science of Tsunami Hazards, 17 (3), 167-172.

Myron, L. Belfer (2006),Caring for children and adolescents in the aftermath of natural disasters International Review of Psychiatry, Volume 18, Issue 6.

National Institute for Health and Clinical Excellence (NICE), (2006), Obsessive-compulsive disorder: core interventions in the treatment of obsessive-compulsive disorder and body dysmorphic disorder. The British Psychological Society and The Royal College of Psychiatrists. Available at: www.nice.org.uk

National Institute of Mental Health, (2000), Helping children and adolescents cope with disasters: http://www.nimh.nih.gov

National Research Council (2006), Facing Hazards and Disasters: Understanding Human Dimensions. Committee on Disaster Reduction in the Social Sciences: Future Challenges and Opportunities, National Academy Press, Washington D.C.

Natural Disasters, (2013), Be Informed, Dec 18.

Nawanant Piyavhatkul, Srivieng Pairojkul, Chanyut Suphakunpinyo (2008), Psychiatric Disorders in Tsunami-Affected Children in Ranong Province, Thailand Medical Principles & Practice 17: 290-295.

NDMA (2012), Report, (www.ndma.gov.in)

Negash, A, Alem A, Kebede D, Deyessa N, Shibre T, Kullgren G (2005), Prevalence and clinical characteristics of bipolar disorder in Butajira, Ethiopia: A community-based study. Journal of Affective Disorders 87, 193-201.

Negash, A, Chotai J, Alem A, Kebede D, Shibre T, Kullgren G (2009), Burden of care of bipolar disorder: Perception of caregiver relatives in rural Ethiopia.

Negash, A, Kebede D, Alem A, Melaku Z, Deyessa N, Shibire T, Fekadu A, Fekadu D, Jacobsson L, Kullgren G (2004), Neurological soft signs in bipolar I disorder patients. Journal of Affective Disorders 80, 221-230.

Newcomb, K.R. and McCann, W.R (1987), Seismic history and tectonics of the Sunda Arc, JGR, 92 (B1), 421-439.

Newman, M. (2004), Helping children cope with disasters and terrorism, Journal of Child Psychology and Psychiatry 45(1): 172.

NICE (National Institute for Clinical Excellence). (2005), Posttraumatic stress disorder (PTSD): The management of PTSD in adults and children in primary and secondary care. NICE Clinical Guideline http://www.nice.org.uk/nicemedia/ pdf/ CG026NICEguideline.pdf

Niculescu, AB, Akiskal HS (2001), Proposed endophenotypes of dysthymia: evolutionary, clinical and pharmacogenomic considerations, *Mol Psychiatry*. Jul; 6(4): 363-6.

Nikapota, Anula (2006), After the tsunami: A story from Sri Lanka, Information Healthcare Volume 18, Number pp. 275-279(5).

Nilamadhab Kar (2009), Psychological impact of disasters on children: review of assessment and interventions, World Journal of Pediatrics 5(1): 5-11.

NIMHANS, (2005), Psycho-social manual for children (www.nimhans.org)

NIMHANS, (2007), Handbook of Psychiatric Social Work (www.nimhans.org)

Nolte, IM, Martin EC, Boenigk S (2012), Cross-sectoral coordination of disaster relief. Public Management Review 14: 707-30.

Olfson, M, Liu SM, Grant BF, Blanco C. (2012), Influence of comorbid mental disorders on time to seeking treatment for major depressive disorder. *Med Care*. Mar; 50(3): 227-32.

Ortiz, M., and Bilham, R. (2003), Source Area and Rupture Parameters of the 31 December 1881, Car Nicobar Earthquake estimated from tsunamis recorded in the Bay of Bengal, J. Geophys. Res- Solid Earth, 108(4), ESE 11, 1-16.

Oxfam International, (2009), Collaboration in crises: lessons in community participation from the Oxfam International tsunami research program, Oxfam.

Parker, D. and Tapsell, S. *et al.,* (2009), Relations between different types of social and economic vulnerability, Final draft report submitted to EU project 'Enhancing resilience of communities and territories facing natural and na-tech hazards' (ENSURE).

Pendse, C. G. (1945), The Mekran earthquake of the 28th November 1945, India Metrological Department, Scientific Notes, 10, 141-145.

Pfefferbaum, B. (1998), Caring for children affected by disaster, Child and Adolescent Psychiatric Clinics of North America 7(3): 579-597.

Portes, A,Landolt P. (1996), The downside of Social Capital. The American Prospect; 26: 18-21.

Prasetiyawan; Eka Viora; Albert Maramis; Budi Anna Keliat (2006), Mental health model of care programmes after the tsunami in Aceh, Indonesia International Review of Psychiatry, Volume 18, Issue 6, Pages 559-562.

Prinstein, M. J., A. M. La Greca, Vernberg, E.M., and Silverman, W.K (1996), Children's coping assistance: How parents, teachers, and friends help children cope after a natural disaster, Journal of Clinical Child Psychology 25(4): 463-475.

Priya, R., and G. Kanaga (2013), A Study on Status of Tsunami Affected Children's in Nagapattinam District, International Journal of Scientific and Research Publications, Volume 3, Issue 6, June.

Putnam, R. (2000), Bowling Alone: The Collapse and Revival of American Community. New York: Simon & Schuster.

Putnam, RD, Leonardi R, Nanetti RY,Raffaella Y (1993), Making Democracy Work: Civic Traditions in Modern Italy. Princeton: Princeton University Press.

Pynoos, RS, Goenjian A, Tashjian M, Karakashian M, Manjikian R, Manoukian G, (1993), Post-traumatic stress reactions in children after the 1988 Armenian earthquake. British Journal of Psychiatry, 163: 239-247.

Rachman, S, Hodgson R, Marks IM. (1971), The treatment of chronic obsessive-compulsive neurosis. *Behavior Research Therapy,* 9:237-247.

Rachman, S, Wilson GT. (1980), *Effects of Psychological Therapy*. London, England: Pergamon.

Rao, K (2006), Psycho-social support in disaster-affected communities, International Review of Psychiatry, Vol. 18, No. 6, pp. 501-505, Inform a world Database.

Rastogi, B. K. and R. K. Jaiswal. (2006), A Catalogue of Tsunamis in the Indian Ocean, India Science of Tsunami Hazards, Vol. 25, No. 3, p. 134.

Reijneveld SA, Crone MR, Verhulst FC, Verloove-Vanhorick SP, (2003), The effect of a severe disaster on the mental health of adolescents: a controlled study, Lancet. Aug 30; 362: 691-695.

Reijneveld, SA., MR. Crone, Verhulst FC, Verloove-Vanhorick SP (2003), The effect of a severe disaster on the mental health of adolescents: A controlled study, Lancet 362(9385): 691-696.

Renn, O, Schweizer PJ. (2009), Inclusive risk governance: concepts and application to environmental policy making. Environmental Policy and Governance; 19: 174-85.

Renn, O, (2008), Risk governance: coping with uncertainty in a complex world, London and Sterling: Earthscan.

Report of the Psycho-social Support Programme in tsunami-affected populations in India (2006), Information Healthcare Vol.18, No. 10, pp. 299-308.

Richard Eiser. J, Ann Bostrom, Ian Burton, David M .Johnston, John Mc Clure, Douglas Paton, Joopvander Pligt, MathewP.White (2012), Risk interpretation and action: A conceptual framework for responses to natural hazards, International Journal of Disaster Risk Reduction, Vol. 1, No. 5-16 June.

Richard Williams (2007), The psycho-social consequences for children of mass violence, terrorism and disasters International Review of Psychiatry, Volume 19, Issue 3, pp. 263-277.

Riolo, SA, Nguyen TA, Greden JF, King CA. (2005), Prevalence of depression by race/ethnicity: findings from the National Health and Nutrition Examination Survey III. *Am J Public Health*. Jun; 95(6): 998-1000.

Rohan, KJ, Lindsey KT, Roecklein KA, Lacy TJ. (2004), Cognitive-behavioural therapy, light therapy and their combination in treating seasonal affective disorder, Journal of Affective Disorders, 80: 273-283.

Roper, G, Rachman S. (1976), Obsessional-compulsive checking: experimental replication and development. *Behavior Research Therapy,* 14:25-32.

Rosati, Michael (2006), Effectively addressing the mid- and long-term needs of young people affected by the tsunami in Aceh:On-site assessment Inform. Healthcare Vol. 18, pp. 271-273(3).

Rotberg, B, Schoen G, Zalsman G. (2008), Anxiety disorders in children and adolescents Geha Mental Health Center, Petah Tikva. Harefuah. Jul; 147(7):628-33, 661, and 660.

Rush, AJ, Kraemer HC, Sackeim HA, (2006), Report by the ACNP Task Force on response and remission in major depressive disorder. *Neuropsychopharmacology*. Sep; 31(9): 1841-53.

Rush, AJ, Trivedi MH, Wisniewski SR, Nierenberg AA, Stewart JW, Warden D, (2006), Acute and longer-term outcomes in depressed outpatients requiring one or several treatment steps:. *American Journal of Psychiatry*, Nov; 163(11): 1905-17.

Rutter, M. (1987), Continuities and discontinuities from infancy, In: Osofsky JD, eds. Handbook of infant development, 2nd ed. New York: Wiley, 1256-1296.

Ryder AG, Schuller DR, Bagby RM. (2006), Depressive personality and dysthymia: evaluating symptom and syndrome overlap. *J Affect Disord*. Apr; 91(2-3): 217-27.

Salkovskis, PM. (1985), Obsessional-compulsive problems: a cognitive-behavioural analysis, *Behavior Research Therapy,* 23:571-583.

SAMHSA (1999), Child and Adolescent Mental Health, Centre for Mental Health Services, Rockville, Maryland.

Sarah Bradshaw and Maureen Fordham (2013), Women, Girls and Disasters A review for DFID, Gender and Disaster Network www.gdnonline.org Retrieved in August 2012.

Saxena, Shekhar; van Ommeren, Mark; Saraceno, Benedetto (2006), Mental health assistance to populations affected by disasters: WHO role Information health care, pp. 199-204(6).

Saylor, C. F., and C. C. Swenson, (1992), Hurricane Hugo blows down the broccoli: Preschoolers' post-disaster play and adjustment, Child Psychiatry & Human Development 22(3): 139-149.

Science of Tsunami Hazards (2006), Vol. 25, No. 3, p. 128.

Sekar, K, Biswas, S. Jayakumar, Bhadra S. Kumar (2005), Tsunami Disaster-psycho-social care for children Manual 3, NIMHANS.

Sekar, K, (2006), Psycho-social support in Tsunami Disaster: NIMHANS Responses. Disaster and development 1(1):141-154.

Shankman, SA, Klein DN. (2002), The impact of comorbid anxiety disorders on the course of dysthymic disorder: a 5-year prospective longitudinal study. *J Affect Disord*. Jul; 70(2): 211-7.

Shannon, MP, Lonigan CJ, Finch AJ Jr, Taylor CM.(1994), Children exposed to disaster: I. Epidemiology of post-traumatic symptoms and symptom profiles, Medical University of South Carolina, Charleston, J Am Acad Child Adolescent Psychiatry. Jan; 33(1): 80-93.

Shaw, R, Goda, K, (2004), From Disaster to Sustainable Civil Society: The Kobe Experience, Disasters 28(1): 16-40.

Shibre, T, Kebede D, Alem A, Negash A, Kibreab S, Fekadu A, Fekadu D, Jacobsson L, Kullgren G (2002), An evaluation of two screening methods to identify cases with schizophrenia and affective disorders in a community survey in rural Ethiopia, International Journal of Social Psychiatry 48(3), 200-208.

Shooshtary, MH, Panaghi L, Moghadam JA (2008), Outcome of cognitive behavioural therapy in adolescents after natural disaster. Journal of Adolescent Health 42: 466-472.

Showalter, E. (1985), The Female Malady: Women, Madness and English Culture, 1830–1980, New York: Penguin Books.

Silva, RR, Cloitre M, Davis L, Levitt J, Gomez S, Ngai I, *et. al.,* (2003), Early intervention with traumatized children. Psychiatric Quarterly, 74: 333-347.

Simpson, HB, Foa EB, Liebowitz, MR, (2008), Randomized, controlled trial of cognitive-behavioural therapy for augmenting pharmacotherapy in obsessive-compulsive disorder, *Am J Psychiatry*, 165: 621-630.

Smith, G, Wenger D (2007), Sustainable disaster recovery: operationalizing and existing agenda. In: Rodriguez H, Quarentelli EL, Dynes R, editors. Handbook of disaster research, New York: Springer; p. 234-57.

Smith, E.M., North, C.S. (1993), Posttraumatic stress disorder in natural disasters and technological accidents. In: Wilson, J.P., Raphael, B., eds. International Handbook of Traumatic Stress Syndromes. (pp. 405-419). NY: Plenum Press.

Somasundaram, DJ, van de Put WA (2006), Management of trauma in special populations after a disaster, Journal of Clinical Psychiatry 67 Suppl 2: 64-73.

Somchai Chakrabhand; Benjaporn Panyayong; Pattama Sirivech (2006), Mental health and psycho-social support after the tsunami in Thailand: International Review of Psychiatry, Vol. 18, No. 6 December, pp 599-605.

Souza, Renato R, Bernatsky, Sasha S, Reyes, Rosalie R, de Jong, Kaz K (2007), Mental health status of vulnerable tsunami-affected communities: a survey in Aceh Province, Indonesia. Published by find-health- articles.com, 30 May.

Stephenson Jr. M (2005), Making humanitarian relief networks more effective: operational coordination, trust and sense making. Disasters; 29:337-50.

Stevens, S and Slone, L (2008), Tsunami and mental health: What can we expect?, National Centre for PTSD, http://www.ncptsd.va.gov/ncmain/ncdocs/fact_shts/fs_ tsunami_mental_health.

Stubenbort, K., G.R. Donnelly and Cohen, J. A. (2001), Cognitive-behavioural group therapy for bereaved adults and children following an air disaster, Group Dynamics 5(4): 261-276.

Sugar, M. (1988), A preschooler in a disaster, American Jl of Psychotherapy 42(4): 619-629.

Sugar, M. (1989), Children in a disaster: An overview, Child Psychiatry and Human Development19 (3): 163-179.

Suresh, BM, Shweta Tandon, Satish Chandra Girimaji, Vivek Benegal, Uday Kumar, G.S., Ameer Hamza, Kavita Jangam, and D. Nagaraja (2008), Psychological Impact of the Tsunami on Children and Adolescents from the Andaman and Nicobar Islands Prime Care Companion Journal of Clinical Psychiatry, 10(1): 31-37.

Suresh, BM; Satish Chandra Girimaji; Vivek Benegal; G. S. Uday Kumar; Ameer Hamza; D. Nagaraja (2006), Tsunami: Psycho-social aspects of Andaman and Nicobar islands. Assessments and intervention in the early phase Int. Review of Psychiatry, Volume 18, Issue 3, pp. 233-239.

Susan, M. Becker, PhD, MPH (2007), Psycho-social Care for Adult and Child Survivors the Tsunami Disaster in India and published in Traumatology, Vol. 13, No. 3, 11-20 (2007).

Swenson, C. C., and C. F. Saylor, (1996), Impact of a natural disaster on preschool children: Adjustment 14 months after a hurricane, American Journal of Orthopsychiatry 66(1): 122-130.

Szrete, S, Woolcock M. (2004), Health by Association? Social Capital, Social Theory and the Political Economy of Public Health, International Journal of Epidemiology; 33(4): 650-67.

Tapsell, S; McCarthy, S; Faulkner, H and Alexander, M (2010): Social Vulnerability and Natural Hazards. CapHaz-Net WP4 Report, Flood Hazard Research Centre – FHRC, Middlesex University, London.

Thienkrua, Warunee, Lopescardozo Barbara somchaihakkrab Andguadamuz Thomas, E. Pengjuntr Wachira, Tipiwatanaskul Prawate and M. Akornsatian Suchada; Ekassawin Supara, Panyayong Benjaporn Varangrat Anchalee, Tappero Jordan Schreiber Merritt, Van Griensven Frits, (2006), Thailand Post-Tsunami Mental Health Study Group, THAILANDE, Symptoms of posttraumatic stress disorder and depression among children in tsunami-affected areas in southern Thailand in JAMA Vol. 296, No. 5, pp. 549-559.

Tierney, K, Oliver-Smith A (2012), Social dimensions of disaster recovery. International Journal of Mass Emergencies and Disasters; 30: 123-46.

Tierney, K. (2012), Disaster governance: social, political, and economic dimensions, The Annual Review of Environment and Resources; 37: 341-63.

Trad, PV and Raine, MJ (1995), The little girl who wouldn't walk: Exploring the narratives of preschoolers through previewing, Journal of Psychotherapy Practice and Research, Vol. 4, pp. 224-236.

U.S. Department of Health and Human Services, Children's Bureau, (1995), Coping with Disasters: A Guide for Child Welfare Agencies, Washington, DC.

Udwin, O., S. Boyle, *et. al.,* (2000), Risk factors for long-term psychological effects of a disaster experienced in adolescence: Predictors of Post Traumatic Stress Disorder, Journal of Child Psychology and Psychiatry 41(8): 969-979.

UNDP (2001), From relief to recovery, UNDP, New York.

UNDP (2011), Post-disaster recovery guidelines UNDP, New York.

UNICEF (2005), Children in tsunami affected countries, Press Centre, http://www.unicef.org/

Uphoff, N. (2000), Understanding Social Capital: Learning from the Analysis and Experience of USA: Wiley.

Ussher, J. (1992), Women's Madness: Misogyny or Mental Illness, University of Mass. Press.

Valderhaug, L, Götestam P. (2007), An open clinical trial of cognitive-behaviour therapy in children and adolescents with obsessive-compulsive disorder administered in regular outpatient clinics. *Behavior Research Therapy,* 45: 577-589.

Van Asselt, M, Renn O. (2011), Risk governance. Journal of Risk Research, 14: 431-49.

Van der Veen, A., Dopheide, E., Parker, D., Tapsell, S., Handmer, J., Gregg, C., Bonadonna, C., Van Griensven F, Chakkraband ML, Thienkrua W *et. al.,* (2006), Mental health problems among adults in tsunami-affected areas in southern Thailand. JAMA; 296: 537-548.

Vernberg, E.M., Vogel, J.M. (1993), Psychological response of children to natural and human made disasters: II, Interventions with children after disasters. Journal of Clinical Child Psychology 22(4): 485-498.

Vijayakumar, L, Kannan GK, Ganesh Kumar B, Devarajan P (2006), Do all children need intervention after exposure to tsunami? International Review of Psychiatry; 18: 515-522.

Vijayakumar, L, Kannan, GK & Daniel, SK (2006), Mental health status in children exposed to tsunami, International Review of Psychiatry, Vol. 18, No. 6, pp. 507-513.

Vijayakumar, L; Thara R; John Sujit; Chellappa Shant; (2006), Psycho-social intervention after Tsunami in Tamil Nadu, India, Information Healthcare, Vol. 18, No. 3, pp. 225-231.

Visanuyothin, Taweesin; Chakrabhand, Somchai; Bhugra, Dinesh (2006), Tsunami and mental health in Thailand, Information, Healthcare Vol. 18, No. 3, pp. 271-273.

Vogel, PA, Stiles TC, Gotestam KG. (2004), Adding cognitive therapy elements to exposure therapy for obsessive compulsive disorder, *Behavior Cognitive Psychotherapy*; 32: 275-290

Vogel, J.M., Vernberg, E.M. (1993), Psychological response of children to natural and humanmade disasters: I. Children's psychological responses to disasters. Journal of Clinical Child Psychology 22(4): 464-484.

Weichselgartner, J. (2001), Disaster mitigation: the concept of vulnerability revisited, Disaster Prevention and Management, Vol. 10 (2): 85-94.

WHO (2002), Gender and health in disasters, Retrieved on 02-03-2013 from www.who.int/gender/other_health/en/genderdisasters.pdf

Wisner, B., Blaikie, P.M., Cannon, T., Davis, I. (2004), At Risk. Natural Hazards, People's Vulnerability and Disasters, Routledge.

Wolmer, L., N. Laor, Ceyda D., Joanna Siev, and Yanki Y., (2003), School reactivation programs after disaster: Could teachers serve as clinical mediators?, Child & Adolescent Psychiatric Clinics of North America 12(2): 363-381.

Wolpe, J (1969), *The Practice of Behavior Therapy*, Ist Edition, New York, NY: Pergamon Press.

Wood, J.J., McLeod, B.D., Sigman, M., Hwang,W. and Chu, B.C. (2003). Parenting and childhood anxiety: Theory, empirical findings, and future directions. Journal of Child Psychology and Psychiatry, 44, 134-151.

Wooding, S, Raphael B (2004); Psychological impact of disasters and terrorism on Children and adolescents: Experiences from Australia, Prehosp Disast Med; 19(1): 10-20.

Woolcock, M, Narayan D. (2000), Social Capital: Implications for Development Theory, Research, and Policy. The WOTU Bank Research Observer; 15(2): 225-49.

Woolcock, M. (2002), Social Capital in Theory and Practice: Reducing Poverty by Building Partnerships between States, Markets and Civil Society, UNESCO; 20-44.

Yarnal, B. (2007), Vulnerability and all that jazz: Assessing vulnerability in New Orleans after Hurricane Katrina, Technology in Society. 29. 249-255.

Yin Yin New (2005), Children and the Tsunami, A Year On, A Draft UNICEF Summary of What Worked, November.

Young, M. A. (1997), The community crisis response team training manual (2nd ed.). Washington, DC: National Organisation for Victim Assistance.

Yule, W, Williams, R and Joseph, S (1999), Post-traumatic stress disorders in adults, in W Yule (ed.), Post-traumatic stress disorders: Concept and therapy, John Wiley & Sons, Chichester.

Yule, W, Bolton D, Udwin O, Boyle S, O'Ryan D, Nurrish J (2000), The long-term psychological effects of a disaster experienced in adolescence, The incidence and course of PTSD, Journal of Child Psychology & Psychiatry 41(4): 503-511.

Yule, William (2006), Theory, Training and timing: Psycho-social interventions in Complex emergencies, Information Healthcare, Vol, 18, No. 6, pp. 259-264.

Zahran, Sammy, Lori Peek and Samuel Brody, D (2008), Youth Morality by forces of Nature, Forces of Nature, Children, Youth and Environments 18(1): 371-388. Retrieved (20-02-2014) from www.colorado.edu/journals/cy

Zenere, F. J., and Lazarus, P.J., (1999), Winds of terror, Children's responses to hurricane and tornado disasters, In A. S. Canter and S. A. Carroll (Eds.), Crisis prevention and response: A collection of NASP resources Bethesda, MD: National Association of School Psychologists, pp. 223-229.

Websites Visited

http://www.ingentaconnect.com/content/routledg/cirp

http:///wwwChildrensHealth.com

http://www.nctsnet.org/nccts/nav.do?pid=abt_ntwk

http://www.nctsnet.org/nctsn_assets/pdfs/parents_guidelines_talk_children_hurricanes.pdf

http://www.nctsnet.org/nctsn_assets/pdfs/reports/ParentGuidelines_SpanishVersion.pdf

http://www.nctsnet.org/nctsn_assets/pdfs/teachers_guidelines_talk_children_hurricanes.pdf

http://www.nctsnet.org/reports/InformationforParentsonChildhoodTraumaticGrief.pdf

http://www.nctsnet.org/nctsn_assets/pdfs/edu_materials/MediaTipsforParents.pdf

http://www.apahelpcenter.org/articles/article.php?id=69

http://www.apahelpcenter.org/articles/article.php?id=107

http://www.apahelpcenter.org/articles/article.php?id=109

http://www.nimh.nih.gov/publicat/violence.cfm

http://www.mentalhealth.samhsa.gov/cmhs/TraumaticEvents/tips.asp

http://www.bt.cdc.gov/mentalhealth/

http://www.imcworldwide.org/pdf/Mental_Health_Guidelines_Katrina_assistance.pdf

http://www.ncptsd.va.gov/topics/katrina.html

http://www.aacap.org/publications/factsfam/disaster.htm

http://www.nmha.org/reassurance/children.cfm

http://kidsaid.com/dougypage.html

http://www.childtrauma.org/CTAMATERIALS/katrina.asp

http://www.nea.org/crisis/images/crisisguide-b3.pdf

http://www.missingkids.com/missingkids/servlet/PageServlet?LanguageCountry=en_US

http://www.familylinks.icrc.org/katrina

http://www.firstgov.gov/Citizen/Topics/PublicSafety/Hurricane_Katrina_Recovery.

http://www.hunter.cuny.edu/socwork/nrcfcpp/disaster_relief.html

http://www.dhr.state.al.us/page.asp?pageid=750

http://www.dhr.state.al.us/page.asp?pageid=750

http://www.mdhs.state.ms.us/

http://www.dss.state.la.us/

http://www.dfps.state.tx.us/About/Releases_and_Newsletter

http://www.socialworktoday.com

http://www.psychologytoday.com

http://www. psychcentral.com

http://www.tn.gov.in/tsunami

http://www.freejournal.net

http://www. tsun.sscc.ru

http://www.iitk.ac.in

http://www.mapsofworld.com/Tsunami

http://www.bom.gov.au › Tsunami Warnings

http://www.wsspc.org/TsunamiCenter/Tsunami

http://www.tn.gov.in/tsunami

http://www.emdat.be

http://*www.ready.gov*

http://www.library.thinkquest.org/16132/frames.html

http://www.wikipedia.org/wiki/Man-made_hazard

http://www.iaea.org

Annexure - I

Impact of Tsunami as Perceived by the High School Students at Kanyakumari District–A Psycho-social Analysis

Mental Health Inventory

Sl. No.	*Mental Health Inventory*	*Yes*	*No*
1.	I am quite content the way I am now		
2.	I am not a good joker		
3.	My job is quite dull and boring		
4.	I am not good adjudging others		
5.	I prefer my habitual way of living		
6.	I am a victim of late		
7.	I am in the habit of disobeying meaningless rules		
8.	I experience a sense of well-being		
9.	I have no fear in doing a task which society criticized		
10.	Mine is a very happy family		
11.	I don't care much for the happiness of others, because most of them care not for mine		
12.	Feel loneliness		
13.	I cannot fully express my affections and genuine feelings		
14.	I try to win feelings of others		

(Contd...)

15.	I am afraid to mix with strangers		
16.	I am happy to have born on this earth in my family		
17.	I like myself		
18.	To my failure mostly other people were responsible		
19.	My weakness which are known to others do trouble me		
20.	I wish to be like him (her)		
21.	I am afraid that my decision may go wrong		
22.	I feel sorry for beggars and the handicapped		
23.	Ugliness and physical defects in others repels me		
24.	Most of the people are selfish and when possible they take advantage over you		
25.	Getting ahead in life is just a matter of luck and pull		
26.	To me life is over the same as before		
27.	I lead a king of life that is satisfying to me		
28.	A sense of fear about future bites me		
29.	I behave occasionally like children–crying, laughing		
30.	I am afraid of people's criticism		
31.	My life is meaningful		
32.	I am habitually dependent on other for idea and decisions		
33.	I am good worker, in my little sphere		
34.	I am well-rounded, square in behaviour and expression		
35.	As a mature individual I withhold my emotions from free expression		
36.	I feel that the most important thing in life is money		
37.	I in the final state trust my own decisions than others		
38.	To me, my small achievement is greater than my gather's glory		
39.	I am so afraid that how I am going to manage all my family problem		
40.	While introducing myself I emphasize parents occupation and status		
41.	I feel that most people are so unreasonable, it is hard to talk to them		
42.	I have never completely revealed about myself to another		

(Contd...)

43.	I have no deep attachment with anyone		
44.	I try to shape my own future and I have faith in that		
45.	I do not act in ways just to please others		
46.	I rarely value others peoples Arguments when it contradicts mine.		
47.	I feel helpless		
48.	In haste I decide and regret later		
49.	New things about life rarely interest me		
50.	To me mere material wealth is not enough for a full life		
51.	I do my work just mechanically		
52.	It is my habit to think about the past very frequently		
53.	I wish to have a comfortable living free of all problems		
54.	I have few talents to use		
55.	I think that other people know more free of all problems		
56.	I think that other people know more about me than myself		
57.	There are some people I don't like		
58.	I am adventurous, testing limits		
59.	There is nothing real in this life		
60.	If I were to be bore again I would like to be the same person.		

Study Habit Inventory

Sl. No.	*Study Habit*	*Yes*	*No*
1.	I frame my own time- table study at home		
2.	I work according to my time-table		
3.	I study regularly in my study–room		
4.	I prepare almost all my subjects before going to school and read them again at home, whatever is done in the class		
5.	I join tuition classes		
6.	I read at place where and get disturbed by radio, people's children's play, relatives, guests etc.		
7.	I cannot study well as I keep myself engaged in the domestic work		

(Contd...)

8.	I make note of important points during reading		
9.	I use dictionary to look up meaning of new words		
10.	I pay more attention to new words while studying		
11.	I take down detailed notes on what is being taught in the class room		
12.	The doubtful points which arise during reading are depend to the subjects teacher of clarity		
13.	I try to solve at once, the difficulties met with while reading		
14.	I miss important points while taking notes in the class room		
15.	I read annotations (guides) rather than text books		
16.	I underline the important points in my text books while reading		
17.	I pay more attention to the subjects I find difficult		
18.	I devote more time to study subjects in which I am weak		
19.	I give priority to studying the difficulty subjects		
20.	I read the same subject for a long time		
21.	I study only that subject I am interested in and leave out the subject which I find uninteresting		
22.	I study with concentration		
23.	I feel I don't study at all		
24.	My mind goes astray when I read		
25.	I understand that I read but don't remember it		
26.	In examination I think of the answers of the questions before		
27.	I get nervous at the time of examination		
28.	I read till late at night at the time of examination		
29.	I read class-notes at the time of examination		
30.	I do not prepare questions occurred (asked) at previous examination thinking that they would not be set again		
31.	I do not study regularly for I get important questions and suggestions at the time of examination		
32.	I memorize definitions, formulas, etc., after understanding them		

(Contd...)

33.	I discuss the subjects read, with my friends		
34.	I read while reclining on a bed		
35.	I read aloud (loudly)		
36.	I try to compare things learnt in one subject with those in another		
37.	I ruminate over all things I read		
38.	Before I start reading new lessons I briefly revise the lesson read		
39.	After reading one paragraph, I at once review it mentally		
40.	I spent my leisure time at school in reading		
41.	I use books from the library		
42.	I read newspapers and other books too		
43.	I participate in the class room discussion		
44.	I answer the question asked by the teacher while teaching		
45.	I cannot progress in my studies due to my dislikes for certain teachers and subjects		

Study Involvement Inventory

Sl. No.	*Study Involvement*	*Strongly Agree*	*Moderately Agree*	*Not at All Agree*
1.	This school has a fine tradition of public service			
2.	I feel this school is dong an important job in showing how school should be managed			
3.	I get the "what is the use" feeling when I do not succeed in my studies			
4.	Most things in life are more important than my studies.			
5.	My teachers correct and check my work			
6.	I feel close to my classmates			
7.	I feel a sense of pride in studying in this school			
8.	Generally speaking my stay in this school has not been satisfactory			
9.	I am very clear about my future career			

(Contd...)

10.	The major satisfaction in my life comes from my studies			
11.	The teachers compliment when my work is outstanding			
12.	My class mates help each other when we need it			
13.	I would advice any youngest to join this school			
14.	The record of this school is an example of what a good school can achieve			
15.	I am confident of my success in my studies			
16.	I have other activities more important than my studies			
17.	If I make any mistakes I am corrected			
18.	I am satisfied with my relationship with my fellow students			
19.	If I had my life to live over again I would still choose to study in this school			
20.	If I hear (or lead) any criticism about my school. I would get very angry.			
21.	When I fall in some study, I stop making future efforts			
22.	To me my studies are only part of who I am			
23.	This school has a fine set of teachers			
24.	I feel that I am unfit for studies			
25.	I used to care about my studies, but now other things are more important to me.			

Taylor's Manifest Anxiety Scale

In this scale, most of these are check lists of the things about which adults are anxious. The Taylor's Manifest scale is currently the most widely used tool to assess anxiety of adults. The subjects answer "TRUE" or "FALSE" to the item that are given. There are 27 such items scored in terms of the numbers answered in the level items. If response coincides with the key, a score of one is given and otherwise nil score. Then the total score is calculated.

Sl. No.	*Description*	*True*	*False*
1.	I am often sick to my stomach		
2.	I am about nervous as other people		
3.	I work under a great deal of strain		
4.	I blush as often as others		
5.	I have diarrhea (the rams) once a month or more		
6.	I worry quite a bit over possible troubles		
7.	When embarrassed I often break out in a sweet which is very annoying		
8.	I do not often notice my heart pounds and I am seldom short of breath		
9.	Often my bowels do not move for several days to a time		
10.	At times I lost sleep over worry		
11.	My sleep is restless and disturbed		
12.	I often dream about things Idol not like to tell other people		
13.	My feelings are hurt easier than most people		
14.	I often find myself worrying about something		
15.	I wish I could be as happy as others		
16.	I feel anxious about some things or someone almost all of the time		
17.	At times I am so restless that I can't sit in a chair for very long time		
18.	I have often felt that I faced so many difficu-lties, I could not overcome them		
19.	At times, have been worried beyond reason about something that really did not matter, I do not have as many fears as my friends		
20.	I am more self conscious than most people		
21.	I am the kind of person who takes things hard		
22.	I am very nervous person		
23.	Life often a strain for me		

(Contd...)

24.	I am not at all confident of myself		
25.	At times, feel that I am going to crank up		
26.	I don't like to face a difficult or make an important decision		
27.	I am very confident of myself		

Depression Inventory

The inventory was first formulated in 1988 and consists of 21 categories of symptoms and attitudes towards depression each category' being a specific behaviour manifestation of depression. The statements are ranked according to the severity of the symptom any one in each alphabet.

A. (Sadness)

0 I do not feel sad
1 I feel blue or sad
2a I am blue or sad a the time and I cannot snap out of it
2b I feel that I won't ever get over my trouble
2 I am so sad or unhappy that I cannot stand it.

B. (Pessimist)

0 I am not particularly pessimistic or discouraged about the future
1 I feel discouraged about the future
2a I feel that I have nothing to take forward
2b I feel that I won't ever get over my trouble
3 I feel that the future is hopeless and that things can not improve.

C. (Sense of Failure)

0 I do not feel like a failure
1 I feel that f have failed more than the average person
2a I feel that I have accomplished very little
2b As I look back on my life all I can see is lot of failures
3 I feel I am a complete failure as a person.

D. (Dissatisfaction)

0 I am not particularly dissatisfied
1 I feel bored most of the time
2a I don't enjoy things the way I used to
2b I don't get satisfaction on the anything anymore
3 I am dissatisfied with everything.

E. (Guilt)

0 I don't feel particularly guilty
1 I feel bad or unworthy a good part of the time
2a I feel quite guilty
2b I feel bad or unworthy practically all the time now
3 I feel as though I am very bad or worthless.

F. (Expectation of Punishment)

0 I don't feel disappointed myself
1 I have a feeling that something bad may happen to me
2a I feel I am being punished or will be punished
2b I feel I deserve to be punished
2 I want to be punished.

G. (Self-Dislike)

0 I don't feel disappointed myself
1a I am disappointed in myself
1b I don't like myself
2 I am disgusted with myself
3 I hate myself.

H. (Self-Accusations)

0 I don't feel I am any worse than anybody else
1 I am critical of my faults
2 I blame myself for my faults
3 I blame myself for everything bad that happens.

I. (Suicidal Ideas)

0 I don't have any thoughts of harming myself
1 I have thoughts of harming myself but I would not carry them out
2 a I feel I would be better off dead-
2 b I feel my family would be better off if I were dead
3a I have definite plan-about committing-suicide
3 b I would kill myself if I could

J. (Crying)

0 I don't cry anymore than usual
1 I cry more now than I used to
2 I cry all the time I can't stop it

3 I used to be able to cry but now I can't cry at all even though I want to

K. (Irritability)

0 I am no more irritated now than I ever am
1 I get annoyed or irritated more easily than I used to
2 I feel irritated all the time
3 I don't get irritated at all at the things that used to irritate me

L. (Social Withdrawal)

0 I have not lost interest in other people
1 I am less interested in other people now than I used to be
2 I have lost most of my interest in other people and have little feelng for them
3 I have lost all my interest in other people and don't care about them at all.

M. (Indecisiveness)

0 I make decisions about as well as ever
1 I try to put off making decisions
2 I have great difficulty in making decisions
3 I can't make decisions at all any more

N. (Body Image Change)

0 I don't feel I look any worse than I used to
1 I am worried that I am looking old or unattractive
2 I worried that there are permanent changes which make me look unattractive.
3 I feel that I am ugly or repulsive looking.

O. (Work Retardation)

0 I can work about as well as before
1a It takes extra effort to get started and going with something
1b I don't work as well as I used to
1 I have to push myself very hard to do anything
2 I can't do any work at all

P. (Insomnia)

0 I can steep as well as usual
1 I wake up more tired in the morning than I used to

2 I wake up one-two hours earlier than usual and find it hard to get back to sleep

3 I wake up early every day and can't get more than five hours sleep

Q. (Fatigability)

0 I don't get any more tired than usual

1 I get tired more easily than I used to

2 I get tired from doing anything

3 I get too tired to do anything

R. (Anorexia)

0 My appetite is no worse than usual

1 My appetite is not as good as it used to be

2 My appetite is much worse now

3 I have no appetite at all any more

S. (Weight Loss)

0 I haven't lost much weight, if any, lately

1 I have lost more than five pounds

2 I have lost more than ten pounds

3 I have lost more than fifteen pounds

T. (Somatic Preoccupation)

0 I am no more concerned about my health than usual

1 I am concerned about aches and pains or upsets or constipation

2 I am so concerned with how I feel or what I feel that it is hard to think of much else

3 I am completely absorbed in what I feel

U. (Loss of Libido)

0 I have not noticed any recent changes in my interest to know about sex

1 I am less interested to know about sex that used to be

2 I am much less interested to know about sex now

3 I have lost interest to know about sex completely

Adjustment Inventory

Introduction

Below are some questions relating to how people feel and act in their day to day life? You are requested to go through them one by one and answer them with 'Yes' or 'No', as it applies to you. You are to indicate your answer by (1) mark. Please note that there is no right or wrong answer to these questions. The true answer is what you feel applies to you. Please answer all questions.

Sl. No.	*Statements*	*Yes*	*No*
1.	Do you have ups and downs in moods without apparent cause?		
2.	Do you get the feeling that you are not competent to do things you are asked to do?		
3.	Have you had any trouble with your heart, kidneys or lungs?		
4.	Have you had unpleasant disagreements with any person or persons with whom you live, over such matters as religion, sex, social and moral code or convention?		
5.	Do you make friends easily?		
6.	Do you frequently suffer from cold, cough, etc?		
7.	Do ideas run thorough your head so that you cannot sleep?		
8.	Are you often the subject of criticism at home?		
9.	Do you hesitate to meet on your own important and highly placed persons?		
10.	Do you frequently have headaches?		
11.	Do you worry over possible misfortunes?		
12.	Do persons with whom you live now understand and sympathize with you generally?		
13.	Do you have unpleasant arguments and disagreements with friends or outsiders fairly often?		
14.	Are you subject to asthma or any other breathing trouble?		
15.	Do you often experience conflicting moods of love and hate for members of your immediate family?		
16.	Do you have any hobbies to occupy your tune?		
17.	Do the actions of any of the members of your home make you irritated of feel depressed?		

(Contd...)

18.	Do you generally prefer to be alone rather than in the company of people?		
19.	Are you subjects to attacks of indigestion?		
20.	Do you think by the large, your life has been a purposeful one?		
21.	Do you think you have fewer friends than others?		
22.	Do you feel tired much of the time?		
23.	Have you frequently felt depressed because of the unkind things that others have said of you?		
24.	Have you been troubled by feelings of insecurity?		
25.	Do you often hesitate to speak out before a group?		
26.	Do you often feel fatigued when you get up in the morning?		
27.	Do things go wrong for no fault of yours?		
28.	Does lack of money tend to make your home life unhappy?		
29.	Are you easily moved to tears?		
30.	Are the matters, pertaining to your home that frequently worry you?		
31.	Have you fallen ill frequently in the last five years?		
32.	Do you often feel lonely even when you are in the midst of the people?		
33.	Are there quite a few things in your life of which you can feel proud of?		
34.	Do you feel that your friends have happier homes than you?		
35.	Do you find it easy to ask others for help?		
36.	Do you feel there is lack of love and affection among members of your person home?		
37.	Have you undergone a surgical operation?		
38.	Do you worry long over humiliating experiences?		
39.	Do you think you are a lonely and unwanted person?		
40.	Do you think you are much better than most of your age mates?		

Conti...

41.	Do you feel that many of your friends don't understand you?		
42.	Does the thought of a snake, earthquake or fire frighten you?		
43.	Have you achieved most of the things you wanted to achieve in your life?		
44.	Do you think people generally are unsympathetic?		
45.	Do you get discouraged easily?		
46.	Do you take on social responsibilities voluntarily?		
47.	Is the home where you now life often in a state of turmoil and dissension?		
48.	Does some particular thought keep coming to your mind to bother you?		
49.	Have you been troubled by the thought that you have been leading an unworthy and useless life?		
50.	Do your friends enjoy your company?		

Annexure - II

Disaster Mitigation Management Towards Child Welfare Services–Tamil Nadu Experience

Mission Statement

To provide immediate relief and long-term rehabilitation; to convert the traumatic challenge into an opportunity and create environment friendly and safe habitations; to provide livelihood options with specific focus on the empowerment of the vulnerable sections of the society especially women; to enhance the effectiveness of the community to face disasters in the future and to obtain sustainable and lasting outcomes by forging strong public private partnerships.

Strategic Intent

- Reconstruct damaged and vulnerable houses using disaster-resistant features.
- Undertake vulnerability-mapping to locate new habitations in safer locations.
- Create new sustainable livelihood options in harmony with environment.
- Form SHGs, especially for the weaker sections to empower them.
- Build capacity of coastal communities to cope more effectively with disasters Restore coastal ecology.
- Provide better physical infrastructure.
- Address psychological trauma and educational needs of children for an improved future.

Response of the Government of India

In view of the devastation and substantial damage caused to the state by the tsunami, the Government of Tamil Nadu (GoTN) sought the help of the Government of India (GOI) for relief, reconstruction and rehabilitation programmes valued at approximately Rs 4,800 crore along with 54,000 mt of foodgrain, through a memorandum in the Ist week of January 2005.

Besides offering the required assistance, the GOI also set up a Core Group Committee and an Inter-Ministerial Central Team, besides a Joint Assessment Mission with the participation of funding agencies such as the World Bank, Asian Development Bank, United Nations and Commonwealth Agencies, to facilitate assessment, development, implementation and monitoring of the immediate, short- and long-term programmes and to provide the necessary guidance/approvals.

The Central Government established a National Early Warning System for Tsunami and Storm Surges in the Indian Ocean at the Indian National Centre for Ocean Information Services (INCOIS), Hyderabad since September 2007. The Interim Tsunami Warning Centre was operational at INCOIS as early as July 2005. As a special gesture, Central Government exempted steel and cement for housing reconstruction from excise duty.

Budget Sanctioned for the Government Built Housing Projects

Districts	***Amount (Crore)***
Chennai	277.98
Cuddalore	6.594
Kancheepuram	11.823
Villupuram	9.45
Nagapattinam	16.485
Thoothukudi	6.2775
Total	**328.6095**

Source: Govt. of Tamil Nadu, 2008.

Psycho-social Support to Children

Govt. of Tamil Nadu and partners felt that people in the community could provide the best possible psycho-social support, as they were aware of social behaviour and practices. The UN team for Tsunami Recovery Support (UNFPA, UNICEF, UNODC and UNDP) led by the WHO India country office developed a community-based sustainable trauma care. The PSS programme was made possible through the active participation of various government departments, UN agencies, private sector, NGOs and other partners. UNODC supported the development of training strategy. Department of Social Welfare was designated as the nodal department for organising the programme.

The Department of Social Welfare took the lead in the programme along with the Departments of Education and Health and district-level institutions coordinated the activity. The preparatory process included extensive consultations and development of a strategy and schedule for training community-level workers (CLWs): identification of master trainers, selection of CLWs from the field and cascade training for 2813 CLWs in 11 districts, under the supervision of District Social Welfare Officers (DSWOs).

A substantial number of training materials and manuals were developed for various aspects of PSS. They are now available for wider dissemination. Among these are a facilitator's manual, handbooks for field workers, pamphlets, a manual for helping children and adolescents, a training manual for prevention and management of alcohol abuse.

Several NGOs and civil society groups were also trained by partner agencies. The trained CLWs were made responsible for 20 families (approximately 100 members) each. They interacted regularly with these families, provided psychosocial support in the form of lay counselling, assistance in social needs and referral to the health system for further care.

A cell with a psychologist, data manager and necessary infrastructure was established in the Directorate of Social Welfare, Chennai, to coordinate the programme. A cadre of trained CLWs, drawn from various sectors, has been made available. District authorities can draw on them for various social support programmes. 13,000 workers have been trained, 275,000 persons supported, 52,000 provided additional counselling and 120,000 children reached.

SCARF has introduced telemedicine as an option for providing expert consultation. There is a dearth of trained mental health professionals, and a wider use of telemedicine can provide expert opinion in disaster situations. So far, 200 patients have received care through telemedicine.

Children

Tsunami has orphaned 241 children and 1513 children lost one of their parents. Education was hampered by the tsunami for an estimated 269532 children. Tsunami had also sharply exposed the orphaned and abandoned children and children whose parents and guardians themselves were in a vulnerable situation, to the risks of child trafficking, child labour, child abuse, violence against children and child marriage.

Children also stood the chance of losing legal rights over land, assets, and property. Children orphaned and separated, children from damaged and destroyed houses and schools had very special needs in terms of psychological and emotional support, socio-economic protection and protection from trafficking and other risks and education. The special needs of children were identified and appropriate models for child support and protection were developed.

Care and Support

Both governmental and non-governmental agencies, made an effort to provide psycho-social care for children affected by the tsunami. Timely provision of such care contributed to reduction in trauma amongst children. UNICEF which was the lead agency working in the children sector involved the Directorate of Teacher Education, Research and Training (DTERT) and the Nehru Yuva Kendra (NYK) along with other partners. NIMHANS, Bangalore, VIMHANS, New Delhi, SCARF, SNEHA and TTRCRF, Chennai provided technical support.

UNFPA provided financial support for training of health workers and community-level workers through NYKs, with special focus on adolescents and youth. Both demand and supply side of psycho-social care was given attention. Frontline staff members of NGOs and social workers directly interacting with children were provided training and resource material on psycho-social care for children.

Interventions Towards Child Care and Support (Govt. of Tamil Nadu, 2008)

Intervention	***Impact***	***Agency and partners***
1,300 teachers and 1,300 youth volunteers were trained in psycho social care	Child-friendly techniques such as puppetry, play therapy, clay modelling and cultural expressions, along with one-on-one counselling, were used to draw out the children	UNICEF and partners
Around 2900 play kits to schools and youth clubs	Approximately 30,000 children benefited from these kits	
2,600 resource persons trained in the care of children and adolescents	Village-level play activities were held in over 250 villages in all the affected districts	Education Department and NYK

Conti...

	Children who need special care and protection were identified and trained volunteers spent time with them	
	The trained volunteers are engaged in village level activities with children and cover both school going and non-school going children	
	Counselling and community-level play activities are estimated to have benefited over 20,000	
	Children directly and another 60,000 children indirectly through schools and through various supplementary programmes	

Child Participation

Participation of children intensified through organised platforms after the tsunami. Such participatory, often adult-facilitated, platforms provided children with a voice; assisted them to overcome their traumas and fear of the sea; gave them an opportunity to develop leadership skills; facilitated peer learning; enhanced their self-worth; and allowed engagement with issues affecting them and their communities. Examples include children's club/ parliament taking up issues of sanitation, and assisting other children suffering from depression or trauma. Organised participation through such clubs, etc. has exposed children to knowledge and information on various issues. For instance, children have received training in disaster preparedness and first aid. UNICEF and its partner NGOs covered 6,000 children through their life skills programmes. Clubs provided children space for creative and recreational activities. In quite another way, participation through clubs demonstrated children's resilience to loss and trauma – either suffered or witnessed.

Child Protection

UNICEF conducted field assessments of separated children and orphans, including tracking and follow-up of these children. Subsequently, UNICEF supported the 'State Consultation on Registration and Tracing of Children'. To prevent trafficking UNICEF agreed to support a strategy development and training workshop for police officers on trafficking, and publication of 5,000 copies of a book in Tamil on trafficking.

Instead of creating new mechanisms, processes were initiated to strengthen existing mechanisms of child protection such as the Juvenile Justice

System, Village Level Watch Dog Committees (VLWDC), intensive networking between NGOs at all levels and between NGOs and government and creation of mechanisms such as Child Protection Committees at the village level. This was achieved through the orientation and training on child rights and child protection issues including trafficking. For instance 1250 VLWDC members were trained as part of capacity-building on child protection. The cumulative outcome of these initiatives was increased awareness on child protection issues and sensitisation of the stakeholders to recognise, identify and respond to the child protection concerns.

Enhanced Protection of Children

Various steps undertaken by government, UNICEF and INGOs contributed towards better protection of children from potential abuse and exploitation such as trafficking, child labour, and dropping out of school. Such steps include opening orphanages, service homes, financial assistance, provision of free education, banning adoption in the first six months after the tsunami and, most importantly, creation of a database of children (including vulnerable children) affected by the tsunami.

The State Department of Social Defence, has completed a home study of 2,240 tsunami-affected children. Creation of a database is singled out by many as a measure of far reaching consequence because of its potential to assist in an evidence-based approach to programming for child protection in Tamil Nadu. On the issue of orphans, it should be noted that the government gave primacy to community-based rehabilitation over institutional care, thereby, pre-empting numerous risks posed to children in an institutional setting. All orphaned children are either in orphanages or in the custody of relatives who are taking care of them as guardians.

Safe Spaces for Children

When Govt. of Tamil Nadu, UNICEF and INGOs rushed in to establish normalcy in the lives of children immediately after the tsunami, their joint focus was on getting schools and Anganwadis back in action. This focus on re-organising schools, starting Anganwadis, announcement of schemes for continuing schooling and fee waiver sought to simulate a routine which emphasised the importance of learning and education. While it had its practical merits in as much as it had a positive impact on children and school drop out rates, its symbolic significance should not be discounted. By giving primacy to pre-school centres and schools, the inextricable link of schooling as a rite of passage from childhood to adulthood was emphasised. It sought to reinforce the message among communities that pre-school centres and schools are safe spaces where children belong.

Restoring Schools

The Department of Education deemed any school that has students from affected habitations as 'tsunami affected'. There were 567 such schools across 13 districts of Tamil Nadu. Within two weeks collective efforts ensured that all children were back in school, after quickly assessing reconstruction, relocation and repair needs of schools even if it meant studying in temporary shelters. All except the four worst affected schools had started functioning within two weeks. Reconstruction of 76 schools and major and minor repair works in 195 schools was undertaken in fully or partially damaged government and aided schools.

Assistance to Students

Within two months following the tsunami, several GOs were issued to enable supply of free textbooks and notebooks, uniforms and duplicate certificates to replace those lost in the disaster. Other measures included allowing affected children to write their school leaving exams later than scheduled and ensuring that no affected child paid any kind of fee. Thanks to the concession in tuition and examination fees they could resume schooling. Besides giving Rs 300 per month as scholarship from PMNRF scholarship schemes for all the students, studying in classes I to X, from tsunami affected families. GoTN implemented various support schemes for children who were orphaned and those whose schooling was discontinued after the tsunami.

All CEOs of affected districts were instructed to monitor the implementation of orders. 1,05,264 children received textbooks and notebooks and 96,723 received uniforms from the government, while a large number benefited from additional supplies from UN bodies and NGOs. UNICEF and other partner NGOs played a vital catalytic role in getting education in the affected areas back on the rails. Kits of various kinds, from student kits to water containers and midday meal utensils, school furniture and play material was provided. UNICEF also equipped bridge course centres, which helped out of school children get back into the mainstream. NGOs supported and participated in a number of government and UNICEF-initiated activities. Resumption of schooling activities played an important role in improving the mental wellbeing of affected children.

A number of activities such as special tuition centres and recreation centres are continuing with an aim to reorient all affected children to their normal studies. Separate public exams were conducted for the children from the tsunami affected families and the pass percentage was higher than the regular exams.

Financial Assistance

The government has sanctioned financial assistance to children/girls who have lost both parents or one parent to the tsunami and the other parent prior to the tsunami and deposited the amount in the name of beneficiaries. Besides that in an effort to support schooling, the following financial packages from the PMNRF were given to students affected by the tsunami.

Child Assistance Scheme

Children who lost one parent in the tsunami and were less than 18 years of age on the day of tsunami are eligible to get this assistance. A sum of ₹ 51,000 is deposited in fixed deposits in Nationalised Banks and the respective banks have been paying the monthly interest to the surviving parent. The deposit will be made available, when the child attains the age of 18 for their further studies or self-employment. With similar arrangements with the nationalised banks; ₹ 3 lakhs each was given to orphaned children above 18 years and ₹ 5 lakhs each was given to orphaned children from 0-18 years.

Scholarship for Tsunami-affected Children

Children whose families were affected by the tsunami through loss of life, or livelihood and who are studying from I to X standard are eligible to get this assistance. Under this scheme, a sum of ₹ 300 per month will be given to the children to defray school going expenses. This assistance will be made available directly to the children through their parents/guardians through individual bank accounts, till they complete X standard. In Nagapattinam alone 25,770 children were benefited under PMSTAC and 1037 under PMCA scheme for the year 2005-06.

Reimbursement of Tuition fees/Special fees

Govt. of Tamil Nadu exempted tsunami-affected students from paying tuition fees/special fees for the period from January 1, 2005 to till the end of academic year 2005-2006. Govt. of Tamil Nadu paid the amount payable by the students. This concession was extended for the academic year 2006-07 from the month June 2006. The tuition-fee waiver from Govt. of Tamil Nadu covers classes from LKG to XII and higher studies in Polytechnics, Engineering colleges, Medicine, Nursing courses etc. So far a sum of ₹ 14.50 crore was sanctioned for the academic year 2005-06 for 33,127 students and ₹ 12.36 crore was sanctioned for the year 2006-2007 for 25,187 students.

To ensure that students get all the benefits offered to them by the state government, necessary orders have been issued by the Education Department to all the concerned educational institutions and individuals. The District Collectors also sent letters to all the Educational Institutions concerned, to send claims for reimbursement of Special Fees and Tuition Fees payable by the tsunami affected students. Care was taken that no eligible person is deprived of the benefits of these schemes.

Progress of Expenditure on the Prime Minister's Child Assistance Scheme as on 31.07.2008

Sl. No.	*District*	*No. of beneficiaries*	*Amount released*	*Amount spent*	*Balance*
1.	Chennai	48	2448000	2346000	102000
2.	Cuddalore	214	10914000	10455000	459000
3.	Kancheepuram	24	1224000	1224000	NIL
4.	Kanyakumari	137	6987000	6987000	NIL
5.	Nagapattinam	1037	52887000	52887000	NIL
6.	Thiruvallur	8	408000	408000	NIL
7.	Tiruvarur	24	1224000	1224000	NIL
8.	Tirunelveli	2	102000	102000	NIL
9.	Thanjavur	1	51000	NIL	51000
10.	Villupuram	18	918000	918000	NIL
	TOTAL	**1513**	**77163000**	**76551000**	**612000**

Source: Govt. of Tamil Nadu, 2008.

Steps Towards Quality Education

UNICEF has been a major player in the Joint UN Initiative and has contributed towards bringing a change in the traditional scenario of rural schooling. Essential school supplies have reached over 76,000 children and 1875 teachers. 281 schools have been equipped with blackboards, furniture, bags and recreation kits. Quality Education Package has reached over 1300 schools and is making a difference to the school environment, teacher training, teaching-learning materials and community involvement. Thirty-first bridge schools with well-equipped classrooms and learning materials are helping to mainstream 620 out-of-school children. So far, 40 have been sent to regular schools. Many NGOs, mobilised communities through awareness campaigns, enrolment drives, bridge courses for dropouts, etc. Organisations like Round Table India focused on restoration and reconstruction of damaged classrooms. The role of village panchayats and particularly headmasters in the revival of some schools has been an inspiring lesson for replication.

Funding Partners with Government of Tamil Nadu: At a Glance

A. Prime Minister's National Relief Fund (PMNRF)

Partners: Government of India and Government of Tamil Nadu.

Goal: overall medium and long-term rehabilitation of the coastal communities including children and economically active population in the tsunami-affected areas.

Locations: all tsunami-affected districts.

Project Cost: ₹ 88.94 crore.

Components:

- Prime Minister's Child Assistance Scheme (PMCAS)
- Prime Minister's scholarship for tsunami-affected children
- Support of social infrastructure
- Support to fisherman scheme
- Universal health insurance scheme

B. Emergency Tsunami Reconstruction Project (ETRP)

Partners: World Bank and Government of Tamil Nadu.

Goal: Repair damaged houses and provides for multi-hazard resistant houses, reclaim agricultural lands, strengthen fisheries infrastructure, strengthen animal husbandry infrastructure, restore damaged public infrastructure, create green shelter belts and undertake scientific studies in the affected coastal areas.

Locations: 13 coastal districts of Tamil Nadu.

Project Cost: ₹ 1852.74 crore ($423 million).

Project duration: 31.10.2008 - likely to be extended till 31.12.2010.

Components:

- Housing Reconstruction (US$596.8 million) about 87
- Restoration of Livelihoods (US$36.4 million) about
- Public Buildings and Public Works (US$19.5 million)
- Technical Assistance and Training (US$11.1 million)
- Implementation support (US$19.0 Million, about 3 per cent

C. Tsunami Emergency Assistance Project (TEAP)

Partners: Asian Development Bank and Government of Tamil Nadu

Goal: Restoration of:

- Livelihoods
- Transportation such as roads and bridges and ports

- Rural and municipal infrastructure such as water supply
- Capacity-building and implementation assistance

Locations: 13 coastal districts of Tamil Nadu

Project Cost: ₹ 629.93 crore ($143.75 million)

Project Duration: Expected date of completion is 30.04.2009

Components and activities: Livelihood ($ 49.99 million or ₹ 218.96 crore)

1. Restoration of livelihoods of affected poor and low-income households organised into SHGs and other similar groups recognised by the state government as affected directly or indirectly by the tsunami, through support by way of capacity-building, establishment and enterprise-training.
2. Formation of new SHGs both male and female for affected households not yet organised in community-based groups to restore livelihoods through micro-enterprise, training and establishment support.
3. Replacement of productive assets (i.e. excluding housing) of tsunami-affected households.
4. Skill up-gradation.
5. Risk-mitigation through group, life and asset insurance as applicable, of affected households receiving assistance under this component.
6. Reconstruction of tsunami-affected community-based infrastructure.
7. Technical support for implementation, monitoring, and impact assessment of this component.

Transportation (US$26.80 million or ₹ 117.39 crore)

8. Roads and bridges (roads sub-sector).
9. Ports and harbours (ports sub-sector).

Rural and Municipal Infrastructure

10. Water supply and sanitation (US$ 23 million or ₹ 100.74 crore).
11. Other rural and municipal Infrastructure (US$ 40.75 million or ₹ 178.49 crore).

Capacity-building and Implementation Assistance ($ 3.21 million or ₹ 14.06 crore)

12. Design and construction, supervision and technical support consultancy.

Implementation support

13. Quality assurance and audit.
14. Project management and evaluation.

Partners: International Fund of Agricultural Development and Government of Tamil Nadu.

D. Japan Fund for Poverty Reduction (JFPR)

Partners: Govt. Tamil Nadu, JPFR and ADB

Goal: Reducing poverty in Tsunami affected areas

Locations: 13 coastal districts of Tamil Nadu

Project Cost: ₹ 16.704 crore(US$ 3.79 million)

Project Duration: 08.03.20011

Components and activities:

E. International Fund of Agricultural Assisted Project (IFAD)

Goal: Medium and long-term rehabilitation and reconstruction of livelihoods of coastal tsunami-affected communities.

Locations: Covers six coastal districts of Tamil Nadu: Kancheepuram, Villipuram, Cuddalore, Nagapattinam, Tiruvallur and Kanyakumari

Project cost: ₹ 129 crore (US$ 30 million)

Project duration: 8 years

Components and activities:

- **Community Resource Management.** Community resource planning, Safety at sea, Community support.
- **Community Institutions.** Support for self-help groups, Formation of fish marketing societies, Support for coastal schools.
- **Micro and Rural Finance.** Venture capital fund Micro-credit for SHGs Financial innovation, Risk management and insurance.
- Micro-Enterprise Development Micro-enterprise training
- Project Management and Coordination
  - Development of a three-tier project management structure consisting of an autonomous not-for-profit Coastal Community Development Society promoted by the state government.
  - District Implementation Office (PIU) at each project district working in close collaboration with the District Collector as Chairperson of the district-level Implementation Advisory Committee.

F. United Nations Assistance

Partners: United Nations and Government of Tamil Nadu.

Goal: Moving from post-disaster relief to recovery, restoring livelihoods and upgrading infrastructure, prospective risk reduction, policy support and co-ordination.

Locations: Coastal areas of Tamil Nadu. **Project cost:** US$ 38.79 Million.

Project duration: Up to 31.12.2008.

Components and activities:

- Moving from post-disaster relief to recovery (US $ 8.5 trafficking, Health and nutrition HIV/AIDS prevention and education.
- Restoring livelihoods (US$ 10.65 Million) Rebuilding sanitation and hygiene.
- Prospective risk reduction (US$ 16.55 Million) Healthy Capacity-building for disaster risk-management.
- Coordination and knowledge networking (US$ 3.05 Million).

Impact of Tsunami in Tamil Nadu at a Glance

- 13 districts affected
- 238 villages and 418 hamlets affected
- 7997 lives lost
- 241 children orphaned
- 1513 children who lost one of their parents
- 846 missing persons
- 3625 injured persons
- 118000 houses damaged
- 0.49 million people evacuated
- 1.078 population affected
- 16082 cattle-loss
- 51078 fishing vessels damaged/lost
- 0.3 million number of families whose immediate livelihood was affected
- US $880 million assessment of damages to infrastructure, including housing 8844.35 agricultural and horticultural lands damaged in Ha
- 775 kms roads damaged
- 608 kms power lines damaged
- 14 damaged ports/fish landing centres

Source: Govt. of Tamil Nadu (2008), Tiding over Tsunami part 2, Oct.

Index

U

V

W

Y